DIVIDED NATION?

MURRAY GOOT & TIM ROWSE

DIVIDED NATION?

Indigenous Affairs and the Imagined Public

MELBOURNE
UNIVERSITY
PRESS

MELBOURNE UNIVERSITY PRESS
An imprint of Melbourne University Publishing Ltd
187 Grattan Street, Carlton, Victoria 3053, Australia
mup-info@unimelb.edu.au
www.mup.com.au

First published 2007
Text © Murray Goot and Tim Rowse 2007
Design and typography © Melbourne University Publishing Ltd 2007

Cover design by Melanie Feddersen
Text design by Sandra Nobes
Typeset by J&M Typesetting
Printed in Australia by Griffin Press

National Library of Australia Cataloguing-in-Publication data:
Goot, Murray.
    Divided nation: Indigenous affairs and the imagined public.

    Bibliography.
    Includes index.
    ISBN 978 0 522 85342 1.

    1. Aboriginal Australians – History – 20th century.
    2. Aboriginal Australians – Government relations.
    3. Australia – Race relations. I. Rowse, Tim, 1951– .
    II. Title.

305.800994

Contents

Tables and Figures

Acknowledgements

Although this book was written mainly in the second half of 2006, we have been working intermittently on the issues it tackles for nearly twenty years.

In the course of our research and writing we have accumulated a large number of debts. Brian Aarons from the Department of Prime Minister and Cabinet, the late George Camakaris from AMR:Quantum, the late Ian Henderson from the Federal Secretariat of the Australian Labor Party, Sol Lebovic from Newspoll, John Mitchell from AGBMcNair, Keith Patterson from Patterson Market Research, the Roy Morgan Research Centre, Irving Saulwick from Irving Saulwick & Associates, and John Stirton from ACNeilsen provided data or answered our questions about their polls; Rochelle Graham, Stephen Gray and Sophie Holloway facilitated our access to the polls in the Australian Social Science Data Archive.

Jeremy Beckett, Kathy Betts, Marion Orchison and John Western helped in diverse ways, as did Wayne Hooper, Rick Ponting, Dennis Shanahan and Mark Textor.

The Department of History in the Faculty of Arts at ANU hosted a seminar in October 2006, at which we presented an early version of our Introduction and parts of Chapters 1 and 2. We are grateful to those who contributed to the discussion, particularly Peter Brent.

Our work was supported initially by a consultancy from the Commonwealth Department of Aboriginal Affairs (1988–89) for Goot. More recently we have benefited from the support afforded by Macquarie University and the Australian Research Council, under Grant DP0559934 (Goot), and by the Australian National University (Rowse).

This support allowed us, among other things, to draw on the skills and dedication, first of Helma Neumann, and later of

Kylie Brass who was responsible for constructing the graph on page 19 and for assembling much of the data on which it depends.

At Melbourne University Publishing Foong Ling Kong, our publisher, Cinzia Cavallaro and Felicity Edge, our editors, helped shape the book.

Clare Coney was not only a careful copy editor, she also made important suggestions about the structure of our Introduction and Conclusion.

We are also grateful to the forbearance of our immediate families—Deb Brennan, Anna Brennan, and Tim Goot-Brennan; Jan Mackay and Anna Mackay—from whom our attentions were divided rather more than usually they are.

Introduction

From the release of the *Bringing Them Home* report in 1997 to the climax of the reconciliation decade in 2000, the question of whether the Prime Minister should apologise to the 'Stolen Generations' was the subject of public debate.[1] The pros and cons of an apology from the Prime Minister seemed to condense and to dramatise some difficult questions about the history and identity of Australians. Had we been at fault, in our dealings with Indigenous Australians, and did we have the courage and the grace to apologise, for the sake of 'reconciliation', through our Prime Minister? Or were Indigenous Australians demanding too much, exaggerating the damage wrought by colonisation, refusing to concede the benefits, pushing contemporary Australians into unfounded admission of guilt and thus putting reconciliation at risk? The nation was divided in its opinion about whether the Prime Minister owed Indigenous Australians an apology on the nation's behalf.

Divided Nation? is about how we can understand the divisions in Australian public opinion about Indigenous issues in this and in other emblematic moments in Australian history over the past forty years. We have chosen four moments in the past fifty years in order to consider two questions: how has Australian 'public opinion' on Indigenous issues been represented and what part have those representations played in the political process? Our first moment is May 1967 when the Australian public voted in a referendum that gave the Commonwealth power to legislate for Aborigines and meant that all Aborigines could be counted within the national population, in the reckoning of electoral boundaries and of Commonwealth grants to the States. The overwhelming vote was understood to be an expression of Australians' desire to 'include' Aborigines and to cease discriminating against them. There were few public opinion polls in 1967, but other research from the late 1960s reveals the nature and limits of the popular disposition to be 'inclusive'.

The 1983–86 national land rights debate is the second episode we examine where public opinion studies began to figure prominently in the ways that governments and others reasoned, publicly and privately, about the policy issues of the day. The Hawke Government backed down from its attempt to legislate national land rights after commissioning public opinion research that suggested that 'middle Australia' was not well disposed to land rights for Aborigines.

Polls were again a feature of political debate in 1993—our third moment—when Australians discussed how best to respond to the High Court's 1992 *Mabo* decision: should the laws of the land recognise 'native title'? If so, on what terms? Public opinion polls, during the native title debate, were weapons of political struggle.

In our final moment, the 1999–2000 climax of the Decade of Reconciliation, the interpretation of polls again became central to political contention.

A Mandate to Apologise?

Public opinion polls taken after the release of the Human Rights and Equal Opportunity Commission's (HREOC) 'Stolen Children' report, in May 1997, placed the Prime Minister, John Howard, in a dilemma: one poll suggested widespread support for a Government apology to Aboriginal people; one suggested widespread opposition to such a course; and one fell somewhere in between (Table 1). Why were there such different results, and what sense could a Prime Minister, or any politically active person, make of these data on public opinion?

Table 1 Opinion on whether the government should apologise for the 'stolen children', 1997 (percentages)

Questions

'Recently a report by the Human Rights Commission has recommended that all Australian Parliaments officially acknowledge the responsibility of previous governments for the laws and policies which led to the forcible removal of Aboriginal children from their families. The Human Rights Commission has recommended that all Australian parliaments formally apologise for the suffering caused by those laws and policies. Do you agree or disagree with this recommendation?' (AGB McNair, 23–25 May 1997)

'Now for a question about the inquiry referred to as the "stolen children" inquiry. Do you think the Federal Government should or should not apologise to the Aboriginal people for the events revealed in the "stolen children" inquiry?' (Newspoll, 30 May–1 June 1997)

'Thinking now about the report into the Government policy which allowed Aboriginal children to be taken from their families between 1910 and 1970 and placed within the white community. The report has been dubbed "The Stolen Children" report. The Prime Minister, Mr Howard, has decided against the Government giving a formal national apology. He said that to do so is [sic] to indicate in some way that the present generations are responsible and can be held accountable for errors, wrongs and misdeeds of earlier generations. Overall, do you agree or disagree with Mr Howard's statement?' (Morgan Poll, 4–5 June 1997)

John Howard believed apology would represent general population incl. present generations not just actions & past parts ??

swayed by HREOC's opinion -

Poll	Apologise	Don't Apologise	Don't Know	n
AGB McNair	65	30	5	(2065)
Newspoll	50	40	10	(1200)
Morgan	37	57	6	(522)

swayed by PM's decided opinion &

statement accepting population responsibility

n = number of respondents

Sources: Wright, 'Majority Wants Official Apology', for AGB McNair; Gordon, 'Black Apology Splits Voters', for Newspoll; Morgan Poll Finding No. 2993.

The highest level of support for an apology was recorded by the first of the polls, taken by AGB McNair before the HREOC report was tabled in the Commonwealth Parliament. Respondents were told of 'the forcible removal of Aboriginal children from their families' and of the recommendations of the 'Human Rights [and Equal Opportunity] Commission', that 'all Australian parliaments acknowledge the responsibility of previous governments' for these events and 'formally apologise for the suffering caused'. Asked whether they agreed or disagreed 'with this recommendation' (strictly speaking, two recommendations), 65 per cent agreed.

The lowest level of support for an apology, 37 per cent, was recorded by the last of the polls, conducted by Morgan. Here respondents were told that 'Aboriginal children' had been 'taken from their families between 1910 and 1970 and placed within the white community'; that 'the report' (no mention of it being a HREOC report) had been 'dubbed' 'The Stolen Children' report. Morgan made sure that respondents knew that the Prime Minister had decided by then against the Government's giving 'a formal national apology'; the Prime Minister, Morgan explained, had decided that to apologise would be to 'indicate in some way that the present generations are responsible and can be held accountable for errors, wrongs and misdeeds of earlier generations'.

Between AGB McNair's high and Morgan's low came Newspoll's result. Newspoll's question informed respondents of neither HREOC's recommendation nor the Prime _most objective ??_

Minister's reaction to it. The Newspoll question simply told of the 'stolen children' inquiry and asked whether the Government should apologise to the Aboriginal people because of 'the events revealed'.

The polls varied in the way they pitched their questions. In particular, they varied in terms of the information about the report that each pollster offered to (or withheld from) respondents. They differed in what they told respondents about the range of reactions to the report, and, in choosing whose reactions to incorporate as background information, the polls chose figures and organisations of different status and reputation. Respondents were influenced by these framings. AGB McNair boosted support for an apology by ensuring that the only information it provided, or recommendations it rehearsed, were sourced to the 'Human Rights Commission'. Morgan, by contrast, helped persuade respondents that the Prime Minister should *not* apologise, not only by offering a misleadingly narrow account of the period covered ('between 1910 and 1970') and by failing to identify authorship of the report, but also, and more importantly, by drawing respondents' attention to the Prime Minister's reaction and to his alone. Morgan rehearsed Howard's reasons for rejecting an apology while not offering any reasons the report ought to be accepted. Newspoll elicited a more even split by not mentioning the source of the report and by not making direct reference to its recommendations; Newspoll avoided arguments for and against the report. Apart from being told of a report on 'stolen children' affecting Aboriginal people, Newspoll respondents were given no cues. The result? A division of opinion weighted slightly towards an apology—an understandable outcome, given the information.

The importance of the cues offered by Morgan is underscored by the response elicited by a second, but almost identical, question asked in the same Morgan poll. Having just said whether they agreed or disagreed with the Prime

Minister's decision, Morgan's respondents were asked 'whether or not there should be a Federal Government apology'. On this occasion, however, the response options were doubled; instead of a two-fold choice they were offered a four-fold choice: 'The Federal Government should formally apologise even if the apology makes it easier to claim compensation' (23 per cent chose this option); 'the Federal Government should formally apologise only if it does *not* make it easier to claim compensation' (chosen by 27 per cent); 'The Federal Government should not apologise because it is enough [sic] individual politicians to apologise' (10 per cent); 'The Federal Government should not apologise because the policy was legal and well meaning at the time' (agreed to by 37 per cent of those interviewed).

In response to Morgan's earlier question—the question that had immediately preceded this—37 per cent had said they favoured the Government's apologising; but with the follow-up question the number jumped to 50 per cent, provided that any apology did not make it easier for Aborigines to claim compensation. In response to that earlier question, 57 per cent had said they favoured Howard's decision not to apologise; now, 47 per cent did so. In short, what had been a margin of 20 percentage points in favour of Howard's position suddenly became a margin of three percentage points against. The explanation, almost certainly, lies not only in the responses allowed by the second of the two questions, but in the second question's omission of any reference to the Prime Minister's position or to his reasons for holding it.

Did one of the three results—AGB McNair's, Newspoll's or the first of Morgan's results—more truly represent public opinion? That depends on what one understands by public opinion—and on whether one treats the polls as a political weapon.

What Is 'Public Opinion'?

It is possible to see a public opinion poll as a referendum or a plebiscite that is not binding on the Government. A poll measures how each person would vote on a specific proposal. Every opinion has the same value, just as in democratic voting procedures. The poll does not measure each person's knowledge of the issue or the strength of their opinion. Nor does a poll ask respondents for their own ideas about the issue. It simply asks whether a person is for or against a proposition formulated by the pollster. One of the originators of public opinion polling, George Gallup, was strongly attracted to plebiscites or referenda as the democratic ideal; his polls modelled referenda, he said, even if they did not bind governments.[2] (Newspoll approached the 'apology' issue in this plebiscite fashion—it simply asked whether the Federal Government 'should or should not apologise'.)

However, there is another view of 'public opinion' that would lead us to discount all three of the polls. Critics of the plebiscite notion of public opinion polls object to the assumption that respondents have informed opinions before the pollster approaches them and that the poll question simply enables the expression of that opinion. For such critics, public opinion about a Government apology could be represented by the polls only if the public was aware of the report, had been given an opportunity to hear it discussed, and had formed some definite opinion on the matter—even if not a well-informed one. None of the three polls on the apology tried to find out whether respondents had heard of the report, were aware of the reactions to it, or had discussed it with others. The first poll was conducted after the report had received some media coverage but before the Prime Minister, officially, had shown his hand; the second came hard on the heels of the official release of the report and the Prime Minister's declaration that there would be no formal apology; even the third poll, which followed a week later, may have been taken before the issues had had time to sink in. The question of an apology bore directly on the interests of very few of the respondents. It is reasonable to infer that even if the respondents had been aware of the report, they probably knew little of its findings, had not given it much thought and certainly had not formed definite opinions about it. In this sense, public opinion on the apology did not exist; its apparent existence was an artefact of the poll process itself.[3]

Some of those who doubt, in this way, the reality of public opinion have attempted to rethink the position of the public in the democratic process. They evoke 'the public' whose opinions result from deliberation. A 'deliberative opinion poll', writes the American political scientist James Fishkin, 'models what the public *would* think, if it had a more adequate chance to think about the questions at issue'. Another American political scientist, James Farr, invites us to think of the jury, a group brought together to hear the evidence, to deliberate on it and to come to a decision. Daniel Yankelovich, a leading American public opinion researcher and another critic of the polls, argues that 'quality' in public opinion depends on consistency, firmness and a willingness to take responsibility for the consequences of one's views.[4] Both the AGB McNair and the Morgan polls attempted to give respondents some background on which they might base their judgments, though both were one-sided in what they offered. McNair's information favoured the HREOC recommendations; Morgan's information raised negative features of those recommendations. A balanced introduction of the apology question would have combined argument and counter-argument. Nonetheless, however deficient in execution, McNair and Morgan allowed respondents deliberation in some form.

John Howard did not apologise. 'If you're going to speak on behalf of the nation', he explained, 'then the nation must support it'.[5] Howard spoke after the AGB McNair poll was published but before the Morgan poll was taken. Labor's former Minister for Aboriginal Affairs, Robert Tickner, saw things quite differently. 'The integrity of the government's position', he would later write, was 'undermined when the *Sydney Morning Herald* published a Herald-AG [sic] McNair poll which found that 65 per cent of respondents agreed that there should be an official acknowledgement and an apology for the suffering caused by the policy of forced removal'.[6] While Howard was at odds with 'the nation' as revealed by the AGB McNair poll, Tickner had ignored Newspoll and the Morgan poll.

Since politicians are concerned not so much with measuring public opinion as they are with managing it, neither Howard's remarks nor Tickner's are puzzling. While some leaders may want to know what a fair survey would reveal, most would be satisfied with a survey that tells them what—given their own preferences—they could get away with. A poll-following politician is sometimes able to choose among polls. The three 'apology' polls revealed an unstable pattern of opinion, with contradictory potentials for political persuasion. Can a politician, using the polls, win 'the nation' to his preferred position? The Morgan poll suggested that if the Prime Minister stuck to the script that 'present generations' could not be 'held accountable for errors, wrongs and misdeeds of earlier generations' he would carry the day. But, on the evidence produced by AGB McNair, had the Prime Minister decided to endorse the HREOC recommendations he might well have carried opinion in that direction, too. Indeed, since the Opposition would have backed any endorsement of the HREOC findings by the Government, persuading the public of the merits of an apology might have been easier than getting electors to agree that the recommendations were best ignored. In 1997 the Prime Minister conceded that his refusal to apologise had 'hurt' his government 'politically'. In 2000, the year that marked the end of the Decade of Reconciliation, he was said to have regretted his decision not to apologise.[7]

Public Opinion and Indigenous Australians

On a number of occasions in Australia's recent past, politicians have justified their positions by referring to 'public opinion' as either mandating their position or acting as a constraint. However, only since 1941 have Australians been subject to public opinion polling. Before then, how was 'the public' made visible? We can understand one of the older notions of public opinion by paying attention to the work of the noted anthropologist A.P. Elkin. Not only an academic but also a public intellectual, Elkin's agitation around Aboriginal issues, from the late 1920s to the 1970s, included presenting himself as both leading and reflecting public opinion. Although he was interested in public opinion research, in his writing about Aboriginal issues he did not cite such research. Elkin drew on an older idea of public opinion as mobilised pressure from concerned people.[8]

Writing shortly before the 'powers referendum' in 1944, when it seemed likely that voters would be asked to authorise a transfer of responsibilities over Aboriginal affairs from the States to the Commonwealth, Elkin sought to outline the 'great stirring of public interest in Aboriginal matters', the 'advance of public opinion' that had occurred in the 1930s. This 'advance of public opinion' supported 'a unified policy and administration' that 'would ensure that each advance in policy or method' within any one State or within the Northern Territory, 'would apply all over the Commonwealth'. Several factors, he argued, had stimulated this 'advance': 'the spread of knowledge based on scientific research, the watchfulness and public work of humanitarian and missionary bodies, and the holdings and findings of commissions of inquiry'; 'an "unnecessary, though legally justified", shooting of an Aborigine by a constable, in Central Australia, that kept public feeling roused'; and 'the newspapers in Sydney, at least'—the *Sydney Morning Herald* and Sydney *Sun*—that had 'helped whole-heartedly in the campaign for justice and a positive policy for Aborigines'. Politicians had noticed this shift in public opinion:'The growing agitation for a unified policy for Aboriginal administration in Australia as a whole was noted by a Conference of Commonwealth and State Ministers which met in Adelaide in August, 1936'. By the late 1930s, 'all the Governments, with the exception of Victoria' had 'yielded to public opinion and overhauled their policies and methods of administration'.[9]

In Elkin's account, 'interested citizens' constituted the public, and to gauge their opinions you observed what they did—the 'meetings' that 'were held', the 'articles and letters' that 'were published in the press', the 'letters and telegrams sent to Canberra'. Sometimes citizens, roused by particular incidents, acted individually; for example, in 1933, in the wake of widely publicised killings of Aborigines at Caledon Bay. Sometimes citizens started groups, such the Australian Aborigines' League (Victoria), formed in 1932. Sometimes groups originally formed for other purposes extended their horizon, as happened in 1939 when 'the Trades and Labour [sic] Council,Sydney,added its weight to the general movement of opinion by endorsing a pamphlet, which advocated the centralization of affairs affecting full-bloods in the hands of the Commonwealth Government, and the granting of full citizenship rights to all mixed-bloods'.[10] In 1944, Elkin identified his own arguments for policy reform as a considered expression of the public opinion whose mobilisation he narrated.

In a subsequent pamphlet, *Aborigines and Citizenship* (1958), Elkin returned to the narration of public opinion, identifying two turning points—one that preceded the stirrings of the 1930s and one that followed it. In the second quarter of the nineteenth century, he remarked, 'the efforts made by sincere persons, missionary and Government, had few if any permanent results, and helped to confirm a growing opinion that the Aborigines could not be civilized'. But over the last quarter of a century,

> one of the most striking facts [has been] the remarkable change ... in attitudes towards Aborigines, and in public interest. To those of us who have been closely connected with the change, it is a veritable revolution—for the better ... citizenship is at hand. In 1933 it was hard even to conceive of such things; but now they are inevitable.

Elkin conceded that there were 'still a considerable number of people who have no time for [Aborigines] and regard them as a curious and inferior race'. Nonetheless, he insisted, 'those who think or speak in this way, now realise that even the full bloods can no longer be treated as a kind of serf, and that citizenship is a birthright that can no longer be denied to the Aborigines'. It was true that 'many difficulties' remained but, apart from the 'ironing out of anomalies', these could not 'be solved by amendments of Acts ... or by public meetings'. Now, 'when an obstacle is raised by prejudice in some locality, citizens in that same locality rise up and work to overcome that obstacle'. Of all the solutions, action at a local level was the '[g]reatest'. Here was a guarantee that 'assimilation will come and Aborigines and ourselves will be truly fellow citizens'.[11]

Elkin's booklet of 1944, *Citizenship for the Aborigines*, was published three years after the birth of the Australian Public Opinion Poll (The Gallup Method)—APOP—but before it had asked any questions about Aborigines. From February 1947 to October 1958, the year in which Elkin published *Aborigines and Citizenship*, APOP asked ten questions about Aboriginal issues: one in 1947; six in 1954; one in 1957, when some thought a referendum 'to permit Federal control of Aboriginal affairs could be carried through within a month';[12]

and two in 1958. However, Elkin did not take the opportunity in *Aborigines and Citizenship* to refer to opinion polls. Central to Elkin's notion of public opinion was the idea of individuals or groups voicing their opinions by performing certain actions: holding meetings, publishing pamphlets, letters and articles in the press, and contacting politicians. It was not only as individuals but also as groups that they took the initiative, expressing their views, and ensuring that these views came to be more widely known. It was the people directly involved in these activities—all pushing, in Elkin's account, in roughly the same direction—who decided, or at least influenced, what the issues were, when they were raised, and how they were framed and expressed.

Public Opinion as Respondent Opinion

In the understandings of public opinion promoted by the use of survey research—including public opinion polls and, later, focus groups—each aspect of public opinion as Elkin described it is implicitly denied or effectively ignored.[13]

First, instead of public opinion being wholly dependent on individuals or groups taking the initiative to express their opinions, and having to bear the costs involved, the expression of public opinion is now dependent on the polls, with most of the costs (other than a small cost in terms of the interviewee's time) borne by the polling organisation—or, as is usually the case, by whoever pays for the poll. Those who are interviewed do not initiate the process: they are described, appropriately, as 'respondents'. Respondents who are not interested in, or who have no real view on, a particular issue raised by a poll, far from being discounted or ignored (as they are in Elkin's view), not only count but may count equally with those who do have views—provided only that they choose a nominated response ('yes' or 'no', 'agree' or 'disagree', and so on).

Notwithstanding reforms proposed by Gallup in 1947, in few of the polls that are the focus of this book have any attempts been made to discover whether respondents know anything about the matter at hand. Gallup, acknowledging critics, had proposed that the polls should first establish whether respondents had 'heard or read' anything about an issue, and that they should then determine the 'knowledge, or lack of it' that respondents brought to the questions.[14] In Australia few polls (or their paymasters) have risen to the challenge. Few polls have invited respondents to say that they have no views. When they do—in some of the polls on land rights, a treaty, and Indigenous rights to self-government—the impact on interpretation can be important. And only recently, roughly since the establishment of Newspoll in the mid-1980s, have polls attempted to distinguish views according to the 'intensity' with which they are held (another of Gallup's 1947 recommendations).

Second, polls treat opinion as though it can be assessed independently of action. Whereas Elkin inferred public opinion from behaviour, pollsters equate public opinion with attitudes, and attitudes with the things polls measure. Polls give governments, political parties and interest groups useful intelligence about how people who are not yet mobilised might be persuaded to mobilise. Polls can be an early warning device in relation to public discontent and a source of reassurance when the public seems acquiescent or on side. Conducted in advance of policy changes, polls can indicate what changes are likely to meet resistance, what changes are a matter of indifference, and what changes are likely to win support. Information of this kind may thus promote what Jacobs and Shapiro call the 'democratic responsiveness' of governments. Equally, polls might generate a form of 'crafted talk': unpopular policies rhetorically reframed.[15] Or unpopular policies might be adopted, as originally presented, because their electoral salience is reported by the polls to be low.

Third, instead of identifying public opinion with the views expressed by group leaders—the labour movement's views on

Aborigines, for example, expressed by the delegates to the Trades and Labor Council—polls equate public opinion with the summed preferences of the group's members, independently ascertained. This enables polls to bypass or undermine the representative claims made on behalf of groups. As a way to deal with trade unions, this was one of the possibilities that most excited Gallup. But it also creates an incentive for lobby groups to commission their own polls. It is a powerful move in contemporary politics, as Australia's mining interests have shown, to report 'the views of the people', as ascertained by polling organisations that present themselves as independent of 'political predilections' and of 'public or private cause[s] no matter how worthy' (Gallup's boast on behalf of his own Institute).[16]

Fourth, public opinion, when equated with respondent opinion, is a commodity to be sold. It is a form of politics that is exchanged in the market. The most important buyers have been newspapers that believe their readers find polls interesting 'news'. From 1941 to 1973, Roy Morgan ran APOP (otherwise known as the Gallup poll or the Morgan Gallup poll) for the Melbourne *Herald* and *Sun News-Pictorial* and for papers owned or controlled by the Herald and Weekly Times in each of the other capital cities, except for Sydney where it was published by the *Daily Mirror*. However, since the early 1970s, when the Morgan monopoly was broken, most of the polling has been done for papers that attract bigger advertising revenues, with a more middle-class, more affluent and increasingly well-educated audience: Irving Saulwick and Associates, and more recently ACNielsen, for the Melbourne *Age* and *Sydney Morning Herald*; Morgan and AGB McNair at various times for either *Time* magazine or the *Bulletin*; and Newspoll for the *Australian*.

Presenting poll results as news items in a newspaper affects the ways that polls are designed and reported. Newspapers have limited space and polls are expensive. Even polls conducted for the broadsheets on complex issues have to be restricted to a small number of questions—sometimes, as with the apology for the 'Stolen Generations', to a single question. While the press determines the issues that the polls are to cover, it is the polling organisations that craft the questions, fix the order in which they are to be asked, and carry out the fieldwork. Pollsters also decide what information, by way of preamble, respondents are to be given. Tailored to the demands of 'news', polls are usually designed so that respondents' choice is limited: most often to two ('agree'/'disagree'; 'approve'/'disapprove'), sometimes to three ('more rights', 'less rights', 'the same rights'), occasionally to more than three (for example, where respondents are given a list and asked to choose the 'most important' item on it). A 'don't know' response is invited only rarely. Open-ended responses, where respondents are invited to reply in their own words—another of Gallup's 1947 recommendations—are expensive to record and time-consuming to code; accordingly, they, too, are rarely offered. As the polls on the apology for the 'Stolen Generations' show, different response options can make a substantial difference to the 'public opinion' that the polls report.

The job of interpreting a poll's findings lies, in the first instance, and sometimes in the last instance, with the polling organisation. Journalists do not necessarily make their own analysis of the data. Sometimes, as in the early Morgan polls, the findings may appear in the press under the pollster's own name; where that doesn't happen, polling organisations may insist nonetheless on checking what a journalist wants to say. At other times, journalists make their work easier by simply repeating the pollster's account. Once the poll is published, others may interpret the findings differently, but first interpretations—sometimes condensed into a sub-editor's headline—can be hugely influential, not on all of the paper's readers, but on other journalists, the politically interested, and politicians.

By fashioning a certain account of 'the public', pollsters and their clients—the press included—become political actors. Once opinion polls become credible parts of the political process, the temptation to deploy the representations of 'the public' that the polls offer becomes highly attractive. Instead of a wide range of activists and groups choosing the issues on which they want to express their views and the terms in which they want to express them, those who run the polls, or who pay for them—the press, governments, powerful political parties or well-heeled interest groups—determine when a poll should be conducted, the issues that should (or should not) be polled, what information (if any) about an issue respondents are to be given, and the terms in which opinions on particular issues are to be expressed. They also determine whether results will be made public; in Chapter 2 we give a vivid example of this tactic. Even where pollsters do not have a direct stake in an issue, they will have their own particular view not only on what questions to ask (at least one pollster thought *Mabo* 'too hard') but also on how the questions should be asked.[17] This has led to polling organisations misleading respondents over the meaning of land rights, 'States' rights', the judgments of the High Court, and so on.

The Benefits of Public Opinion Polls

If the polls produce contingent and even tendentious accounts of 'the public', and if, as one social theorist famously insisted *à propos* of the polls, 'public opinion does not exist',[18] why should we pay the polls any attention? And if we do attend to them, should we prefer their understanding of 'public opinion' to the 'public opinion' to which Elkin's pamphlets bore witness?[19]

Three features of the polls are appealing. Each points to a different kind of democratic inclusiveness. First, polls attempt to represent an entire population (people over a certain age, voters, or whoever), not just the part of the population whose activities are reported by the press or noticed by politicians.

Second, by rejecting the notion that what people believe or feel can be inferred from what they do, polls recognise those not engaged in political activity. The significance of their views is open to debate, but at least, through polling, we can get some idea of their thinking. It is good democratic practice to suppose that the views of those not engaged are as worthy of enumeration as the views of the activist.

Third, polls offer one way to study popular culture systematically. By asking the same questions of all respondents at more or less the same time, polls represent opinions, however constructed, on all manner of things in terms that allow these opinions to be added and subtracted, compared and contrasted; and they allow this to happen over time. For example, they enable careful study of the contrast between opinions that are reasonably consistent across a series of interrelated questions and those that are quite inconsistent or 'mushy'.[20] In Australian political culture there are some deep and abiding structures of belief about the place of Indigenous Australians in the nation. In particular we show the persistence of alternative ways of framing Indigenous issues. If Australians are 'divided', it is not necessarily into opposed sectors of public opinion. While there are many issues over which people are divided, what we show is that Australians are divided as well *within themselves*; hence, in the polls, respondents can make sense of Indigenous matters according to more than one way of framing the issues. The polls show this 'internal' division—our collective philosophical ambivalence—over and over again.

It is increasingly the polls that call Walter Lippmann's 'phantom public' into being.[21] However, even where polls are equated with public opinion—and this is not an equation we make—they should not be taken at face value. Like evidence of any other kind—including evidence of the kind Elkin adduced about 'public opinion'—the polls need to be interrogated, their strengths noted and their weaknesses understood. Carefully interpreted, the data shed light on

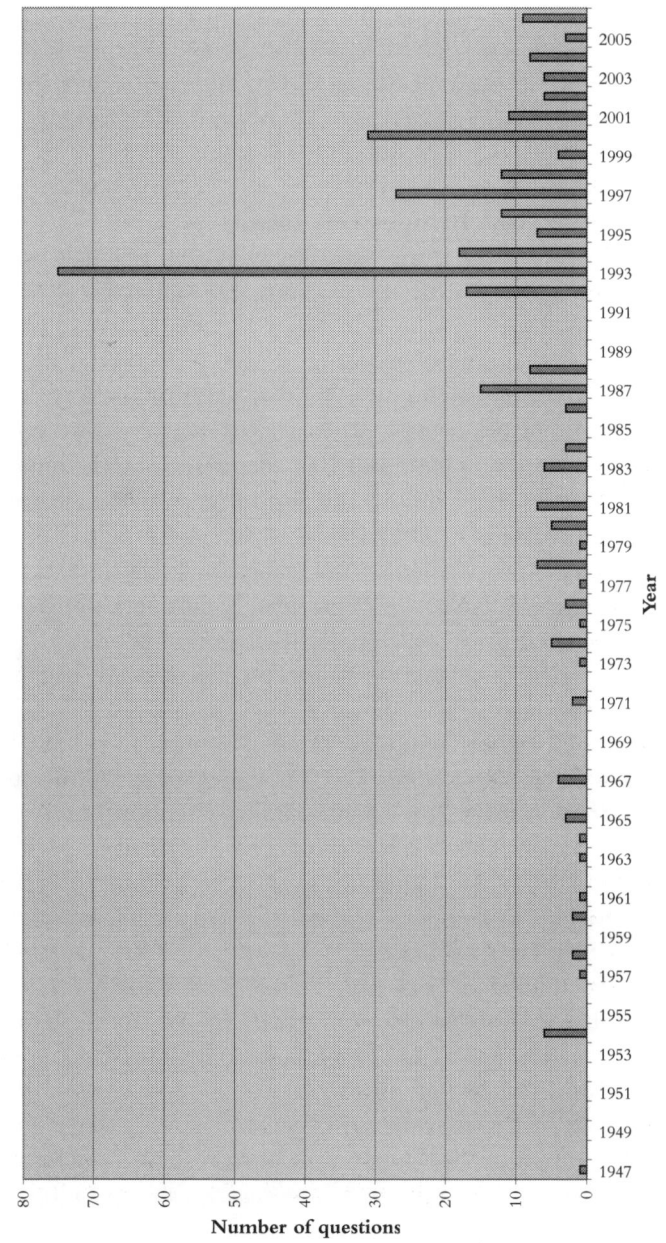

Figure 1 Media commissioned polls on Aboriginal issues, 1947–2006

popular views—views that would otherwise remain almost entirely out of sight. With few exceptions, historians of race relations in Australia have shown little interest in public opinion and even less interest in the polls.[22] We take this to be a blind spot—one for which there is a cure.

Polling and Indigenous Issues

In Figure 1 (page 19), we have plotted the rise of polled opinion on Indigenous affairs as a commodity purchased by media organisations.[23] The graph shows a more or less steady rise from 1957 until 1987; a period of zero interest after the 1988 Bicentennial, reviving in 1992; a spectacular jump when the 'native title' debate took place in 1993; and two lesser spikes in media interest in 1997 and 2000, occasioned by the report on the 'Stolen Generations' and by the end of the Decade of Reconciliation.

There was a time when Indigenous affairs (back then, 'Aboriginal affairs') were determined by the interaction between governments and 'mobilised opinion' (churches, humanitarians, Aboriginal organisations, pastoralists' associations, petitioners, letter writers). When public intellectuals such as A. P. Elkin and W. E. H. Stanner wrote as advocates of reform in Indigenous policy, from the 1940s to the 1960s, they presented themselves as speaking for 'mobilised opinion', whose history they sometimes recounted as part of what they had to say. It was important to their authority, as they understood it, that they could present their ideas as products of an articulate movement among concerned citizens.

Such advocacy has sometimes achieved notable results. In the 1960s, 'mobilised opinion' persuaded the Government that a referendum was necessary largely without backup from 'respondent opinion'. By the end of 1965, the year in which the Menzies Government was persuaded to conduct the 1967 referendum on Commonwealth powers and on the terms for reckoning the numbers of the Australian population, only eighteen questions on Aboriginal affairs had ever been put to the Australian public by the country's sole national polling organisation, Roy Morgan's Gallup poll. Of these eighteen questions only three were in reference to the referendum. One simply asked respondents to predict the consequences of a 'Yes' vote, but did not ask them their opinion on the issues; the other two, in May 1965 and in December 1965, asked about 'including aboriginals in the census'.[24] The 'mobilised opinion' that persuaded Menzies to hold a referendum would have been able to cite poll evidence on Aborigines in the census to boost the argument for a referendum on deleting Section 127 from the Constitution, but there were no polls to test the popularity of the suggestion—made since 1910—that Aboriginal affairs be made a national government responsibility. That the Menzies Government agreed to a referendum on Section 51 (xxvi) as well as on Section 127 was a testament to the effectiveness of 'mobilised opinion'—in particular, the 'dogged campaigning' of the Federal Council for the Advancement of Aborigines and Torres Strait Islanders (FCAATSI).[25]

In the politics of Indigenous affairs, 'mobilised opinion' continues; there are still organised groups that petition, criticise and pressure governments, often from radically different points of view; for example, Australians for Native Title and Reconciliation (ANTAR), and the Bennelong Society. However, the rise of public opinion polling as a political technology has added 'respondent opinion' to the policy process. More and more 'respondent opinion' has been produced since Morgan Gallup asked the first question about Aboriginal affairs in February 1947, at a time that Paul Hasluck, a former Minister for Territories, later recalled as a 'reawakening' of interest in the 'social or racial problem'.[26] Thereafter, especially in recent times, Figure 1 understates the amount of polling about Indigenous issues; it shows only those items commissioned by media organisations, notably the press. It does not include the research for political parties, corporations and governments, some of which is sometimes made public. We estimate that the inclusion of such private polling in the graph would have made the upward curve both smoother and steeper.

Public opinion about Indigenous affairs nowadays is assumed to be 'respondent opinion'—precisely measurable polled opinion, or the more impressionistic opinion gathered through carefully constructed focus groups or via other techniques of a qualitative kind. The possibility that 'public opinion', in either of these senses, could be taken into account has meant, at times, that politicians have made sure that it *had* to be taken into account.

We can identify exactly when an Australian government first made it necessary for reformers in the field of Indigenous affairs to cite the support of 'respondent opinion': 1984–85. In Chapter 2 we examine how the Minister for Aboriginal Affairs, Clyde Holding, had to deal with a Prime Minister—Bob Hawke—who was hearing from Western Australia's Premier, Brian Burke, about Labor Party polling in Western Australia. The Western Australians' advice emphasised the risk to Federal Labor if it went ahead with a national Aboriginal land rights law that included the mining veto. To defend his original model, Holding sought funds for a pro-land rights media campaign. But the Hawke Cabinet decided that before it signed off on such a campaign the Department of Aboriginal Affairs should commission a survey of public attitudes. The firm the Department hired, Australian Nationwide Opinion Polls (ANOP), produced a report that included not only recommendations for a marketing campaign but also an analysis of the attitudes of what it called 'middle Australia'. Responding to leaks of poll results and to one another's leak-based news stories about 'public opinion', politicians and journalists promoted 'middle Australia' as a threat to be conquered. Whereas Holding, in 1983, had conceived his political task as finding a consensus between Aboriginal interests, mining interests and the State governments, based on some sort of compromise, by winter 1985 he and the Hawke Government imagined their task as persuading 'middle Australia' to accept land rights.

Never before in Indigenous affairs had a pollster's representation of 'public opinion' become so explicitly part of a government's reasoning about its policy intentions. When the Government—for whatever reasons—abandoned its national land rights policy, it included among its reasons a speculative narrative of the Australian public's disposition towards Aborigines and land rights. Public 'backlash' became an unquestioned part of the story that political actors told about the mid-1980s.

This sequence—from attending to 'mobilised opinion' to attending to 'respondent opinion'—was recapitulated in 1999–2000. The Council for Aboriginal Reconciliation had developed, by the second half of 1999, a procedure for public consultation that effectively engaged people who had become interested in the reconciliation process. However, the Council—encouraged by the Howard Government—judged that this process was not a sufficiently convincing way to produce an account of what the Australian public wanted. So they commissioned public opinion research, a combination of focus group and survey studies. The focus group study using non-Indigenous participants was leaked, almost certainly in pursuit of a political end, and an impression of 'public opinion' was quickly disseminated as a combination of politicians and journalists offered convergent readings of the 'facts' in the focus group report. The survey results soon followed—released and recounted as a portrait of the public. By March 2000, the Prime Minister and his critics were framing their observations about the politics of reconciliation with reference to what 'the Australian public' thought. 'Respondent opinion' had again displaced 'mobilised opinion'.

We are not saying that politicians, journalists and the public should take no notice of public opinion studies (though we wish that the limitations of focus group studies were more widely understood). Indeed, we think that public opinion studies can be valuable as evidence for the writing of the history of Australian political culture. However, the relevance of public opinion to the political process should not be taken as predetermined. And, to the extent that one does take public opinion to be relevant to the policy process, there are no rules for preferring 'mobilised' to 'respondent' opinion, or vice versa. That is, 'the public'—however represented—is a variable element in politics. Sometimes it is an excellent idea to make sure that a policy has strong public support; sometimes it hardly matters.

From the Referendum to 'Reconciliation'

Public interest in Indigenous issues since the 1940s has been stimulated by particular events, such as the calling of a referendum, the release of reports, and controversial judgments of the High Court. The need to find out what the public thinks has not been constant. Those who are concerned with the government of Australia can go for long periods without having to consider the relationship between their work and 'public opinion'. However, every now and then—though more 'now' than 'then'—'the public' enters into the calculations of politicians and political activists, and at these moments pollsters' research produces an account of 'the public' that politicians and political activists must somehow address.

For most of the last forty years Australians have been invited to recall the 1967 constitutional referendum as a high point in popular goodwill towards Indigenous Australians. By voting 'Yes' to two amendments to the Constitution, more than nine out of ten voters expressed inclusive and egalitarian sentiments towards Aborigines (a term that in that context included Torres Strait Islanders). In our first chapter we seek to show the texture of this popular feeling as revealed in a variety of academic surveys carried out variously by John Western, Ronald Taft and Lorna Lippmann, and in polls conducted by Morgan. Popular feeling, we argue, was not significantly shaped by official distinctions between Aborigines based on descent (half-caste, full-blood). What mattered, instead, was the distinction Australians made between extending 'political' inclusiveness to Indigenous Australians and maintaining a 'social' exclusiveness that kept Indigenous Australians at arm's length. That is, while Australians accepted that Aborigines were part of the Australian nation, with equal citizenship rights, they were much less accepting of the idea that Aborigines should share public space, and they mostly opposed the idea of Aborigines as marriage partners. Elkin's intuitive distinction, drawn years before the referendum, between *political assimilation* (proceeding rapidly, as an effect of assimilation policy) and *social assimilation* (inhibited by Aborigines, and non-Aborigines' perceptions of one another as alien) had proved valid.

One of the myths of the referendum has been that the vote was an expression of support for 'land rights', an issue just beginning to be politically significant at the time. There was no nationally based survey research on the popularity of land rights legislation until the 1980s. However, beginning with the Dunstan Government in South Australia in 1966 and continuing in the Northern Territory in 1975–76, under the Whitlam and Fraser Governments, under Tonkin in South Australia in 1981, Labor and non-Labor politicians assumed that land rights enjoyed support, as a just principle, among most Australians who cared enough to have an opinion about it. This comfortable assumption was called into question from 1983 to 1986, when the Hawke Government, asserting the power that the 1967 referendum had created, committed itself to legislating land rights for all States and Territories. Suddenly, 'land rights' was said to threaten both 'States' rights' and the prosperity of the mining industry, with the mining industry, the Western Australian Government and the Hawke Government deploying public opinion surveys as part of the political play.

The 1991 parliamentary commitment to reconciliation, like the parliamentary commitment to a 'Yes' vote in the 1967 referendum, enjoyed bipartisan support. Just as the 'Yes' vote of 1967 was without clear policy content, so 'reconciliation' was a popular and bipartisan idea in the 1990s only as long as its policy implications remained vague and open to diverse interpretations. The High Court made it more difficult to pursue a consensus-seeking approach to 'reconciliation' when it ruled, in June 1992, that many Indigenous Australians held 'native title'. Did the Court's controversial endorsement of Indigenous rights point the way for governments to give 'reconciliation' substance? Or would the public be turned off 'reconciliation' if it were defined as 'the Aboriginal agenda'? In the 1993 debate about how the Government should legislate on native title, 'public opinion' was a persistent news story. Much of the polling on native title, far from being disinterested, was research into the potential utility of hostile framings of native title. And one effect of the native title debate was that the meaning of 'reconciliation' became more clearly contested between those whose advocacy linked it with the recognition of Indigenous rights and those who argued that 'reconciliation' was being undermined by the persistence of Indigenous grievance.

The emergence of this contest is a theme of our fourth chapter, which draws heavily on unpublished market research commissioned by the Council for Aboriginal Reconciliation. In February 2000, parts of the press and the Prime Minister interpreted this research, which had been leaked to the press, as casting doubt on the willingness of the public to embrace 'reconciliation', especially its willingness to have the Prime Minister offer an apology to the 'Stolen Generations'. We question this interpretation. In particular, we argue that in the 1990s the struggle to define 'reconciliation' became a contest over the meanings of the term 'responsible'. The question of an 'apology', we argue, is best understood as but one instance of the contested implications of what it is to be 'responsible'.

1

The 1967 Referendum and the Politics of Inclusion

The 1967 referendum was an outstanding expression of public sentiment about Aborigines. Over 90 per cent of voters agreed to remove two clauses of the Constitution deemed to discriminate against Aborigines: the first, Section 51 (xxvi), that enabled the Parliament to make laws for '[t]he people of any race, other than the aboriginal race …'; and the second, Section 127, which stipulated that '[I]n reckoning the numbers of people of the Commonwealth … aboriginal natives shall not be counted'. The unanimity of opinion registered in this referendum was unprecedented, and nothing like it has been seen since.

Public opinion polling on the attitudes of Australians to Aborigines and to Aboriginal policy commenced in 1947 with a question about 'assimilation'. One way to understand the early research is to ask what it reveals about the public's approach to the policy of assimilation. While policy eras rarely terminate at a clearly defined moment, we will define the period 1947–70 as the era of assimilation policy. During this period Roy Morgan was the only pollster to produce polls, based on national samples, for the Australian press.[1] But alongside the Morgan polls were the early stirrings of sociologists and social psychologists committed to the techniques of survey research and interested in 'white' attitudes to Aborigines.

The data from the early polls and other studies, we argue, show the emergence of two distinct strands of public thinking about what was sometimes called 'the Aboriginal problem'. One strand dwelt on what Aborigines had in common with all other Australians; this strand was receptive to the argument that the entitlements of Aboriginal citizens were, or should become, equal to the entitlements of all Australian citizens. The other strand of thinking dwelt on the differences between Aborigines and other Australians. The two strands co-existed. There are several ways of naming the two, and more than one way of evaluating their implications. The interplay of one discourse, around sameness or universality, with the other discourse, around difference, was made complex by the ways in which both styles of thinking remained relevant to Australians concerned with the issues raised by assimilation.

Assimilation: From Difference to Sameness

It is best to distinguish 'assimilation' as a *doctrine* about the sameness and permissible differences within a national population, from 'assimilation' as a diverse array of *governmental practices* aimed at people whose difference is understood to be a 'problem'.[2] In this book we are concerned with assimilation as a doctrine; we will only refer to the assimilation practices of governments or missions when we need to make sense of a particular question about them in an opinion poll or survey.

The classic formulation of assimilation as a doctrine is the formulation to which a Commonwealth–States conference of ministers, the Native Welfare Conference, agreed in January 1961:

The policy of assimilation means in the view of all Australian governments that all aborigines and part-aborigines are expected eventually to attain the same manner of living as other Australians and to live as members of a single Australian community enjoying the same rights and privileges, accepting the same responsibilities, observing the same customs and influenced by the same beliefs, hopes and loyalties as other Australians. Thus, any special measures taken for aborigines and part-aborigines are regarded as temporary measures not based on colour but intended to meet their need for special care and assistance to protect them from any ill effects of sudden change and to assist them to make the transition from one stage to another in such a way as will be favourable to their future social, economic and political advancement.[3]

The statement combines the notions of 'sameness' and 'difference' in a particular way: the difference between Aborigines and 'other Australians' is a residual and temporary condition, for Aborigines will eventually become the 'same'. The same as what? The doctrine is silent on what 'manner of living' is typical of other Australians. But whatever that 'manner of living', departures from it by Aborigines were to be tolerated only as long as those departures would eventually cease. To be Aboriginal was a condition to be remedied over time and by authoritative guidance. Government policies and community effort would assist all Aboriginal people to change, notwithstanding that Aborigines would change at speeds that varied according to region, descent and historical experience.

It is widely agreed, among historians and others, that this philosophy was promoted successfully from the late 1930s not only by politicians, intellectuals, and church personnel, but also by many Aborigines and Torres Strait Islanders, until it became, in the 1950s, the driver of all Australian governments' policies. Until the 1940s, the heritage of over 150 years of law and administration had seen the substantial abridgment of

Aborigines' citizenship rights. The task of assimilation was to endow Aborigines with the capacities that would make it no longer necessary to discriminate against them. That much was widely agreed. If in the cause of 'assimilation' some government interventions in the lives of Aborigines were controversial, this was because the practical implications of the doctrine were open to debate.

For example, the practice of child removal: did 'assimilation' warrant the continuation of this practice, or was child removal one of the discriminatory policies that promoters of 'assimilation' would seek to abolish? One historian of child removal, Anna Haebich, has shown that although the public had long regarded the removal of Aboriginal children from their families and their placement in institutions and foster families as 'normal', the critics of this practice became influential in the 1950s 'as a response by federal and state governments to both international pressures ... to abandon race-based discriminatory policies, and to mounting political action by Aboriginal people and their supporters demanding citizenship rights'.[4] If we accept that the goal of 'assimilation' was equality of citizenship, then we can credit 'assimilation' with assisting this challenge to child removal.

Assimilation was an ideological framework in which practices of discrimination were open to question. Other discriminatory policies, too, were reviewed critically in the name of Aborigines' 'citizenship'. From the 1950s to the 1970s, in every jurisdiction, legislative and policy reform gradually standardised the citizenship entitlements of Aboriginal Australians. Assimilation, understood as an assault on discrimination, was a popular and progressive cause.

If, as we will demonstrate, the Australian public's approach to 'assimilation' has never been simple, the dilemmas of the doctrine of 'assimilation' must bear much of the blame. Our reading of public opinion studies conducted from 1947 to 1970 shows that those who conducted these studies employed a variety of vocabularies for naming what made Aborigines 'different', and they deployed a number of ways to evoke the 'sameness' or equality Aborigines shared with other Australians. 'Difference' could be evoked as a matter of morality, way of life, culture or race. Some kinds of Aborigines ('full-blood') could be understood to be more different from Australians than other Aborigines ('part-Aborigines'). Equality could be evoked by reference to entitlement, responsibility or humanity. Our key point is the persistence in the construction of public opinion of two parallel themes—equality and difference.

From Blood to Capacity

Until the 1960s, Australians had learnt from legal statute and government policy not to think of Aborigines as enjoying any kind of collective entitlement. Instead, Australians were invited to consider Aborigines as both a different race and a differentiated population—one with no distinctive entitlements or needs. Their only general entitlement was to be admitted, eventually, to the full rights of individual citizenship.

Australians made two kinds of distinctions among Aborigines. One involved distinctions in terms of descent. The other distinguished among Aborigines according to whether or not they had become 'civilised' or remained 'tribal'. Often these two distinctions were conflated: in official and in popular thought there has been a deep heritage of equating 'social conditions with racial origin'.[5] This facile calibration of descent with way of life was embedded in official thought and practice when governments began to enumerate the Aboriginal population as 'full-blood' or 'half-caste' in the late nineteenth century, a practice reflected in the Census enumeration prior to 1967.[6] For much of the twentieth century, governments treated 'blood' or 'descent' as if it were a reliable guide to a person's character, and public attitudes often followed this distinction.

However, because it was possible not to equate 'blood' or 'descent' strictly with 'way of life' there was sometimes a tension within the way Australians thought about descent. How important was it? On the one hand, 'half-castes' seemed to have a lot in common with 'full-bloods'. At times governments defined 'half-castes' loosely to include anyone of Aboriginal descent; 'half-castes' were classed as 'Aboriginal', and it was assumed that their tendency to associate and to intermarry with 'full-bloods' confirmed—for better or for worse—their Aboriginal heritage. A reader could still find this emphasis on the common Aboriginal heritage of 'full-bloods' and 'half-castes' in a book by an 'expert' published in 1961: J. W. Bleakley, Queensland's Chief Protector and Director of Native Affairs from 1914 to 1942, wrote of the 'hereditary Aboriginal temperament' that it was 'often likely to assert itself, even where the person has been brought up in infancy amongst whites or rescued from the degrading atmosphere of camp life'. 'With this type', he added, 'it was not so much a matter of the colour of the skin as the colour of the mind'.[7]

On the other hand, the tendency to include 'full-blood' and 'half-caste' as 'Aboriginal' (sometimes the legal term was 'native') was increasingly vulnerable to the thought that half-castes were different because they had a different genetic potential and/or enjoyed the benign influence of a non-Aboriginal parent. Legislators recognised that a half-caste might cease to be 'Aboriginal' by ending his or her associations with other 'Aboriginals' and by living like a 'white man'. In the 1930s and 1940s, most Australian jurisdictions amended their laws to grant exemption to such people. From the point of view of constitutional law, 'half-castes' were not 'Aborigines'. The Attorney-General had consistently advised the Commonwealth Statistician and the Chief Electoral Officer that 'Aboriginal native' in the Constitution did not refer to half-castes.[8] In the 1940s, 'half-castes' in the Northern Territory mobilised to demand that they no longer be covered by the Commonwealth's laws regulating Aborigines: as a category they saw themselves as deserving of citizenship.[9] The

Commonwealth revised its Northern Territory legislation in 1953 so as to confirm what had become customary in Territory law enforcement: that 'half-castes' were not to suffer the abridgment of citizenship that would continue to apply to 'wards' (effectively, 'full-bloods').[10] In these and in other ways, the idea that a 'half-caste' was much closer than a 'full-blood' to being a citizen was reinforced.

The Morgan poll explicitly tested the significance of the 'full-blood'/'half-caste' distinction in October 1954 by asking respondents whether they thought 'half-castes should be treated as full blooded Aborigines or as white people'. One-third (35 per cent) refused to answer the question on its own terms, most being recorded as 'undecided' (20 per cent) or as offering 'no response' (3 per cent), and the others (12 per cent) apparently saying 'neither'. But most (65 per cent) answered as if they found the 'full-blood'/'half-caste' distinction relevant, for they were willing to answer in the terms that Morgan had set. Most (52 per cent) thought that 'half-castes' should be treated like 'white people'. Relatively few (13 per cent) wanted 'half-castes' treated like 'full-bloods' and therefore treated differently.[11]

'Assimilation'—as both principle and policy—helped to undermine racial determinism. Advocates of 'assimilation' drew attention to the ways that experience determined a person's capacities. When A. P. Elkin recommended a national Aboriginal citizenship policy in 1944, he illustrated the transition from one way of thinking to the other. Among 'full-bloods', Elkin differentiated between 'the incurably nomadic full-bloods' and 'full-blood children and young adults'. As his language implied, he did not propose that any educational effort be applied to 'incurably nomadic full-bloods', but the lives of the young could be transformed by settling them on government or mission stations. There they would be educated 'in the "how" and "why" of all new activities; in the "three R's"; in moral and social life; and in health and hygiene'. He offered this age-differentiated prescription for 'Aborigines of mixed-blood in isolated regions'.[12] Aboriginal people of 'isolated regions' had much in common, notwithstanding that some were 'full-blood' and others 'mixed', because of their isolation from the main social and economic institutions of Australia. So if we take Elkin as exemplary of the progressive thinking behind assimilation policy in the post-war era, we can see economic and social factors beginning to rival racial factors as the supposed determinants of Aborigines' ability to integrate into Australian society.

Although Elkin wrote as if he would treat all Aborigines from isolated regions in the same way, he was not ready to abandon all consideration of descent: 'the advance [of Aborigines of mixed-blood in isolated regions] might be more rapid', he conceded.[13] Thus, in 1944, Elkin equivocated about the importance of interbreeding: to effect a program of assimilation it was desirable, but certainly not essential, that Aborigines interbreed with Europeans, for people of any descent could be trained in the ways of citizenship.

Elkin continued to pay attention to differences of descent, but later he attached a different significance to them. In the 1964 edition of *The Australian Aborigines*, he conveyed the latest research about Aboriginal 'colour and caste'. He noted that Aborigines classed as 'quadroon-three eighths' degree of Aboriginal descent were tending to intermarry, rather than marry Europeans and produce children even 'whiter' than themselves.[14] However, this was significant to Elkin not because he himself thought that Aborigines' capacities could be measured according to how 'white' they were in descent. Rather, he attributed this idea to *others*. Australians, he suggested, generally thought intermarriage (or miscegenation) promoted 'assimilation'.

It has been forgotten that, perceptively, Elkin distinguished four kinds of assimilation—economic, political, social and religious. In 1964 it was 'social assimilation', with its litmus test of intermarriage, that particularly concerned him. He argued that this could be eased or inhibited according to the degree to which Aborigines differed 'in appearance and some customs'. It worried him that Aborigines of mixed descent were identifying as Aborigines rather than losing that identity as, generation by generation, they interbred with Europeans. Their Aboriginal identity was inhibiting their moral development: they were continuing to feel aggrieved as 'Aborigines', and 'only very slowly do they learn that rights imply responsibilities'.[15]

The trajectory of Elkin's thought illustrates how the language of descent (half-caste/full-blood) could persist in Australian consciousness while changing its significance. 'Colour' and descent were no longer thought *by social scientists* to determine behaviour, but they were *popularly* perceived as important characteristics of individuals and groups. Elkin worried that both European and Aboriginal Australians were remaining caste- and colour-conscious. 'Social assimilation' required that an increasing number of Europeans would have children with people of Aboriginal descent. Their progeny would be increasingly 'white'. Colour prejudice—on both sides—seemed to have set limits to that process.

Against this background of scientific and (inferred) popular thinking about the racial aspects of 'assimilation', we can consider those post-war polls that used 'full-blood' and 'half-caste' in their questions. Were Australians less confronted by a 'whiter' Aboriginal person? Were people of mixed descent more easily welcomed as friends and neighbours?

Degrees of Descent and Social Acceptability

In 1965, social psychologist Ronald Taft set out to discover what sort of 'social distance' non-Aboriginal people living in Perth wanted to maintain between themselves and Aborigines. To that end he asked 186 respondents in Perth whether, according to their 'first feelings', they 'would willingly admit' either 'part-Aborigines' or 'full-blood'—considered 'as a class and not just as the best or worst ones you have known'—to various social situations or 'classifications' (see Table 1.1). His results show a consistent favouring of 'part-Aborigines' over 'full-bloods'; but the gap (8–19 percentage points) is not large.[16]

Table 1.1 Social-distance scale, Western Australia, 1965 (percentages)

Question

'According to my first feelings I would willingly admit members of each of the following groups (consider them as a class and not just the best or the worst ones you have known) to one or more of the classifications below.'

	Part-Aborigines			Full-bloods		
	Perth	**Big-town**	**Small-town**	**Perth**	**Big-town**	**Small-town**
A relative by *marriage* if of the right religion	35	24	20	24	14	10
A family *friend*	76	76	64	62	61	56
To *eat* at the same table as me in a café	81	82	82	62	80	60
To *serve food* to me in a café	83	74	74	66	76	58
To be one of my *neighbours*	78	62	80	63	64	66
To *work* alongside me in a shop	88	84	92	79	84	74
To *serve* me in a shop	85	84	86	75	84	76
To *live* in my part of WA	90	94	96	82	96	92
n	(186)	(50)	(50)	(186)	(50)	(50)

Sample: Perth, Bigtown (Narrogin, WA) and Smalltown (York, WA); male householders or their wives; interviewed face-to-face.

n = number of respondents

Source: Taft, 'Attitudes of Western Australians Towards Aborigines', pp. 11, 56.

The Taft study also involved 100 other respondents from Western Australia, fifty from 'Smalltown' (York) and fifty from 'Bigtown' (Narrogin). The Smalltown respondents followed the Perth pattern: they preferred associations with 'part-Aborigines' to associations with 'full-bloods'. The Bigtowners, by contrast, mostly did not. Only in their feelings about 'relative by marriage' (a difference of 10 percentage points between 'part-Aborigines' and 'full-bloods') and about 'family friend' (15 percentage points) did they distinguish 'part-Aborigines' from 'full-bloods'. The Bigtowners did not discriminate in favour of 'part-Aborigines' when asked about eating 'at the same table as me in a café', serving 'food to me in a café', working 'alongside me on my job', serving 'me in a shop', being 'one of my neighbours' or living 'in my part of Western Australia'. What is striking about Taft's results is the differences in the proportions that would accept Aborigines as relatives by marriage (a minority) and the proportions that would accept Aborigines in less intimate situations (the majority).

Interviewing in 1969–70, after the referendum, in two Victorian and two New South Wales towns, Lorna Lippmann also asked questions about 'social distance' that differentiated 'part-Aborigines' from 'Aborigines'. And she asked about the same range of situations (except that instead of asking about living 'in my part of Western Australia' she asked about living 'in my town'). In each town she interviewed fifty people. Because Lippmann presented her results in the form of a graph, without giving the percentages, we cannot make a precise comparison with Taft's results. However, her results are consistent with those for Perth and 'Smalltown': 'part-Aborigines' were favoured over 'Aborigines' ('full-bloods'), but with relatively small differences (2–10 percentage points). And, as with Taft, Aborigines (both kinds) were much less widely accepted (25–45 per cent) across the four towns as relatives by marriage than Aborigines in the seven less intimate contexts (75–90 per cent).[17]

From these results we can draw three conclusions about attitudes to mixing with Aborigines in the second half of the 1960s: first, by a slight margin, respondents favoured 'part-Aborigines' over 'full-bloods'; second, by substantial majorities, they rejected the idea of an Aboriginal person marrying into their family; but third, they overwhelmingly accepted the idea of less intimate relationships with Aborigines. By far the biggest distinction that respondents made was not a distinction based on considerations of descent, but a distinction between more intimate and less intimate forms of association, between having an Aboriginal person ('full-blood' or 'half-caste') marry into one's family and having an Aboriginal person ('full-blood' or 'half-caste') as a friend, neighbour, work colleague, café/restaurant worker or shop assistant.[18] We can put this another way. Out of every three respondents willing to accept social contact with Aborigines as friends, neighbours or in forms of impersonal encounter, only one would also go so far as to countenance an Aboriginal person as a relative by marriage. The Taft and Lippmann results suggest that most Australians were making a distinction between the inclusiveness of society at large and the exclusiveness of their own family. In this sense, there was indeed a 'social colour-bar' in the 1960s.[19]

What perceived features of Aborigines might have made them undesirable members of one's family? Another question that Taft asked in 1965 throws some light on this. He presented respondents with twenty-one antonyms ('trustworthy/untrustworthy', 'sensible with money/wasteful with money', and so on) and asked: 'Of each of the following pairs of descriptions, underline the *one* which you consider applies more than the other to the Aborigines and part-Aborigines in your district. If you really feel that both members of a pair apply equally, then underline both.' The most frequently chosen qualities of Aborigines included 'make good parents' (28 per cent of Perth respondents, 24 per cent of Smalltown respondents)—a result that helps explain why critics of child removal were gaining political ground in the 1960s.[20] However, the other relatively high-frequency answers were negative: Aborigines were 'wasteful with money' (Perth 34 per cent, Smalltown 54 per cent, Bigtown 62 per cent), 'lazy' (Perth 32 per cent, Smalltown 30 per cent, Bigtown 58 per cent), 'unambitious' (Perth 27 per cent, Smalltown 36 per cent, Bigtown 34 per cent), and 'dirty and slovenly' (Perth 22 per cent, Smalltown 26 per cent, Bigtown 30 per cent).[21] Taft's findings were particularly disturbing when one considers that he offered respondents twenty-one 'positive' adjectives, but apart from 'good parenting' they were not frequently endorsed.

Taft 'required' his respondents to attribute general qualities to 'Aborigines and part-Aborigines', so his research does not reveal how many respondents found it difficult to generalise—positively or negatively—about this category of Australian.[22] But how willing were Australians to generalise? In another set of surveys conducted in 1965, sociologist John Western asked two groups of respondents, drawn from Canberra and the New South Wales country town of Condobolin, to say whether they agreed or disagreed with the proposition that 'There may be a few exceptions, but in general Aborigines are pretty much alike'. In Canberra, where 58 per cent of respondents disagreed, he found widespread resistance to the idea that one could generalise. However, in Condobolin the same proportion agreed that 'in general Aborigines are pretty much alike'.[23]

When Lippmann conducted her interviews, she did not assume that people stereotyped Aborigines. Rather, she noted the proportion of respondents who 'mentioned attributes which they considered characteristic of Aborigines in general'. Fifty-two per cent made an unsolicited generalisation: all were negative. Some 24 per cent of her interviewees saw Aborigines as typically 'dirty', 15 per cent saw them as 'drunken' and 'irresponsible', and 10 per cent as 'inferior'.[24]

Can we say that Australians were prejudiced against Aborigines in the 1960s? The results of these three studies do not converge on one answer. Taft's methodology required stereotyping; Lippmann's did not. Of Taft and Lippmann, which is the better guide to Australians' attitudes in the latter part of the 1960s? We can report Lippmann's results in at least three ways: she found no evidence of the positive stereotyping of Aborigines (whereas Taft found some); she found that the willingness to stereotype was a feature only of people with negative views of Aborigines, about half her sample; but she did not make clear whether her stereotypers failed to distinguish between 'part-Aborigines' and 'Aborigines' or whether she simply failed to report it when they did. Western asked people if generalisation (stereotyping) was possible, and many said it was not.

At the time of the 1967 referendum, with its affirmation of inclusiveness, the Australian public appears to have been 'inclusive' in the following ways. In thinking about Aborigines, it did not necessarily distinguish between 'part-Aboriginal' and 'full-blood'; when it made this distinction it only marginally preferred 'part-Aboriginal' to 'full-blood'. While many Australians rejected stereotypes, an equally large proportion subscribed to stereotypes about Aborigines—most of them negative. Australians were inclusive of Aborigines when it came to public spaces and impersonal association but generally drew the line at sharing intimate spaces and forming close family associations.[25] The 'inclusiveness' expressed in the 1967 referendum was not only unspecific about the policies that would bring about inclusiveness; it was also 'inclusive' in abstract and impersonal terms, the terms of a common citizenship, not shared kinship.

Advances in Political Assimilation

In 1964, Elkin contrasted 'political assimilation', which he thought had recently been rapid, and 'social assimilation', which he judged was still slow.[26] If by 'social assimilation' Elkin included intermarriage, the Taft and Lippmann studies on social distance in the mid- and late 1960s support Elkin's view that social assimilation was not as far advanced as he might have wished; only a minority in any study thought that they would like an Aboriginal person to marry into their family. What about 'political assimilation'? Are there studies that show public support for its rapid advance? We can start with a study that measured people's awareness of the defects in Aborigines' citizenship entitlements.

When Western studied attitudes and opinions in Canberra and Condobolin, he measured agreement or disagreement with ten statements about the position and status of Aborigines; the recorded responses to these 'factual statements' demonstrate the unevenness of people's knowledge about the laws restricting the citizenship of Aboriginal people. Western's results, while showing the residents of Canberra as better informed than those living in Condobolin, suggest that Australians were not well informed about the position and status of Aborigines. In order to make our point about the extent of ignorance, we restrict our reporting of his findings to the better informed, the respondents drawn from Canberra. (The proportion that got the answers right is in brackets.)

Responding to the following *true* statements, the majority said they did not know or thought the statement must be false:

> 'In some States Australian half-caste Aborigines do not have full citizenship rights.' (45 per cent)

> 'In some States there are literacy tests which Aborigines have to pass before they are entitled to certain rights.' (34 per cent)

> 'In some States control is exercised over how Aborigines spend their wages.' (41 per cent)

Responding to the following *false* statements, the majority thought them true or admitted that they did not know:

'There are no restrictions imposed on the buying of land by Aborigines.' (38 per cent)

'Aborigines living on Reserves are free to leave when they wish.' (29 per cent)

'There are no restrictions imposed on the land which the Welfare Board may buy for Aboriginal settlements.' (38 per cent)

At the same time Western found that the large majority were well enough informed to declare correctly that the following propositions were *false*:

'All Australian full-blood Aborigines have full citizenship rights.' (73 per cent)

'Aboriginal workers are paid wages equal to those of white people doing the same work.' (72 per cent)

'Aborigines have the right to vote in State and Federal elections.' (66 per cent)

'All Aborigines have the right (by law) to drink in any Australian hotel.' (63 per cent)

Western's work shows that among relatively concerned and knowledgeable citizens (such as Canberra residents) the following defects in Aborigines' citizenship entitlements were well known by 1965: discrimination against 'full-bloods', and a lack of equal rights to receive award wages, vote, and drink in an hotel.[27] Each of these three inequalities had been the subject of discussion and legislative change in the early 1960s.

The Franchise

In 1961, domestic and international criticism of Australia's discriminatory laws stimulated a House of Representatives Select Committee to review the voting rights of Aborigines. In keeping with the increasingly respected theory that ability was not determined by race, the Committee made no use of the language of 'caste' or 'descent' when prescribing the future distribution of the right to vote. Instead the report was imbued with the idea of citizenship as a set of capacities that a person of any racial origin could be taught. It was on safe ground as far as public opinion was concerned. Asked by Morgan, in October 1954, whether 'an Aboriginal' with 'the same upbringing as you ... could have learnt to do your work, or not?' 90 per cent of respondents answered 'yes'.[28] Not so great a majority (70 per cent in Perth, 63 per cent in the two country towns) agreed with a proposition that Taft put to them in 1965 that 'if Aborigines really had equal opportunities with Whites they would be able to hold their own in every way'.[29]

The Committee acknowledged that distinctions of descent, up till then, had affected the Commonwealth's thinking about the franchise. The Commonwealth Electoral Officer had been obliged to accept the enrolment of any person of Aboriginal descent as long as he or she was not an 'aboriginal native'. As defined by the Attorney-General in 1929, an 'aboriginal native' was a person in whom 'aboriginal descent preponderates'. 'Half-castes', on this definition, were not 'aboriginal natives' so they should have been allowed to enrol. However, the traditions of Aboriginal administration had not honoured the Attorney-General's rule: many people of Aboriginal descent who were entitled to vote were not yet voting. 'Thousands of [half-castes or less] in Queensland and Western Australia', the Committee observed, 'who are already integrated into the community and are not living in the tribal state, have the right to be enrolled and to vote at Commonwealth elections but are not aware of that fact'. The Committee believed that in New South Wales many people of Aboriginal descent were excluded as well.[30]

There were various courses of corrective action open to a government whose policy was that 'the aboriginal people ... be gradually integrated into the European community'.[31] The least adventurous option would have been to correct the existing anomaly: to urge the electoral authorities to follow the Attorney-General's narrow definition of 'aboriginal' and continue to exclude them, while reaching out to enrol the people of Aboriginal descent who, in the Government's judgment, were integrated into the community. The most adventurous option would have been to make enrolment for voting in Federal elections compulsory for all adults whatever their degree of Aboriginal descent, and to give the State and Commonwealth electoral officials the resources to educate all newly enrolled Aborigines about the common duty of Australian adults to participate in elections. The middle way recommended by the Committee was to allow, but not require, such enrolment by any Aboriginal adult.

> That the right to vote at Commonwealth elections be accorded to all aboriginal and Torres Strait Islander subjects of the Queen, of voting age, permanently residing within the limits of the Commonwealth.
>
> That, for the time being, the enrolment of aborigines and Torres Strait Islanders be voluntary, but when enrolled, compulsory voting be enforced.[32]

Suggesting that enrolment be optional, recognised that in some regions (the Committee mentioned the north-western part of South Australia) Aboriginal people were 'primitive, illiterate, nomadic, periodically nomadic, or associated only loosely or periodically with missions, or with government agencies for native welfare'.[33] The electoral law in South Australia said that these people were entitled to enrol, but State authorities did not seek to enrol people for whom voting was an unknown or meaningless practice. There was an arguable case, in other words, for limiting enrolment on the basis of Aboriginal citizens' *functional characteristics*, including, most importantly, their interest. The Committee recommended that 'the proce-dures of voting and the structure of the Parliament be explained to aborigines on government settlements and on missions and other convenient locations. In this connection well-prepared visual aids and publications would be helpful.' While acknowledging the relevance of 'capacity', the Committee advocated a non-judgmental approach to it. The Committee 'dismissed proposed tests of literacy, housing standards, permanency of employment or the possession of a bank balance, on the ground that they are not applicable to the electorate at large'. Electoral officials were recommended to help any Aboriginal person complete an enrolment card upon their 'voluntary expression of a wish to enrol'. As the Committee explained, it was 'better that a right be granted before there is a full capacity to exercise it on the part of some individuals, than that others should suffer the frustration of being denied a right that they can clearly exercise'.[34]

In acknowledging that not all Aborigines possessed the same capacities for citizenship, the Committee did not find it necessary to use the language of 'blood' or descent. In promoting a non-racial vision of the Australian political community was the Committee in advance of public opinion, in step with it, or lagging behind? Should the reformers of the franchise have paid more attention to 'blood'?

When asking about the franchise, Morgan did not differentiate between 'full-bloods' and 'half-castes' as potential voters. In October 1954, he asked 'do you think Aborigines should or should not have the right to vote at Federal elections?'. One can only wonder what respondents thought the term 'Aborigines' referred to: did it include all persons of any degree of Aboriginal descent or just those known as 'full-bloods'? Since both the narrow constitutional and the wider understanding of the term 'Aborigines' include 'full-bloods' it is significant that only 15 per cent said that Aborigines should not have the right; 77 per cent said they should.[35] In November 1961, after the Select Committee had recommended that all Aborigines be allowed to enrol, but not be compelled, Morgan again asked whether 'all Australian Aboriginals should or should not be given the right to vote at Federal elections?'.

Now, however, twice as many (30 per cent) were against that reform. Perhaps the word 'all' had made a difference. It may be, too, that public debate about enfranchising Aborigines had helped to increase opposition to it.[36] The reform was nonetheless popular, nearly two-thirds (64 per cent) of respondents supporting it.

When Taft administered a 'civil rights questionnaire' in 1965, he included two propositions about the right to vote. In response to one, he found that only 58 per cent of Perth respondents agreed that 'All Aborigines should have the right to vote for Parliament, whether they are citizens or not'. It is difficult to know what respondents made of the idea that some Aborigines were not necessarily citizens, but perhaps 'citizen' here referred to their recognised capacities. If that were so, then the level of agreement was still quite high: the majority were not in favour of placing any test of functional capacity on the right of Aborigines to vote. The second question can also be interpreted as raising the question of 'capacity'. The committee had recommended that Aborigines not be compelled to vote, but 84 per cent of Taft's Perth respondents thought that 'As long as it is compulsory for Australian citizens to vote, so should it be for all Aborigines who are citizens'.[37] Citizenship, to those who endorsed the statement, evidently implied a common and universal obligation. Still, there were some (16 per cent) who, like the Committee, were prepared to make a concession to Aboriginal differences—or else did not want Aborigines voting at all.

Western measured support for Aborigines' voting by asking respondents from Canberra and Condobolin whether they agreed or disagreed with the statement: 'I have nothing against people of another culture but allowing Aborigines to vote and to drink in public places is going a little too far'. The measure was hardly ideal: respondents opposed to one but not the other might have been unsure what to do. Nonetheless, opposition to the statement was almost unanimous. In Canberra, 85 per cent disagreed; in Condobolin, 82 per cent disagreed.[38]

In short, in the 1950s and 1960s there appears to have been wide support for the enfranchisement of Aborigines.

Citizenship and Alcohol

In choosing to link voting and drinking, Western followed a widespread view that a common set of citizenship capacities underlay the successful performance of both. The House of Representatives Committee, while noting that many Australians linked the right to vote with the right to drink, rejected this link.

> Your Committee considers that the Commonwealth Parliament should refuse to involve [sic] its franchise, in any State or Territory, on a concept of rights which are determined in part by an assessment of a person's fitness to consume alcoholic drinks. Your Committee does not question, in any way, the justification of State and Territory liquor laws but merely asserts that they have no bearing on an entitlement to the Commonwealth franchise.[39]

Morgan's questions about the regulation of Aborigines' access to liquor illustrate a division in the public over the extent to which considerations of cultural difference affected judgments of citizens' responsibilities as drinkers. In October 1958, Morgan asked respondents whether they had 'read or hear[d] about the six months gaol sentence' Namatjira had received 'for giving liquor to another aboriginal'. Virtually all (95 per cent) of those interviewed said they had, 'the widest spread of a news item ever recorded by the Australian Gallup poll'. Namatjira, respondents were told, had been 'given full citizenship two years ago, and there's a penalty of at least six months gaol for a citizen who supplies liquor to an Aboriginal'. Did they 'think', therefore, 'that law should or should not apply to Namatjira?'

Behind the question was an argument that, as an Aboriginal person, Namatjira was subject to contradictory obligations: the customs of kinship and the white man's law. A bare majority (50 per cent) said the law should apply to him, 36 per cent said it should not, and 16 per cent were undecided.[40]

Here is a good example of the tension between understanding Aborigines in the framework of an equalising discourse—in which citizenship entitlement implied a common responsibility to uphold the law, no matter who the citizen was—and a differentiating discourse that recognised the relevance of Namatjira's tribal affiliations to those to whom he supplied the liquor: culture as extenuating circumstance. The same issue—whether the law on supplying liquor should be applied differently to culturally different citizens—was canvassed again by Morgan in February 1960. Respondents were told that '[u]nder Northern Territory law, both white men and Aboriginal citizens must be sent to gaol for at least six months if convicted of giving drink to Aboriginals who are not citizens'. Morgan then asked whether respondents 'approve[d] that, or should the court have the power to impose lighter sentences on Aboriginal citizens for giving drink to Aboriginals who are not citizens?' The majority (58 per cent) wanted to give the court discretionary power; only one-quarter (26 per cent) did not. The difficulty of the issue was again measured in the high (17 per cent) proportion 'undecided'.[41] In December, Morgan's question specified a type of Aborigine: 'Do you think full-blooded Aboriginals should or should not be allowed to buy beer and other alcoholic drinks, the same as other people?' A bare majority (51 per cent) supported Aborigines' right of access. One in three respondents (35 per cent) was opposed. And again, the 'undecided' (14 per cent) were relatively numerous—certainly compared with those 'undecided' about the right to vote.[42]

Segregation

One way to think about citizenship rights is to presume that all citizens have the same rights of access to public spaces. The laws that 'assimilation' was dedicated to amending included restrictions on where Aborigines could go. For example, some statutes had given Ministers and Chief Protectors powers to restrict Aborigines' access to towns and to order an Aboriginal person to live on a 'reserve'. Even as these powers were repealed, an informal structure of restrictions remained. Autobiographies of Aboriginal people able to recall the 1950s tell of managers who partitioned their cinemas so that whites sat with whites and blacks with blacks. J. H. Bell, Malcolm Calley, Ruth Fink, Marie Reay and Charles Rowley document local practices in the 1950s and/or 1960s designed to maintain segregated clothes shops, cafés and hairdressers as well as housing, hospitals and schools, while the 'Freedom Rides' of 1965 and beyond targeted customary restrictions on Aborigines' entry into municipal swimming pools.[43] Customary segregation paralleled and, in some parts of Australia, outlived statutory segregation.

What did Australians think of segregation? Taft's surveys in Western Australia reveal some support for it. Again, some respondents differentiated between 'full-blood' Aborigines and 'part-Aborigines'. Half (52 per cent) of the Perth respondents favoured the segregation of at least one of the spaces nominated by the poll (see Table 1.2). More than one-quarter nominated hotels (29 per cent), public toilets (28 per cent) and bars (27 per cent); one in five nominated swimming pools (22 per cent); and one in six or seven nominated public dances (16 per cent) or cafés (15 per cent).

The pattern is broadly consistent with the responses noted earlier in relation to questions of social distance (Table 1.1). If we average the social distance responses in the Perth sample to 'full-bloods' and 'part-Aborigines', the proportion of respondents rejecting the idea of Aborigines eating 'at same table as me in a café' was 29 per cent, the proportion rejecting the idea of Aborigines serving 'food to me in a café' was 26 per cent, and the proportion rejecting the idea of Aborigines serving 'me in a shop' was 20 per cent. That is, the proportions in favour of these forms of segregation was roughly halfway between the higher percentage favouring social distance from 'full-bloods' and the lower percentage favouring social distance from 'part-Aborigines'. One might have expected a higher percentage of the respondents to want cafés or public dances segregated. But

Table 1.2 Support for segregation, Western Australia, 1965 (percentages)

Question

'Tick any of the following in which you consider Aborigines should be kept separated from white people.'

	Perth#	Bigtown	Smalltown
Residential hotels	29	36	50
Hotel bars	27	30	46
Public toilets	28	38	34
Swimming pools	22	28	26
Public dances	16	26	20
Picture theatres	★	22	22
Cafés	15	★	★
Total for some segregation	52	54	70
Average number of places chosen	1.95	2.54	2.44
n	(186)	(50)	(50)

Notes: The following, potential sites of segregation, less widely supported, are not listed: at sporting events (e.g. races, football); in public transport (e.g. trains); schools and kindergartens; infant health centres; post offices; parks; and church seating.

★ Figures not published, but less than 15 per cent.

The Perth list included hospitals and social clubs, and also invited respondents to add other places to the list.

Sample: as for Table 1.1

n = number of respondents

Source: Taft, 'Attitudes of Western Australians Towards Aborigines', pp. 13, 56.

the range suggests that those who wanted segregation were selective. Sites where people consumed alcohol, or sites of relative intimacy (public toilets, followed by swimming pools), were of more concern than sites where alcohol was not available or contact was not as close. A tendency to 'drunkenness' and to be 'dirty and slovenly', Taft's study showed, were among the more popular fears about Aborigines.[44]

In Bigtown and Smalltown the relationship between the approval of segregation and the expressed desire for social distance was not as strong. Generally, respondents from these towns were more in favour of segregation than their expressed views on social distance might have led one to expect. In Bigtown 38 per cent wanted public toilets segregated, 36 per cent wanted residential hotels segregated and 30 per cent wanted hotel bars segregated; but only 19 per cent, on average, said they would not like to eat at the same table as Aborigines, only one-quarter (25 per cent) disdained being served food by an Aborigine, and only 16 per cent objected to Aborigines serving 'me in a shop'. However, support for segregation did correlate with concern about Aborigines being 'drunken' (32 per cent) or 'dirty and slovenly' (30 per cent).

In Smalltown no fewer than 70 per cent of the respondents favoured segregation of some kind; especially notable was the level of support for segregating residential hotels (50 per cent favoured this) and hotel bars (46 per cent). But support for the social distance measures was hardly commensurate: the proportion not wanting to be served food by Aborigines averaged 34 per cent, the proportion not wishing to eat at the same table as Aborigines averaged 29 per cent, and the proportion objecting to Aborigines serving them in a shop averaged 19 per cent. Nor were Smalltown respondents especially likely to consider Aborigines 'dirty and slovenly' or 'drunken'.[45]

It is possible that for many 'white' Australians who were adjusting to the equalities that assimilation decreed, 'citizenship' and 'segregation' were not in contradiction. That is, it was possible to think that as long as the rest of the population did not have to mix with Aborigines, it did not matter that Aborigines were coming to enjoy the same entitlements as they enjoyed. Many of Taft's respondents might have regarded such distancing devices as segregated public spaces as the price that both kinds of Australians had to pay for living in a condition of harmony and equality. In that model of race relations, social distance is the condition for the coexistence of such different peoples, not the antithesis of it. The idea that segregation might secure tolerance and equality is probably not one most readers of this book in 2007 would want to contemplate. (In 1954, the US Supreme Court ruled the doctrine of 'separate but equal' unconstitutional.)[46] But faced with the challenges of assimilation, segregation may well have been the model that came easiest to many Australians in the 1960s. Assimilation could confer rights on Aborigines, without compromising the customary separation of Aborigines and non-Aborigines in their daily lives.[47]

The Universality of Political Community

For Taft, commenting on his 1965 poll results, there was a divergence between what people said about Aborigines as people with whom they might mix, and what they said about Aborigines' citizenship entitlements. Taft speculated that, while there were 'increased feelings of tolerance for Aborigines and greater advocacy of their civil rights', images of Aborigines had changed little.[48] Whether his observation about 'change' was correct we do not know, as he presented no data about the past, but he was right to distinguish what made Aborigines the same as non-Aborigines in entitlement from what made them seem different—and less—than non-Aborigines in their qualities as people. Clearly, commitments to civic equality could sit alongside personal reservations about or distaste for those to whom civic equality was to be extended.

In his survey, Western also identified two dimensions to his respondents' views about Aborigines. One had to do with their images of Aborigines—what qualities they thought were typical of Aborigines. Ten of his 'opinion statements' (listed below) tried to tap into the image respondents had of Aborigines (the numbers in brackets are the percentages of Canberra residents and Condobolin residents who respectively 'strongly agreed' or 'agreed', though overwhelmingly these figures represent agreement rather than 'strong' agreement):

14. The trouble with letting Aborigines into a nice neighbourhood is that they gradually give it a typical Aboriginal atmosphere. (19, 42)

17. Restrictions should be placed on the Aborigine to protect him from his own lack of responsibility. (33, 55)

15. Because the Aborigine can never escape from the limits of his culture, he will always adapt the white man's materials to his old ways. (18, 45)

12. The incorporation of Aborigines into our communities could well lower our standards of hygiene. (24, 29)

16. There may be few exceptions but in general Aborigines are pretty much alike. (22, 58)

19. One reason white and black races can never merge is because the white culture is so much more advanced. (24, 50)

18. No matter how much one might support it on idealistic grounds, there have been too many unfortunate consequences of racial mixing for me to be willing to agree with it. (18, 38)

13. Aborigines expect to get more out of life for nothing than white people. (21, 47)

21. When all is said and done Aborigines probably prefer not to mix with whites. (40, 72)

20. Manual labour and unskilled jobs seem to fit the Aboriginals' nature and ability better than more skilled or responsible work. (45, 55)

10. I have nothing against Aborigines but can never see myself being really friendly with one. (17, 35)

Western also identified a second dimension to his respondents' opinions: their views about what Aboriginal people were entitled to. Seven of the items tried to tap this dimension. (Again, the numbers in brackets are the percentages of Canberra residents and Condobolin residents who respectively 'strongly agreed' or 'agreed', and where the proportion agreeing was large, one-quarter to one-third of the agreement was 'strong'):

8. If an Aborigine sat next to me in a bus or train I would feel uncomfortable. (3, 6)

2. If I had decided to vote along party lines in an election I would still vote for my party if they elected [sic] an Aborigine. (91, 88)

3. All Aborigines should possess Australian citizenship automatically. (89, 90)

4. There should be no difference between rates of pay for Aborigines and whites engaged in the same work. (90, 85)

9. I have nothing against people of another culture but allowing Aborigines to vote and to drink in public places is going a little too far. (12, 14)

6. Aborigines should have full use of all public facilities which are used by whites. (82, 76)

1. Aborigines should be encouraged to join local organizations so that they can play their full part in the life of the town in which they live. (94, 87)

The significant features of the second series of items are: first, that the level of support for 'rights' was generally very high; and second, that respondents from Canberra and Condobolin differed little—their very different responses to the 'image' items notwithstanding. In 1967, when Western re-ran both sets of items in Melbourne, Brisbane and five country towns (two with substantial Aboriginal populations) the pattern of response was similar to the pattern in Canberra and Condobolin. That is, he found large urban/regional differences on 'image' questions' but smaller urban/regional differences on 'rights' questions. While the 'image' of Aborigines in Melbourne and Brisbane was not as favourable as it had been in Canberra, support for 'rights' was virtually the same.[49]

If what respondents thought of Aborigines did not determine the rights they accorded them, then the failure of 'assimilation' as a social project was not holding back assimilation as a political project.[50] Western's results vindicated Elkin's 1964 distinction.

The 1967 Referendum

The constitutional changes made by the overwhelming vote of Australians on 27 May 1967 had no direct or obvious policy consequences. The referendum was not a test of the electorate's support for any clearly stated approach to Indigenous policy. Eighteen months after the referendum, one astute observer commented: 'No one knows or can say exactly what message that signal sent.'[51] Voters supported a greater role for the Commonwealth, but the issues on which they voted gave no indication of what they wanted the Commonwealth to do. Historians of the campaign in favour of voting 'Yes', such as Bain Attwood, Andrew Markus and Sue Taffe, agree that the propaganda was broadly affirmative of 'Aborigines' and broadly hostile to 'discrimination' against them.[52] By voting 'Yes', the campaign frequently implied, the electorate would mandate Aboriginal rights, equality, full citizenship for Aborigines, and positive and practical aid to the Aboriginal people.

Historians differ in their accounts of what the 'Yes' campaigners understood by the central concept—'discrimination'. According to Attwood and Markus, underlying the campaign waged by the Federal Council for the Advancement of Aborigines and Torres Strait Islanders (FCAATSI), was a set of liberal principles which emphasized individual rights and equality, casting the referendum as a means of realizing the ideal of a homogeneous 'modern' and 'progressive' society which incorporated all peoples as citizens. In the campaign this vision was barely distinguishable from the Australian State's widely accepted assimilationist programme.[53]

However, Taffe has argued for a different reading of FCAATSI's intentions in the 'Yes' campaign: from 1958 to 1967 FCAATSI activists concluded that the rights of Indigenous Australians could not be fully acknowledged within the then-dominant paradigm of citizenship for Indigenous Australians.[54] She compares a series of petitions for the amendment of Section 51 (xxvi) and finds in the wording of the later petitions the concept of 'positive discrimination'.

Increasingly through 1965 and 1966, reports, letters and addresses argued for a referendum on the ground that it would allow the Commonwealth to deliver compensatory programs to Aboriginal Australians, as a means to their equal citizenship. This activity culminated in yet another petition drafted in 1966. Unlike the 1957, 1958 and 1962 petitions, the 1966 version was forthright in requesting positive discrimination, asking: 'That specific provision should be made in the Constitution for the advancement of Aboriginal people'.[55]

The concept of 'positive discrimination', she concludes, was known and embraced by some of the organisers who favoured 'Yes'.

The official definition of 'assimilation' from the 1961 Native Welfare Conference, quoted at the beginning of this chapter, included a general justification of discriminatory policies (unspecified), provided they were temporary:

any special measures taken for aborigines and part-aborigines are regarded as temporary measures not based on colour but intended to meet their need for special care and assistance ... to assist them to make the transition from one stage to another in such a way as will be favourable to their social, economic and political advancement.

Some people who saw the point of these words would have had in mind such 'temporary measures' as *restricted* Aborigines' citizenship rights. However, it was equally possible for 'discrimination' to be understood as the 'special measures' that Shirley Andrews, a FCAATSI activist, had evoked in 1963 in that organisation's publication, *Smoke Signals*. Aborigines, she said, had 'special needs' that justified 'special facilities'. 'Aborigines who took advantage of the "special facilities"', she argued, 'would not suffer any restriction of their rights' as they did 'under existing legislation'.[56] Andrews quoted approvingly the International Labour Organization's Convention 107 on 'Indigenous and Tribal populations' which promoted 'equal status' while also giving its blessing to special measures for 'promoting the social, economic and cultural development of these populations and raising their standard of living'.

Taffe argues that, although the idea of 'positive discrimination' was prominent in the thinking of some of the architects of the 'Yes' campaign, such as Andrews, the concept was not deployed in the campaign. Rather, 'the 1967 campaign strategy was to appeal to a sense of fairness in the electorate'. The campaigners thought that the unsophisticated Australian public would best be won to a 'Yes' vote if the promotion of 'fairness' cast all 'discrimination' in a negative light. 'The campaign goal was an increase in public awareness of legalised discrimination and the building of a community resolve to do something about it.'[57] If the 'Yes' campaign was vague about the policy implications of a 'Yes' vote, Taffe argues, this was a deliberate tactic. She thus points to what was and was not achieved ideologically by the referendum. Voters were not asked to endorse a liberalism in which 'positive discrimination' was acceptable; they were invited to endorse the far less challenging position that 'discrimination' against Aborigines was no longer acceptable. Anyone whose liberal heart warmed to the word 'same' in the Government's statement on 'assimilation' would have strong reasons to vote 'Yes'—and they did.

If Taffe is right, then the 'Yes' campaigners may have underestimated the public's warmth towards 'positive' discrimination'. Certainly in the lead up to the referendum Morgan pointed to wide support for governments spending more on Aborigines. 'Do you think we are doing enough to educate and house Aboriginals or should more be spent on them?', Morgan asked in August 1964. While 16 per cent thought that enough was being spent, three out of every four respondents wanted some authority to spend 'a little more' (19 per cent) or 'a lot more' (56 per cent).[58]

Morgan asked only three questions about the referendum issues themselves. In May 1965 respondents were reminded that 'Under the Constitution' Aborigines were 'excluded from the population counts which decide electoral boundaries' and that the Government now planned 'a referendum to include Aborigines in the census'. Asked how they would 'probably vote', 88 per cent said they would vote 'yes'.[59] Again in December 1965, 87 per cent said they would vote 'yes' at a 'referendum to include Aboriginals in the census'. Morgan predicted 'big "Yes" majorities on this question in all States'.[60] In the month of the referendum itself, Morgan once again asked respondents how they would vote, and found opinion unchanged: 86 per cent said they would vote 'yes'. 'What', respondents were then asked, 'would you say the chief effect will be if the referendum on Aboriginals receives a "Yes" vote and is carried?' Only 4 per cent anticipated bad effects ('drinking, more discrimination') and only 6 per cent expected 'no effect'. Overwhelmingly, the predicted effects would have been regarded as desirable: 'better opportunities, improved conditions, better housing, education' (38 per cent); 'equal rights as citizens' (22 per cent); and 'higher morals, improved status, freedom' (14 per cent).[61] Almost every respondent in this poll owned to having 'very favourable' (35 per cent) or 'fairly favourable' (53 per cent) rather than 'unfavourable' (5 per cent) 'feelings about Aboriginals in general'.[62] Nonetheless, the mention of 'morals' among the anticipated effects of the referendum's passing suggests that some of those who were to vote for constitutional reform harboured negative perceptions of Aborigines.

Conclusion

As we will see in the next chapter, much of the commentary in the 1980s on Australian attitudes to Aborigines looked back on the 1967 referendum as a high-water mark of pro-Aboriginal sentiment. Not only that, the later commentators saw that sentiment as being well defined in its policy preferences: the referendum, some people said, recorded strong support for land rights. We agree with Taffe, Attwood and Markus that this is a misreading of the referendum. The 'Yes' campaign did not cultivate support for any specific policies that the Commonwealth might exercise. Instead, it promoted 'inclusion' and non-discrimination as general principles for the nation to live by. Elkin's distinction between 'political' and 'social' assimilation is relevant to our understanding of the different ways that Australians enacted these principles. As the research reviewed in this chapter showed, a larger proportion of Australians expressed support for 'political' assimilation—that is, for allowing Aborigines the same citizenship rights as other Australians—than for 'social' assimilation. The support for abstract equality expressed in the high 'Yes' vote in the referendum was not necessarily matched by warmth towards Aborigines in social settings. Within 'social' assimilation we can see a further difference between impersonal and intimate social interaction. The research showed that a significant minority of Australians felt more comfortable if certain public spaces remained segregated, and that a majority of Australians were more comfortable if the composition of their own families was not changed by intermarriage with an Aboriginal person. And many respondents—though not all—deployed negative stereotypes of Aborigines. In the late 1960s, in short, there was a disjunction between what Australians thought Aborigines were like and what they thought Aborigines were entitled to.[63]

2

Land Rights, the 'Backlash' and 'Middle Australia'

In March 1983, the Australian Labor Party led by Bob Hawke was elected on a platform that included granting 'land rights and compensation to Aboriginal and Islander communities, using the principles and recommendations of the Aboriginal Land Rights Commission (Woodward Report) as a basis for Legislation, subject to continuing review'.[1] The 1974 Woodward Report had been the basis for both the Labor Party's and the Coalition's approach to land rights in the Northern Territory. Federally, Labor had introduced a bill in 1975 before losing office and Malcolm Fraser had reintroduced the bill, with revisions, in 1976. Both the Whitlam and the Fraser bills set out a process for recognising certain Aborigines as owners of land and allowed these owners a mining veto; both Whitlam's intention and Fraser's legislation were confined to lands in the Northern Territory.

Although there was no doubt that after the 1967 constitutional referendum the Australian Government had the power to determine Aboriginal policies and laws for every State, the Fraser Government (1975–83) had refused to use this power against States that had been hostile to Aborigines' demands for land rights. Between 1979 and 1981 the defiant stances of the Court Government in Western Australian and the Bjelke-Petersen Government in Queensland (both non-Labor) had embarrassed the Fraser Government, without provoking its intervention. Proponents of land rights in every State had found Federal Labor more sympathetic, and by 1982 Labor had moved beyond the Fraser (and Whitlam) position. As President of the Labor Party (1973–78) before entering Parliament in 1980, Hawke had chosen to 'confess', in the first of his 1979 Boyer Lectures, that 'I do not have any idea what "States' Rights" are'.[2] On land rights, Labor's platform promised that where a State or Territory failed to follow the Woodward 'principles' it would 'use Commonwealth constitutional powers and legislation to achieve these objectives'.[3]

Confronting the States—the Western Australian and Queensland governments in particular—Hawke's Minister for Aboriginal Affairs, Clyde Holding, anticipated a struggle. In April 1983, when newspapers reported a University of Queensland study that showed the poor physical and mental health of Aborigines on Queensland's reserves, Holding commented (in the *West Australian*'s 19 April paraphrase) that 'the only solution was to give Aborigines their own land and the skills to manage their affairs'. In an interview he remarked that he hoped 'to bring Australia to terms with itself'. As he explained, 'the history of white domination of Australian society, the genocide that took place upon our Aboriginal citizens I think has scarred the Australian community. It leads to latent and overt forms of rac[ism] …'.[4] He thus foreshadowed that he would interpret opposition to Labor's policy as an expression of the racist strain in Australian society.

In this chapter we show how Holding's anticipation of racist opposition was vindicated. Public opinion research in the mid-1980s persuaded politicians and journalists that Australians were too racist to accept the Hawke Government's national land rights policy. We will trace the steps by which their reading of public opinion became established as truth. In particular, we will tell a story about two ideas that became political orthodoxies: one, that Australia in the 1980s was in the grip of a 'backlash' against the land rights policies of the 1970s; the other, that land rights policy needed, but lacked, the support of 'middle Australia'. We set out reasons for doubting that there was a backlash, for not accepting the category 'middle Australia', and for rejecting the idea that the support of 'middle Australia' was necessary for Labor's project to succeed.[5] That the 'backlash' thesis and the importance of 'middle Australia' were accepted as keys to thinking about 'the Australian public' is a testament to the frequent repetition of these ideas by politicians, political activists and journalists for whom these ideas 'worked'.

Holding's anticipation of racist opposition was, in a sense, self-fulfilling. By imagining his task in a certain way, Holding —with the help of pollsters, journalists and his political opponents—turned his fearful anticipations into 'facts'.

Reconciling Conflicting Interests

A month after the election of the Hawke Government, the *Age* reported that Clyde Holding planned to proceed by four steps: first, he would get a report from Mr Justice Toohey on the strengths and weaknesses of the Commonwealth's Northern Territory *Land Rights Act* (because this Act might have to be amended to be consistent with any national statute); then he would constitute a panel of lawyers, under the supervision of the National Aboriginal Conference, to draft legislation; third, he would move a parliamentary motion reaffirming the powers of the Federal Government to create national legislation (though not constitutionally necessary, this would put pressure on the Opposition); finally, armed with a bill and a resolution affirming Commonwealth powers, he would consult the States.[6] In a speech given on 8 July, Holding warned that 'if we cannot achieve these objectives by agreement, I am not prepared, and the Government is not prepared, to allow the constitutional prerogatives of the Commonwealth and the rights of the Aboriginal people, which clearly rest upon these prerogatives, to be further eroded by recalcitrant State Governments'.[7] The *Sydney Morning Herald* quoted him as saying: 'I don't want to twist anybody's arm but there may be occasions when we have to break a few'.[8] Later, the *Australian* quoted the Minister's claim that the Government had received the electorate's mandate to grant national land rights.[9] A keen writer of letters to the editors of Australian dailies, Holding subsequently repeated this point in a letter to the *Sydney Morning Herald*.[10]

It soon became clear that the States would not be the only critics of a national land rights bill. Aborigines, too, were publicly wary of Holding's promises. The Northern Land Council chairman, Gerry Blitner, was quoted in the *Northern Territory News* predicting that if the Government attempted a national Act it would not be as strong a law (from an Aboriginal point of view) as the Northern Territory *Land Rights Act*.[11] The Northern Territory Land Councils were watchful of any weakening—in the interests of national consistency—of Northern Territory Aborigines' rights to veto mining. These fears were reasonable: the New South Wales Labor Government had released a land rights bill in December 1982 that would not allow land councils a say over the mining of gold, silver, coal or petroleum. Soon after the Hawke Government was elected, New South Wales Koories demanded that Holding use the Commonwealth's powers to force Frank Walker, Wran's Aboriginal Affairs Minister, back to the negotiating table regarding the bill's provisions.[12] On 27 March 1983 Holding asked the Wran Government to delay introducing the bill for twelve months, but he refused to use Commonwealth powers to compel the Wran Government to alter the bill to conform to the intended national standards of landowners' rights. Aboriginal critics took this as a sign that Holding was not willing to confront the States with a strong form of land rights.[13] A test of a bill's strength, from an Aboriginal point of view, was whether landowners had the right to refuse mining on their land. Were Labor to follow Woodward's recommendations (embodied in Whitlam's bill and Fraser's law), Aborigines would have a mining veto. But would Federal Labor, under pressure from a State Labor Government, adhere to Woodward's model? By April 1983, Aboriginal leaders were wondering whether Holding had the nerve to 'twist the arms' of the mining industry and of its sympathisers in State governments.

By November 1983, before he had published an outline of his bill, Holding was responding to sceptical Aborigines and foreshadowing that, when his bill was ready, he might also be at odds with recalcitrant States. To a Government that had frequently used the words 'consensus' and 'reconciliation' to project its mission, the language of conflict did not come easily.[14] 'We'll be looking for consensus because we are a government of consensus', Holding had said. 'But in the final analysis the constitutional responsibility in these matters rests with the Commonwealth'.[15]

To address both his Aboriginal critics and the anticipated critics from the States, Holding commented on the extent and limits, as he saw it, of public sympathy for Aborigines and their grievances. On 22 November, in a speech at the Australian National University, he warned his Aboriginal critics not to arouse public hostility by overstating their rights. To assert Aboriginal 'sovereignty' risked provoking a

> fairly ugly white backlash … And the problem about opening the bottle and letting out the racist genie, it's bloody hard to put it back, once it's out. And it carries over in a way which I think is quite poisonous and destructive, not merely of Aboriginal political objectives, but in terms of what ought to be effective race relations in this country.[16]

This was the first public mention in Holding's campaign—as far as we can trace—of the notion of a 'white backlash'. It was soon to become an influential idea.

The *Courier Mail* warned Holding that on the issue of land rights 'consensus seems almost impossible … [Holding] runs the distinct risk of white resistance, not just from those people opposed to land rights, but from others who might feel, rightly or wrongly, that the Government is moving too far, too fast'.[17] When Ray O'Connor, the former Liberal Premier of Western Australia, predicted that land rights would split the nation between 'black and white', Holding responded that 'the Liberal Party's attitude in WA has the potential of developing attitudes which are essentially racist'.[18] As a gesture of his serious commitment to land rights, Holding announced in November 1983 that the Government would grant the traditional owners of Uluru and Kata Tjuta title to the Uluru–Kata Tjuta National Park, on the understanding that they lease the park back to the Commonwealth. When Radio 3SR (Shepparton) asked him to respond to critics of that decision, Holding used the word 'backlash' and referred to attempts 'to arouse fears and racism in the community'.[19] It was later reported that early in 1984 officers in the Department of Aboriginal Affairs had begun to alert their Minister to a 'backlash'; certainly Holding believed that 'opinion surveys were starting to show that people thought enough was already being done for Aborigines'—something polls had shown for a long time, though more markedly at the end of 1983 than at any time since the Whitlam years.[20]

Holding was also being warned about a 'backlash' by his colleague Graeme Campbell, the Labor member for Kalgoorlie in Western Australia. In a letter to the caucus, circulated before Labor's Biennial National Conference in July 1984, Campbell warned that land rights would arouse racist sentiment within Labor's working-class constituency.[21] Aborigines in his electorate, Campbell told the *Bulletin*, 'already sense the backlash', as he himself did: 'I know the backlash is there and I am concerned to see that it does not become an irresistible groundswell'.[22] Six months later, the Opposition spokesman on Aboriginal Affairs, James Porter, used the same rhetorical ploy when he accused Holding of 'inflated rhetoric' that had provoked a 'community backlash'.[23]

We do not know whether Holding had been briefed by Labor's Federal secretariat on the polling it had commissioned on land rights. Conducted in May and June 1984 by Australian Nationwide Opinion Polls (ANOP) in six marginal seats—Calare (NSW), Deakin (Victoria), Leichhardt and Bowman (Queensland), Kingston (SA) and Franklin (Tasmania)—and presented to the secretariat in July, the Labor Party's polling showed greater support 'for' (47 per cent) than 'against' (39 per cent) 'Aboriginal land rights'. Focused, if only implicitly, on land rights as a potential problem for the party, ANOP's report pointed to where opposition was greatest: in one of the Queensland seats, Leichhardt (62 per cent). The lowest level of opposition to land rights was found in Bowman (43 per cent) and in Calare. ANOP did not measure the *strength* of either the opposition or the support, but it did find that 'potential swinging voters' divided 47:36 in favour of the policy—an encouraging level of support if the Government were resolved to act.[24]

The political fortunes of Labor's land rights policy should have been helped by the fact that in 1977 the Parliament under a Liberal government, led by Fraser, had passed the Northern Territory *Land Rights Act*. Could policy principles applied by the Liberals to the Northern Territory constitute a political risk if Labor were to apply them more widely? Bipartisan support for land rights was quickly fading, however, as critics of Fraser's leadership began to gain strength within the Liberal Party.[25] By July 1984, even Andrew Peacock, an MP reputed to be in sympathy with Fraser's liberalism, admitted to a Liberal Party gathering that 'with hindsight the coalition would not now legislate as it did for land rights in the Northern

Territory'.[26] A week earlier, Holding announced that he was getting advice from journalist Ken Gott about the activities of a racist and populist group, the League of Rights, whose influence over non-Labor politicians the Minister was beginning to find worrying.[27]

To maintain his credibility as a champion of Aborigines, it became necessary for Holding to be seen to be campaigning to reverse the perceived 'backlash' by cultivating public support for land rights. The day before Peacock's speech was reported, Holding foreshadowed that 'to defuse the growing backlash against land rights' the Hawke Government would mount an advertising campaign promoting land rights.[28] He hoped not only to defuse 'the growing backlash' but also to defend himself from critics such as the Aboriginal leaders who had suggested in August that the Government—in fear of a 'white backlash'—was softening its stand on issues like land rights, sacred sites and self-determination.[29] However, the Hawke Cabinet did not back Holding's proposed publicity campaign. Instead, it asked for research into community attitudes, so that the Government could be better informed about the extent of the problem.[30] Holding, who may have sensed a fatal weakening in Hawke's resolve, was frustrated. 'We have failed in not picking up early enough the intensive organisation of some of the frankly racist organisations and the kind of anti-Aboriginal propaganda being mounted in the community', he told the ABC on 16 August.[31] He was furious, too, that his opponents were not so constrained. The 'terror campaign' in the media conducted by the Chamber of Mines of Western Australia (CMWA), he was quoted as saying, was the 'biggest single conning on racist grounds since Adolf Hitler discovered the Jews'.[32]

Nevertheless, Holding did as the Cabinet wished and in August 1984, through the Department of Aboriginal Affairs, commissioned ANOP to 'undertake a community attitude research program as the basis for development of a communications strategy which would maximise public support for the Federal Government's policy on Aboriginal land rights'. ANOP's research proceeded in stages. First, it convened seventeen group discussions composed of adults aged 20–55 of both sexes and 'a range of class groupings', in 'NSW, WA and Qld (primary) and Victoria and SA (secondary)' who were found, 'on the basis of a screening questionnaire', to be 'not strongly committed in their attitudes towards politics in general, and land rights in particular'. It also interviewed twenty-eight 'opinion leaders'—chief executives or key operatives in his or her organisation or institution—with a variety of stances on Aboriginal issues. In late September 1984, it conducted a national survey of 2000 adults. Then, in November and December, it attempted to 'evaluate the effectiveness of a number of communication themes' via a further ten group discussions and interviews with sixteen 'opinion leaders'. By this mix of methods ANOP generated both qualitative and quantitative data. In January 1985 it reported the results of its research to Holding.[33]

Western Australian Pressures

In Western Australia, the Burke Government was also developing a land rights policy and testing public opinion. Between March and May 1984, and again from July to September, the CMWA had conducted an advertising campaign against land rights.[34] This lifted the issue up the political agenda and affected Burke's judgment about what voters in his State would accept.[35] Rejecting 'the major mining provisions in Holding's five principles for land rights'—including the principle that 'Aborigines were to have control of mining on their land'— because the principles were not acceptable to the mining industry, Burke set out to legislate a form of land rights that 'did not jeopardize his government electorally'.[36]

In mid-1984, during the lull in the CMWA's campaign, the Western Australia branch of the Labor Party asked ANOP to survey opinion in Perth's northern suburbs. ANOP reported that among 'potential swinging voters', 15 per cent volunteered that 'land rights' was 'a worry or concern' that they had 'about a Labor State government for another term' (only issues to do with 'state taxes and charges', nominated by 23 per cent, rated more highly); 22 per cent suggested that its 'approach to land rights' was one of 'the two main things that the State government "has done or is doing that you don't like or that worry you"' (again, only issues to do with 'increases in state taxes and charges', nominated by 34 per cent, were rated more highly); and no more than 12 per cent agreed that in 'making decisions on land rights' the State Government had done a 'good or fairly good job' (making it the lowest ranked of ten performance measures).[37] 'Land rights', the report concluded, in relation to '4 key concerns for defusing', was '[a] much misunderstood issue' that was 'causing real electoral problems among middle class voters who have recently supported Labor'. There was 'little sympathy' for 'land rights' and 'if the Liberals are "smarter" in W.A. than they were in Canberra over immigration, their strategy will be to have this issue quietly and unsensationally brew and become distorted in the suburbs by local rumour and grass roots action'.[38]

Armed with WA Labor's ANOP research on Perth voters, Burke lobbied hard—and successfully—against any national land rights model which upheld Woodward's insistence that Aboriginal land tenure include the right to veto mining; according to one report, he told Hawke that land rights 'could cost up to eight Labor seats in Western Australia'.[39] In October 1984, at the beginning of a long Federal election campaign, and despite Holding's argument that 'the Burke Government was exaggerating the electoral threat the land rights issue posed to it', Hawke issued a statement in Perth 'to the effect that the federal government would not over-ride Western Australia's land rights legislation'.[40] In November, when he delivered Labor's policy speech, Hawke acknowledged 'land rights' as a 'vital matter … for Aboriginal people', noted that 'land rights' was 'currently the subject of extensive consultations by the Government', and reassured his listeners that his Government was 'well on the way to a just, equitable and enduring solution which ensures that the interests of all parties are adequately protected'. But gone was the pledge in the 1983 policy speech 'to use, where necessary, the constitutional powers of the Commonwealth to provide the Aboriginal people with the land which has for years been set aside for them'. Gone, too, was the idea that 'land rights' were 'central' to 'truly' bringing the country 'together'. Hawke, says Kelly, had 'retreated on Aboriginal land rights'; he 'was chasing more swinging voters'. Others, however, stress the pressure coming from Burke. Far from being mutually exclusive, these two explanations were mutually reinforcing: Burke would have argued not only that he was under electoral threat in Western Australia but that Hawke was too.[41]

Already, Hawke's statement in Perth had weakened Holding's ability to insist that the national land rights model include Woodward's principle of an Aboriginal veto over mining. Burke and Hawke had instead negotiated a version of land rights that placated the mining industry. In late 1984, ANOP was asked again by the Western Australian Labor Party to determine whether voters 'were basically in favor or not in favor of land rights for Aborigines'. ANOP polled two of Labor's marginal seats, Bunbury and Mitchell, and reported that 'a staggering 90 per cent' were either 'Strongly Opposed' (47 per cent) or 'Opposed but Soft—Lean to Opposition' (43 per cent). However, its assessment of the politics of the issue was 'somewhat different'. Now that Burke had won 'the support of the miners and pastoralists for his state land rights legislation', the issue 'had been "temporarily defused"': land rights were only 'a small vote loser', the skew of opinion notwithstanding. Were the Federal Government, in 1985, to commission an information campaign of 'mammoth proportion and impact', ANOP argued, it would 'lay the issue to rest'.[42]

Knowing, by January 1985, something of the pressure that the Hawke Government had been under to accommodate the Western Australian Government's approach to land rights, journalists began challenging Holding to deny that Hawke was giving up altogether on legislating a national land rights law. Holding denied this, but his words were only partly supported when the Government released a paper in February setting out the terms of the bill that would be introduced to the House in August. Aboriginal landowners would not be given the right to veto mining; rather, a tribunal would arbitrate between a mining lessee and the Aboriginal owners. This provision was widely interpreted as a concession to Western Australia and to the mining industry; it confirmed Gerry Blitner's prediction, two years earlier, that 'national land rights' would entail an amendment to the Northern Territory *Land Rights Act* to reduce the rights of Northern Territory Aborigines. The Hawke Government, in an effort to appease opponents of land rights, was retreating from a principle to which the Fraser Government had been committed in 1976.

'Backlash'—the Enemy of 'Consensus'

Holding defended the proposed bill by returning to the theme of 'consensus'. And, for the first time, as far as we can trace, his idea of consensus explicitly included the notion of majority support. In March 1985, he told the Catholic Commission for Justice and Peace in Sydney that 'if national land rights legislation is to be enduring and successful, it must have the support of the majority of Australians. It cannot ignore the rights, aspirations or concerns of the majority of Australians.'[43] Previously, Holding had used the word 'consensus' to refer to the reconciliation of the views articulated by the State governments, the representatives of Aborigines and the mining industry. Now, through his invocation of 'public opinion' the

Minister was adding the task of attracting majority support to the task of finding consensus between political interests. The *Sydney Morning Herald*, in an editorial, judged that the majority of Australians were neither opposed nor in support; they were 'at best, indifferent to Aboriginal land rights'.[44] This, the paper implied, was an insufficient basis for the Government to proceed. One journalist, Mungo MacCallum, commented that the Hawke Government was now having to respond to a 'backlash, which found its way through the mining lobby into the electorate, into the state governments and into Cabinet … and Mr. Hawke—not for the first time—[had] decided that policy was no substitute for political consensus'.[45]

Though Holding did not refer to the ANOP study in detail until September 1985, he seems to have disclosed part or all of its findings to journalists before then. He was not the only one to do so. From 1 March, newspaper readers were offered glimpses of this poll, and of others, including some commissioned by the Liberal Party. In turn, journalists gave new emphasis to 'the public' as a key player. Amanda Buckley reported that Burke had argued against national land rights partly by telling his Labor colleagues in Canberra about poll research that predicted that five Federal seats would be at risk if land rights included an Aboriginal veto over mining.[46] The *Age* told its readers in March that 'some ministers would prefer the Government to ignore the contentious commitment to land rights especially in the light of public surveys which show little support'.[47] In April, the *Advertiser* disclosed that 'public opinion polls conducted by the Liberals have consistently shown strong opposition to land rights'.[48] 'Public opinion polls sponsored by the State Liberal Party', the *Australian* reported in August, 'have shown that most voters vehemently oppose land rights'.[49] On the 'National Today Show' in October, Sue Kellaway referred to a 'Government commission-ed survey' that revealed '76 per cent of the electorate is against [Aboriginal land rights] … And furthermore, the survey warns that the handing back of Ayers Rock, and the land rights issue generally, is one of the most divisive and potentially explosive issues facing the Australian community'.[50] The figure and her phrases are very close to the terms of the ANOP report. Holding featured the ANOP results in his National Press Club speech on 13 September. Within the public, he said, there were 'deeply held misconceptions and prejudices about land rights'. He quoted two ANOP findings in particular: 'less [sic] than one in five Australians had strong feelings of support for Aboriginal people and their aspirations; and most Australians saw the range of special government programs for Aborigines as largely a waste of money'.[51]

How had this apparently adverse public sentiment come about? In the winter of 1985, as fragments of public opinion research became available through such news stories and seemed to confirm a 'backlash', two historical narratives began to circulate. One put the emphasis on the distant colonial past, the other on the very recent past.

In February, the ABC's Catherine Job had asked Pat Dodson of the Central Land Council if he was 'afraid that the political climate has turned against Aboriginal land rights, that the support just isn't there in the community'. Dodson replied that 'the climate's always been against Aboriginal people getting land rights ... The whole history of this country has been against recognition of Aboriginal rights.'[52] When Holding addressed the Press Club in September, he remarked that recent campaigns around land rights did not entirely account for the disappointing state of public opinion.[53] In the same month, in an interview for *Penthouse*, he ruminated on racism as an underlying theme of Australian history. Although Australia was a multicultural society whose 'level of racial tolerance generally shown towards ethnic communities is now much higher than it was when I was a kid', Aborigines had not benefited. Multiculturalism 'has by-passed Aboriginal people. There is a latent racism which is directed towards Aboriginal people that really goes back to the old days when the colony was founded.' In colonial times the violence against Aborigines was 'genocidal'. The

> perception of Aboriginal people as being something less than human was a necessary ingredient in the psychology of what occurred. And when we look back on it I think that many people find it easier to maintain that perception. That's an easier thing to do—it's almost built into us in some ways.

The interviewer invited him to comment on Western Australia, where 'there is a backlash about land rights'. Holding replied that 'in the West the war has never ceased … in many ways the State's perceptions are those of a frontier society'.[54]

The alternative story was that until recently there had been substantial support for Aborigines and their aspirations, but that something had caused this sympathy rapidly to decline. Without referring to any research other than the most recent polls, Buckley offered such a narrative in the *Sydney Morning Herald* in March 1985.

> For a brief period in Australia's recent history, the shame associated with the bloodier aspects of white settlement overtook the pragmatism of the traditional attitude to the blacks due to a unique combination of economic growth, resurgent Aboriginal activism and the flowering of liberalism and social imagination associated with the Whitlam years. The benign attitude to the blacks just survived the Fraser years. When Clyde Holding became Minister for Aboriginal Affairs in the first Hawke government in 1983 he spoke of land rights as restitution for white Australia's crimes towards the indigenous people, likened to Hitler's persecution of the Jews … You don't hear talk like that around Canberra corridors these days. That was the last vestiges [sic] of the pre-backlash rhetoric of the sixties and seventies describing beliefs that fostered the freedom rides in outback NSW to halt racism, the tent embassies outside Parliament House and the Woodward

Report, commissioned by Gough Whitlam. The latter led to the landmark Northern Territory land rights legislation which Malcolm Fraser enacted on taking power and stood by for his entire prime ministerial career. It was not until the Hawke Labor government, with its promise of national land rights based on the NT model, came to office that the backlash took firm hold with Hugh Morgan, and to a lesser extent John Stone and Geoffrey Blainey, publicly voicing what middle Australia probably believed all along—that the black population ought not to be granted rights unavailable to everyone else.[55]

By suggesting that the critics of land rights were voicing 'what middle Australia probably believed all along', Buckley presented the 1970s flowering of a more positive view as superficial and transient. As we will show, ANOP's characterisation of Australia also included a 'middle Australia' whose opinions were relatively shallow but susceptible to mobilisation into a 'backlash'. It is likely that Buckley had been supplied with all or at least some of the ANOP report.

During this year of partly informed discussion of the dynamics of Australian public opinion, the Hawke Government's national land rights proposal was the object of competing lobbying. The Northern Territory Land Councils opposed it because they did not want to lose the mining veto; the mining industry argued that the bill imposed an unacceptable burden on their enterprise; and the Burke Government feared that the voters of Western Australia would blame it in the next election for jeopardising the prosperity of the State. The 'consensus' for which Holding had striven had not emerged; nor, according to the ANOP and other public opinion research, had majority support. So it was not a surprise to most interested observers that on 3 March 1986 the Hawke Government abandoned its uniform national land rights package.[56] The Prime Minister accepted Premier Burke's congratulations and Aborigines in the Northern Territory kept their mining veto.

In the days following this decision, both the Government and its critics produced histories of the 'backlash' that converged in an interesting way. Opposition spokesperson David Connolly asserted that 'ever since the 1967 referendum', it had been 'accepted that land rights in some form were an essential element for the development of Aboriginal people'. And 'this bipartisan position' had 'remained in place until the Hawke Government and the Federal party conference decision to push for national land rights legislation'.[57] The Prime Minister, addressing the National Press Club on 5 March, said that 'Australians as a whole weren't as compassionate as they were in 1967, when the Federal Government was given power over Aboriginal affairs'. A few days later, Holding agreed with this assessment. 'Nowadays', he told a television interviewer, 'there is a lot less sympathy around for Aboriginal hopes and aspirations' and 'the tension, the disbelief, the latent racial sentiments that are there in many parts of Australia are easily exploited'.[58] 'Aboriginal people', Pat Dodson told the ABC's Andrew Olle, 'view the spirit of the '67 Referendum going down the drain'.[59] In these accounts, the 'benign' recent past to which Buckley had referred was given a specific date and expression—the 1967 referendum that empowered the Commonwealth to make policy and law for all Aborigines in Australia and that allowed the Commonwealth's statisticians to include in the national population 'people of the Aboriginal race'.

The suggestion that the 1967 referendum had been a test of the Australian voters' support for land rights was an old one. Whitlam had first put this interpretation to the House of Representatives on 13 August 1968.[60] However, as we noted in Chapter 1, this reading of the 1967 vote is without foundation. The 'Yes' campaign did not affirm land rights or any other policy innovation; certainly, it did not align 'Yes' with the contentious theme of positive discrimination. It is difficult to use the 1967 referendum vote as a benchmark of anything more than a vague goodwill that demanded no specific concessions by non-Aborigines to Aborigines.

But what of the view that since the Fraser Government's land rights legislation in 1976 there had been a 'backlash' against land rights? And what of ANOP's notion of 'middle Australia' as the key to consensus-based policy? These two questions, pivotal to the politics of land rights in the mid-1980s, remain to be addressed.

Land Rights and the 'Backlash' Hypothesis

The first survey of opinion on land rights, as far as we know, was conducted in November 1972, on behalf of the Australian Council for Overseas Aid Education Committee. The survey followed the McMahon Government's response, on Australia Day 1972, to the Aborigines at Yirrkala mission, who had demanded in 1971 that the government legislate to recognise their customary rights to land. By offering Aborigines on Northern Territory reserves only a weak and conditional form of land title, the McMahon Government had kept the land rights issue very much alive in the months leading up to the Federal election in December 1972. That 'the Government should recognize the principle of Aboriginal Land Rights' was affirmed by 81 per cent of those interviewed, and denied by only 8 per cent.[61] However, the respondents (n = 190) lived in Melbourne, a city known to be relatively favourable to Indigenous rights.

The press did not commission public opinion research on the idea of Aboriginal rights over their land until 1978, the year after Fraser's law giving Northern Territory Aborigines the right to claim vacant Crown land or land held by them as pastoral leases took effect. Their communal, inalienable title to such lands—the result of Fraser's law—included the right to refuse minerals exploration and mining on their land. In November 1978, Irving Saulwick and Associates, on behalf of the *Age* and the *Sydney Morning Herald*, asked a national sample:

'Do you personally think that Aboriginal communities should have the right to refuse to allow mining on their traditional Aboriginal land?' Some 58 per cent said 'yes', 38 per cent 'no'; in South Australia, respondents divided 60:36 on the issue.[62] Eighteen months later, Peter Gardner and Associates were able to reverse the South Australian figures, apparently, by asking something along the following lines: (a) whether Aboriginal tribes should have complete control over their land, decide who should go on the land and whether to permit mining; or (b) whether the State Government should ensure the protection of Aboriginal rights, by deciding who is allowed on to the land and whether to permit mining.[63] Note that in Gardner's way of posing the issue, respondents were asked to view land rights not as an exercise of State authority (in Aborigines' favour) but as an alternative to State authority (and thus, perhaps, as a dereliction of State responsibility). The difference between the two South Australian results within such a short time demonstrates the difference that can be made by changing the terms in which an issue is posed.

There are more examples of this phenomenon. In September 1980, Saulwick introduced a question about drilling on Aboriginal land by telling respondents that recently the Western Australian Government had ordered 'that drilling for oil be started on an Aboriginal cattle station at Noonkanbah'. Respondents were told that the 'Aborigines say that the drilling is too close to an important sacred site'. They were then asked: 'Do you feel that the Federal Government should have tried to use its power to stop this drilling; or do you feel the Federal Government should not have tried to use its powers to stop this drilling?' Opinion was evenly divided: 45 per cent in favour of Federal intervention, 47 per cent against.[64] Should we conclude that support for the Aboriginal position, as re-ported by Saulwick in 1978 and in 1980, had diminished? To do so we would have to suppose that the two questions were measures of the same thing. But consider the differences between the two. One engages respondents' opinions about the proper extent of Federal Government power; the other does not raise this issue. One refers to 'traditional Aboriginal land', the other to 'sacred sites'. One refers to 'drilling for oil', the other to 'mining'. If the two results are not necessarily measures of the same thing, can they be interpreted as measuring a decline in 'support for land rights'?

In July 1983, Morgan introduced a question on Aboriginal rights over minerals by telling respondents that 'At present, owners of land do not own the minerals on their land unless they have a mining lease' (a statement that was not strictly speaking true, as freehold title in some parts of Australia did include ownership of minerals). 'It's been suggested', the preamble continued, 'that with Aboriginal reserves the Aborigines should own the minerals obtained from their reserves'. Asked whether they agreed or disagreed with this suggestion, 40 per cent said they agreed. A few months later, Morgan asked a similar question (as part of the Australian Values Study Survey), and 38 per cent agreed.[65] Can these results be compared with either of the Saulwick results, to show a decline? The Morgan and Saulwick questions are about the same issue only in the sense that they have something to do with mining on Aboriginal land. But whereas Saulwick made no reference to the rights of non-Aboriginal people, the Morgan question implied that to grant Aboriginal ownership over minerals on Aboriginal reserves was to grant a right not available to others. The Morgan poll worked hard to 'educate' respondents and to raise the question of equality of rights between Aborigines and others; Saulwick's questions did not.

The phrase 'land rights' was used in September 1981 when McNair Anderson, conducting the Australian Gallup Poll on behalf of the Herald & Weekly Times, asked whether 'Aboriginal people on Aboriginal reserves' should 'be given land rights—that is, be given freehold land—or should the land on which they live be leased to them?'. On this occasion,

53 per cent of those interviewed supported the idea of land rights for Aborigines.[66] Though subsequent polls (examined below) did not show as high a proportion of support, explanations other than 'backlash' are possible—explanations that again focus on the differences in the questions.

Land Rights and the Principle of 'Equality'

In July 1983, Morgan framed a question on land rights in terms of whether Aborigines should have 'more, the same, or less [sic] land rights than other Australians'—eliciting once again the respondents' opinion about a certain criterion of justice (identical rights for all Australians). The notion of 'the same' proved very appealing: 72 per cent of Morgan's sample supported it. Repeated in the Australian Values Study in August–October, 'same rights' elicited 78 per cent support. Notice, however, that while only 13 to 14 per cent of respondents in these polls supported 'greater' land rights for Aborigines, 38 to 40 per cent—about three times as many— favoured the idea of Aborigines owning the minerals on Aboriginal reserves, a right accorded to very few owners of land in Australia (as the question made clear). Clearly, many respondents who embraced the abstract idea of all Australians having the same rights also endorsed the concrete idea that Aborigines should, in specified circumstances, enjoy rights that other Australians did not enjoy. Again we see the power of the terms of the question to elicit 'opinion' in one form while leaving 'opinion' in another form lying dormant. The readiness of respondents to depart, in specific instances, from the principle of 'same'-ness is also demonstrated in another question posed by Morgan in July 1983. It asked respondents whether they agreed or disagreed that: 'When mining companies explore for minerals on Aboriginal reserves, they should pay an additional fee [beyond the lease fee] which goes to the Aboriginals'. This was a clear and specific departure from the idea that Australians should have identical rights, yet opinion was evenly divided.

There is no doubt that the Australian public likes the idea of 'equality'. In its advertising campaign against the Burke Government's proposed land rights legislation in Western Australia, the CMWA sought to mobilise public support around the view that 'Land rights should be equal rights', and it asked the public: 'Can you afford to pay the price of unequal land rights?'[67] ANOP's research for the Department of Aboriginal Affairs in 1984 confirmed the attractiveness of such appeals to 'equality'. It identified 'equal rights' for all Australians as one of the most 'powerfully emotive' Opposition slogans.[68] However, evidence from the polls shows that, while 'equality' is appealing in the abstract, it is subject to specific qualification in the minds of many. On the issues of land rights, these qualifications are very important indeed.

One way to solicit respondents' departures from the principle that all Australians should have the same rights, as we have seen, was to raise the possibility of Aborigines owning the minerals on Aboriginal reserves, or being paid an additional fee when the minerals on these lands were mined. Another way was to specify that the Aboriginal right would be restricted to certain people—those least affected by colonisation. To grasp this point it is helpful to go back to times when 'land rights' was not in the pollsters' (or anybody's) vocabulary.

In 1947 and 1957, Morgan found, in two measures of public support for 'assimilation' programs, that there was significant public support for Aborigines remaining different.[69] When asked to focus on those Aborigines who were still 'living in their native state' or who were 'tribal', respondents were divided about what governments should do. In February 1947, they split down the middle over whether government responsibility lay in 'help[ing] Aborigines to live their tribal lives' (47 per cent) or in 'educat[ing] them toward white standards' (46 per cent); 7 per cent were undecided. Ten years later, in February 1957, a similar question yielded a similar result. 'In your opinion, should we help the Aboriginals in

Central Australia live their tribal lives, or educate them to live like white men?' (The key word linking this question to its predecessor was 'tribal'.) Again, those with a view were divided equally: 47 per cent preferring that Aborigines be left in their 'tribal' condition, and 45 per cent wanting them educated to live like 'white men'.

In the period 1947 to 1957, a large minority of those polled did not think that 'assimilation' should apply to a certain category of Aborigine: tribal people. This willingness to allow at least some remote and 'tribal' Aboriginal people to remain different seems to have continued among many Australians. We should not assume that this perception of these Aborigines was respectful. The 1947 and 1957 polls do not allow us to see whether respondents were simply dismissing certain Aborigines as candidates for assimilation because of their perceived primitiveness.

Whether the different qualities of remote Aborigines were being admired or deplored in the 1947 and 1957 polls, they were certainly being taken as a reason not to assimilate such people. The high rates of approval, in the 1980s, for land rights in which the land at stake was specified as 'reserves' is a continuation of that older perception that remote Aborigines are significantly different. Australians have long understood reserves, and the 'tribal' people for whom they were declared, as exceptional. Reserves were where Aborigines were allowed to go on being different.

Thus, as we have seen (page 80–1), in a 1981 Gallup Poll 53 per cent of respondents endorsed 'land rights' (equated with 'freehold') for 'Aboriginal people on Aboriginal reserves'. In 1984, when the Gallup Poll asked whether 'Aboriginal people should be given land rights—that is, be given freehold land—or should the land on which they live be leased or sold to them?', only 29 per cent appeared to endorse land rights.[70] But the difference between the two results is arguably a measure of the difference between respondents' perceptions of

'Aboriginal reserves' (specified in the 1981 question) and their perception of land generally (the terms in which the 1984 question was couched). Reserves have long been conceded to the ('tribal') people that occupy them.

There were other ways to distinguish among Aborigines in their entitlement to land. As we showed in the previous chapter, some Australians, following decades of official distinctions between 'full-blood' and lesser 'castes', remain sensitive to distinctions of 'descent' and associate degrees of descent with cultural difference.[71] In February 1984, Tasmanian Opinion Polls (TOP) mobilised this association when it asked whether 'descendants of full-blooded Tasmanian Aborigines should be granted rights to land which they consider to be of special historical or religious significance?'. The idea appealed to 56 per cent of those interviewed. Later that year, in the Gallup Poll, no more than 26 per cent of respondents from Tasmania wanted Aboriginal people to be given land rights; that is, given freehold land. The difference may partly be an effect of sampling variance (the number of Tasmanians in the national survey was small). However, it is also likely that the difference can be explained by TOP's specification of the land (culturally significant) and the people (descendants of 'full-blooded') and by its spelling out the relationship between the two.[72]

'Descent' also figured in the ANOP's 1984 study for the Department of Aboriginal Affairs. Asked 'if there are to be land rights, should all people of Aboriginal descent be able to share or should land rights apply only to certain types of Aborigines?', 55 per cent wanted restrictions. Asked 'Which types?' about half said 'full bloods only', and about one-third 'tribal, rural, outback Aborigines'. About half of ANOP's respondents supported the idea that 'Aborigines should get land rights because it's important for their traditional way of life'.[73] Majority support for land rights could be elicited, ANOP found, if land rights were presented as 'based on Aborigines' traditional association with some areas of land (reserves, tracts or deserts) because of their "real" cultural links with it'.[74] We suggest that ANOP was tapping into a popular perception of Aboriginal difference in 1984 that the very first Australian poll on Aboriginal policy (in 1947) had elicited: the differences between tribal and non-tribal, between reserve land and unspecified land, between 'full-blood' and 'part-Aborigines'. There is an abiding concession to (if not respect for) those Aborigines whose difference from other Australians is signified by such terms as 'tribal' and 'full-blood'. In this tradition of poll results, a mixture of evaluations may be present: from racial superiority to sentimental regard for the 'noble savage'. What matters is that the remoteness of such Aborigines from the way of life lived by most Australians puts them in a special category, as far as public policy goes. They have to be treated differently. This abiding significance of their difference co-exists with a strong belief in the abstract equality of all Australians.

Another line of departure from the principle of equality (less significant than the culture/blood/reserve theme, we think) was discovered by the CMWA. Early in 1985, a poll commissioned by the Chamber showed that people distinguished 'land rights' from 'land grants': those polled were opposed to 'land rights', but evenly divided (45:45) over 'land grants'.[75] Perhaps 'land rights' implied the 'alienation' of more land than would be likely under a system of 'land grants'; or perhaps the notion of charity, control or *noblesse oblige* appealed more than the language of 'rights'. After all, certain Australians—soldier settlers, for example—have long been judged worthy of 'land grants'.

ANOP's 'Middle Australia'

Early in 1985, as we have shown, Holding began to formulate his political task not only as establishing 'consensus' between mobilised interests such as the Aboriginal lobby, the mining lobby and the State governments, but also as cultivating a 'majority' of the public—consensus in a quite different sense. In early 1984, he was conscious of polls 'starting to show that people thought enough was already being done for Aborigines'. In August his Department of Aboriginal Affairs (DAA) asked ANOP how the Government could 'maximise public support for the Federal government's policy on land rights'.[76] It would have been possible to make this a study of the connections between issues, opinions and voting intentions, but ANOP's research for the Department (unlike its research for WA Labor) was not strategic in this electoral sense. Nor, legitimately, could it have been. Commissioned by the public service, not by a political party, the study was bound by convention that excluded questions about past voting behaviour or future voting intentions. (In 1983, questions had been raised in the South Australian Parliament and in the press about ANOP's practices in relation to a poll on drugs conducted for the Minister for Health.)[77] Thus, ANOP's study for the DAA in 1984 paid no attention to the way political representation fragments the nation into electorates of greater or lesser political importance; apart from reporting opinion State by State, distinguishing different parts of a State, or referring to 'communities' defined by industry or by their relationship with the cities, it ignored political boundaries. Nor did it measure the salience of the land rights issue to that small proportion of the voting public whose votes would decide the contest in marginal seats; the closest ANOP came was in its observation that 'the issues' were 'noticeably more salient for Western Australians as a result of the Chamber of Mines campaign', though whether ANOP included a measure of *salience* as against opinion *strength* is unclear.[78] In short, the ANOP study for the DAA was not about whether Labor's land rights policy would jeopardise its majority in the House of Representatives.[79] Rather, ANOP defined the problem as overcoming the resistance to land rights within an imagined Australian community it named 'middle Australia'. For ANOP, 'middle Australia' was not a social or economic category but a curious, quasi-statistical, survey-generated artefact: the proportion of its sample (52 per cent) occupying the 'middle ground' on land rights and 'softly prejudiced' against it.[80]

How, exactly, was this group identified? Respondents, it appears, were asked, first, whether 'they had a view about land rights for Aborigines'; and, if they did have a view, 'whether this was basically in favour or opposed'. (The questionnaire, treated as a confidential document by ANOP, is not included in the report.) 'Those without a view' (an unspecified number) 'were probed' (by means not disclosed) 'as to whether they were inclined one way or the other and why'. This process yielded the following distribution: 'strongly opposed' (24 per cent); 'strongly in favour' (18 per cent); and 'tending to opposition or in favour with reservations' (52 per cent).[81] This last group was 'middle Australia', and ANOP described it in the following terms: 'that majority of white Australians who are not firmly committed one way or the other on Aboriginal issues'; 'resident adults who reveal soft forms of prejudice or ignorance to our screening questions on black rights, land rights and other Aboriginal issues'; and 'the middle leaning increasingly to opposition and prejudice through fear, ignorance, mis-information and soft racism'.[82] Respondents who failed to express firm, clear views on land rights aroused ANOP's anxiety. The attitude of 'middle Australia', far from being 'apathetic', was 'an expression of "soft prejudice" which has a greater propensity to harden than to turn to sympathy'. This potential was presented by ANOP as a test of the Government's ideological nerve and leadership mettle. 'Black rights generally, and land rights in particular, represent the most divisive and potentially explosive issues we have ever dealt with—and we suspect that this country has faced in the post war period.' A campaign was 'definitely, if not desperately needed'. Indeed, ANOP (estab-lished in 1971) had 'never recommended so strongly' the need for 'a government campaign ... in any area'.[83]

However, ANOP's portrait of 'middle Australia' was empirically problematic and its advice to the Government politically naïve. First, its report assumed that 'middle Australia'—those who declined to express an opinion when first asked—would be crucial to the way any land rights policy was received. ANOP noted that 'middle Australia' did not have a '"couldn't care less" attitude'[84]; what it failed to consider was the possibility that since land rights was of low salience to these respondents the Government could discount them as a group from which they had anything to fear. ANOP did not explore the strategy of ignoring 'middle Australia' on the grounds that whatever made them vote for or against the Government it was hardly likely to be the Government's policy on land rights. What ANOP's report did instead was to set the Government the formidable challenge of making a large number of Australians—half the electorate, no less—care enough about land rights to have a definitely held opinion about them, and to understand land rights in a way that favoured the Government's position, not the position of the mining industry and other vested interests that were sure to mount a counter-mobilisation.

Second, ANOP referred to 'middle Australia' as if the reservations that these respondents expressed about land rights were the only significant things they had to say. The survey acknowledged that the 52 per cent were 'tending to opposition or in favour with reservations', but it discounted the significance of those elements that favoured land rights. Probing by interviewers apparently revealed that both those not strongly 'for' and those not strongly 'against' expressed the same reservations about land rights. Accordingly, ANOP referred to them all as the 'softly prejudiced', highlighting their common stock of reservations about land rights rather than any tentatively stated support. Indeed, the report presents a puzzle as to why many of those 'in favour but with reservations' actually supported land rights at all.[85]

A third weakness in ANOP's notion of 'middle Australia' was its decision to pay 'special attention' to 'rural and provincial town dwellers; residents of North Queensland and North-West W.A.; farming and mining communities'. The report fails to say what 'special attention' amounted to, but there is an implication that these locales were among the heartlands of 'middle Australia'.[86] We are left wondering whether ANOP treated these three regional populations as non-Aboriginal Australia's quintessence and, if so, why. Rather than representing the heartlands of 'middle Australia', the areas to which ANOP paid 'special attention' would have been among the areas in which opposition to land rights was highest. As the report makes clear, opposition to land rights was higher in Western Australia (43 per cent 'strongly opposed') and Queensland (36 per cent) than in other states and higher outside the capital cities (30 per cent) than inside them (21 per cent).[87]

On ANOP's own evidence, 'middle Australia' was divided in significant ways. For example, while a substantial minority (40 per cent) of 'middle Australia' admitted that they did not know or were unsure what the Federal Government was 'actually proposing regarding land rights for Aborigines', the remainder said they did. While one-third (34 per cent) agreed that if there were to be 'land rights for Aborigines', they 'should apply to all people of Aboriginal descent', more than half (59 per cent) said they should 'apply only to certain types of Aborigines'. And while half (52 per cent) of 'middle Australia' did not want Aborigines to have 'the power to stop mining on land they own', if there were to be land rights, almost as many (43 per cent) said Aboriginal owners 'should be able to stop mining' (27 per cent 'on parts they live on or that are sacred sites', and 16 per cent 'on any parts of the land they own').[88]

While we could reasonably expect 'middle Australia' to be as muddled as these figures indicate, how consistent was opinion within either of ANOP's two strongly opinionated groups? As Table 2.1 shows, among those strongly in favour of

Table 2.1 Arguments for and against Aboriginal land rights, among those strongly in favour, strongly against, and 'middle Australia', 1984 (percentages)

Question

Twelve statements on land rights—six 'pro' and six 'anti'—were put to respondents in a randomised order who were asked to indicate their agreement or disagreement.

Land rights arguments	Strongly Favour	Middle Australia	Strongly Oppose
Pro			
Land rights will help Aborigines *keep their culture* and help the survival of the race	96	53	21
Aborigines should get land rights because it's important for their *traditional way of life*	93	50	22
Land rights will help Aborigines *improve their lives* and help solve some current problems	81	41	16
Aborigines should get land rights because they *were here first*	93	31	4
Aborigines should get land rights because land has a *special meaning* for Aborigines	84	30	12
We should *compensate* Aborigines for the way they've been treated by giving them land rights	74	26	6
Anti			
Land rights may lead to racial tension and a *separate Aboriginal state*	26	48	75
Land rights for Aborigines means that Aborigines would *own too much of Australia*	15	55	76
Giving land rights to Aborigines means that a lot of land won't be used for *productive purposes*	42	59	78
Giving land rights means that some people could *lose their private land*	52	59	77
Giving land rights to Aborigines is *unfair* to white Australians	11	65	86
Aboriginals shouldn't be *given* land rights; they should have to buy or *work for land*	21	64	88

n =2000; national; 18+; face-to-face; late September 1984

Source: ANOP, 'Land Rights: Winning Middle Australia', Table 11.

land rights there were many, apparently, prepared to stomach some strikingly negative consequences of the policy: half (52 per cent) thought (wrongly) that 'some people could lose their private land'; close to half (42 per cent) thought 'a lot of land' would not be 'used for productive purposes'; one-quarter (26 per cent) were willing to countenance the risk of 'racial tension and a separate Aboriginal state'; a similar proportion (21 per cent) thought Aborigines shouldn't be given land rights at all—they 'should have to buy or work for land'; some (15 per cent) accepted that when given land rights Aborigines would 'own too much of Australia'; while others (11 per cent) wanted land rights to be granted even though, in their opinion, land rights were 'unfair to white Australians'.

On the other side, roughly one-quarter of those 'strongly opposed' to land rights did not agree that private land might be lost (23 per cent); that Aboriginal land use would not be 'productive' (22 per cent); that Aborigines would 'own too much of Australia' (24 per cent); or that there would be a risk of 'racial tension and a separate Aboriginal state' (25 per cent). Some 14 per cent 'strongly opposed' to land rights did not endorse the view that land rights would be 'unfair to white Australians'. And, most bizarre of all, one in ten (12 per cent) of those 'strongly opposed' to land rights did not agree that land 'shouldn't be given' to Aborigines—'they should have to buy or work for land'. ANOP did not comment on these counterintuitive results. Had they done so, it might have undermined the idea that people of 'strong' opinion had worked out internally consistent positions on land rights. Middle Australia was not distinguished by its muddled views. Anyone can produce muddled views if a poll presents them with questions that mobilise different rhetorical themes and frameworks of thought.

One student of Australian political culture, Judith Brett, has argued that 'Aboriginal and Torres Strait Islander claims to a special relationship with the land make their political demands unassimilable to a liberal democratic discourse of equality of opportunity and citizen's rights'.[89] We suggest that Australian respondents to opinion polls on land rights have shown less respect than Brett for the logic of 'liberal democratic discourse'. In order to make sense of the emerging political compromises between Indigenous and non-Indigenous Australians—such as land rights legislation—they have made sure that the notion of Aboriginal difference is 'assimilable' to their frameworks of 'equality'. Does this mean that respondents who employ the discordant frameworks of 'equality' and 'difference' are being illogical? We do not think so. Rather, they are realists who face up to the political fact that the social world embodies compromises between competing values—in this case, the equality and the difference to which Aborigines are widely conceded to have a right. To discern the logic of 'liberal democratic discourse' we must notice not only the relationships between concepts but also the uses to which people put the concepts of liberal thought as they make sense of a world of political trade-offs. (And this is a point to which Brett has shown herself fully alive in her studies of political culture.)[90] We return to the theme of respondent rationality in our Conclusion.

Its weaknesses notwithstanding, the ANOP report appears to have impressed the Department of Aboriginal Affairs.[91] In April 1985, the Department approached advertising agencies with copies of both ANOP's report and 'the Government's preferred land rights legislation model', and a request that the agencies 'submit a proposal for a national communications campaign ... aimed at creating greater public awareness of the need for Aboriginal advancement'.[92] In the attached brief tenderers were advised that the campaign would need: 'to challenge the myths and misconceptions about Aboriginals that are entrenched in the minds of the general public'; 'to encourage positive interaction between Aboriginal and non-Aboriginal people'; 'to supply factual information on

Government policies and programs in such a way that expenditure does not become part of the backlash'; 'to include, but not deal exclusively with, land rights'; and 'to promote an understanding of the need for positive discrimination for Aboriginals'. In its background notes, the Department warned that 'the general climate of opinion on Aboriginal matters is worsening', and that this worsening was due to the 'emergence' of 'racism' that was 'usually latent', and that what had 'trigger[ed]' the worsening were 'the recent anti-land rights campaign waged by lobby groups' and 'the handover of Uluru (Ayers Rock) to the traditional land owners'.[93]

While a campaign along these lines tempted the Ministerial Committee on Government Advertising, the proposal was stillborn. Any campaign, agencies had been advised, would be contingent on 'legislation being introduced and passed by the Parliament'.[94] What the agencies could not be told, though they might have worked it out for themselves, was that ANOP's report itself had made the chances of (uniform) land rights legislation distinctly less likely. While some argued that 'the government's failure to conduct a publicity campaign allowed the opponents of land rights to succeed',[95] members of the Government sympathetic to land rights might have thought a campaign of the kind ANOP had argued for would do more to mobilise opposition to land rights than to galvanise support.

Conclusion

The evidence to 1985—when politicians and journalists began confidently to offer narratives of a 'backlash' against the policy philosophies of 1967 and of Whitlam and of Fraser—does not point to a trend in public opinion about land rights. Rather the evidence suggests a different conclusion: that 'equality', 'Aboriginal tradition' and 'rights' are concepts open to rhetorical manipulation. When 'land rights' was presented as the antithesis of 'equality', 'land rights' came off second best. When land rights was linked to terms which positively evoked Aboriginal difference—some notion of 'Aboriginal tradition' (spirituality, purity of descent, continuity of occupation of reserves)—it received far more support, sometimes majority support. The ANOP research for the Department of Aboriginal Affairs argued correctly that the popularity of 'land rights' depended on the rhetorical context of its presentation. However, public references in 1985 to ANOP and to other polls did not report this insight. Journalists' and politicians' references to these polls gave them another, fanciful, meaning: the polls were said to have demonstrated that the public's support had sunk or that the public's opposition had strengthened; in short, there had been a 'backlash'.

That reading of the mid-1980s polls quickly became an orthodoxy uniting supporters and opponents of the Hawke Government's national land rights policy. The 1985 *Report of the Committee of Review of Aboriginal Employment and Training Programs* referred to the 'apparent backlash from the wider community'.[96] Political scientist Christine Jennett later described the tendency of public opinion in the 1980s as adverse to land rights, suggesting that this 'radically altered climate of public opinion' had 'led the Hawke government to withdraw from its promised national land rights legislation'.[97] Secretary of the Department of Aboriginal Affairs, Charles Perkins, commented that 'in today's generally comfortable Australia, there is a growing number of Australians who believe that Aboriginal people already receive too much government assistance'.[98] Former Chair of the National Aboriginal Congress and energetic critic of the Government's decision to drop national land rights, Rob Riley, explicitly assented to what he cited as Hawke's view that 'attitudes have changed since the heady days of the seventies'.[99] When the Australian Institute of Aboriginal Studies created a research project on 'public attitudes to Aborigines' in 1986—'At a time when public attitudes are said by some to be hardening (the so-called "White backlash") …' it recycled the 'backlash' hypothesis.[100] Thus, in 1987, Fred Chaney, Western Australian Senator for the Liberal Party that had removed 'land rights' from its platform in 1984, could refer to 'the now well-established white backlash which will limit support for Aboriginal advancement programs'.[101] And in his history of the Australian federation, the political journalist Paul Kelly reproduced this orthodoxy when he averred that the Hawke Government's failure to 'establish a national land rights policy' was caused in part by 'a deep public backlash against the steady campaign for Aboriginal rights'.[102]

In the end, the Hawke Government's failure to establish a national land rights policy had more than one cause. In 1983, Labor's platform, for the first time, distinguished between the 'short and long-term aspirations for the ALP', and the commitment to 'uniform Aboriginal land rights', as Hawke's speech-writer was to note, was among a long list of commitments that Hawke would have 'little difficulty or remorse in culling' from 'Labor's herd of sacred cows'.[103] If the platform was one factor that allowed Hawke to cull the Party's commitment to 'uniform Aboriginal land rights', and the perceived 'backlash' in Western Australia was another, the forbidding challenge posed by ANOP's research played its part as well.[104]

'Middle Australia' was (and remains) an important phrase in the language of Australian politics. It refers to the voters—variously defined—that governments must keep on side. Pollsters, journalists and politicians (and sometimes academic social scientists) refer to 'it' as if it were a real sociological entity whose views can be studied, measured and known. We do not share that belief. For ANOP, 'middle Australia' was a category of respondent defined by their failure to state a clear position on land rights. Were their views likely to have been taken into account, in the absence of this sort of research? As a latent interest, perhaps. Were their opinions on land rights likely to turn them against Labor in swinging seats? We do not know. What we do know is that, to his undoubtedly important task of reconciling 'interests' (Aborigines, mining companies, State governments) that were clearly manifest, Holding chose to add the far less important but enormously difficult task of engaging the uninterested public. In January 1985, ANOP produced 'middle Australia' as if it were a crucial actor, an interest to be addressed and persuaded. Intended to help the Government, ANOP's research simply helped frighten the Government off.

3

Native Title and Reconciliation

The lead up to the 1967 referendum was not the last occasion on which the nation's Parliament seemed unified around a positive view of Indigenous Australians. On 5 June 1991, the House of Representatives unanimously passed the Council for Aboriginal Reconciliation bill. That there was no significant dissent from 'reconciliation', it soon became clear, depended on the word being open to diverse interpretations. In this way, June 1991 recapitulated May 1967: both were moments of unspecific national commitment. With 'reconciliation', optimism revived and the nation's political vocabulary was renewed. As Angela Pratt has shown, the frequency with which MPs referred to 'reconciliation' jumped remarkably.[1] Throughout the 1990s, the word would be often used and its meanings diversely understood.

The bill set up a Council for Aboriginal Reconciliation. It did not take the Council long to engage a communications consultant: Donovan Research began its work for the Council in September 1991. Donovan's opening briefing of the Council in January 1992 embodied the political dilemma that promoters of 'reconciliation' would face throughout the 1990s.

On the one hand, the Council's work had to reflect Indigenous aspirations. To this end, it was advisable to 'pre-test' any communication campaign 'against members of the Aboriginal community to ensure that the message strategy is consistent with, or at least not contradictory to, Aboriginal aims and expectations for Reconciliation'. On the other hand, it was important for the Council to define 'reconciliation' initially in terms that associated it with ideas about which '*a majority of the population*' is known to be '*positive*', for 'it is quite clear that many Aboriginals' expectations are … inconsistent with what many non-Aboriginals favour as part of a Reconciliation Process'.[2] Accordingly, the Council should avoid associating 'reconciliation' with 'land rights', until 'other attitudes and beliefs are more conducive'. 'A point of entry for discussion of land rights would be the protection of Aboriginal sacred sites, where, in the absence of conflict with economic development, there is majority community support for such protection.' Later, Donovan added: 'The granting of land rights needs to be justified as assisting Aboriginal self-esteem and self-supporting enterprises'. And: 'Aboriginal spiritual links with the land need to be communicated in a way that is credible and in a way that creates empathy and understanding of these spiritual links as per the Western Australian Land Rights Campaign in 1984'. However, at the beginning of the Council's campaign for reconciliation, 'specific details of goals, especially those relating to Aboriginal demands, should not be stated'.[3]

Within six months of the Council's receiving these cautions about 'land rights', the High Court delivered a judgment that put land at the top of Australia's agenda of public debate. The Court was responding in the first week of June 1992 to a plaintiff from the Torres Strait island of Mer (one of the Murray Islands), Eddie Mabo. The case—indeed, the whole issue of 'native title'—became known by his name. To have a view on *Mabo* was to hold an opinion about the High Court's judgment and/or about the subsequent efforts of legislators to pass a law on native title. *Mabo*, in this sense, made it impossible for the Council to heed Donovan's advice to tiptoe around the issue of land until it judged the public 'ready'.

In the *Mabo* case, inhabitants of the Murray Islands declared that they had property rights in these Islands before the British colony of Queensland annexed the islands of the Torres Strait in 1879. Their property right—native title—was based on their customary law; Queensland law had not extinguished their customary law. The judges agreed: in Australia's common law, native title to land continued after the British Crown became the sovereign power. But the Crown could lawfully extinguish native title by granting someone a proprietary interest in that land. Where the Crown had not granted such a right, native title remained. Claimants could present themselves as the holders of native title by showing that, in their surviving customary law, they were the land's owners.

The wisdom of this judgment was fiercely debated. Part of that debate focused on the legitimacy of the Court's 'now' seeing itself 'as an interpreter of public opinion', to quote the historian Geoffrey Blainey, and its argument that '"the contemporary values of the Australian people", as the judges put it, called for a new deal for Aborigines'.[4] The debate soon included arguments about how the Commonwealth and State governments should legislate to recognise—or to extinguish— the native title that remained. From June 1992, when the Court handed down its judgment, until December 1993, when the *Native Title Act* was passed, politicians, the natural resource lobbies and Indigenous leaders engaged in vigorous and often heated debate. The Act was passed in a Parliament as passionately divided over native title as it had been benignly unified over 'reconciliation' two and a half years before.

We will not retell the story of this debate.[5] Rather, our intention in this chapter is to highlight the part that the pollsters played in it—the issues or themes they raised, the methods by which these were framed, and the ways in which the results were interpreted. We conclude by showing how the Council's market research tracked the impact of the High Court's judgment and by noting the impact this had on Donovan's initial communications strategy.[6]

Polled Reactions to the High Court Judgment

A year after the Court's judgment, when the Commonwealth released its discussion paper, *Mabo: The High Court Decision on Native Title*,[7] and the mining industry set out to discover what the public thought of the judgment, surveys showed that Aboriginal dispossession was widely recognised. In June 1993, when those who claimed to be aware of *Mabo* (four-fifths of the sample) were asked to say what they believed the judgment was 'all about' few betrayed negative understandings. The most frequently mentioned explanations were positive: 'Aborigines reclaiming land they owned before European settlement' (18 per cent); 'restores land rights/native title to Aborigines' (16 per cent); 'acknowledged Aborigines were original owners' (14 per cent); 'recognising Aboriginal title to traditional land they have occupied continuously' (12 per cent); 'Eddie Mabo's success in court/proved title to Murray Island' (10 per cent); 'compensation for Aborigines/loss of land' (5 per cent). Of the rest, most might be classified as neutral (e.g. 'Aboriginal land rights', mentioned by 26 per cent) rather than hostile.[8]

Asked whether they thought 'Aboriginal people have been disadvantaged in any way by the arrival of European and other races in Australia', 70 per cent of those interviewed said that Aboriginal people had been disadvantaged. Elaborating on the nature of the 'disadvantaging', many of the comments were sympathetic to the vocabulary of Aboriginal understanding: 'dispossessed of their land' (27 per cent); 'loss of identity/ culture' or 'forced to live European lifestyle' (48 per cent); 'genocide/many killed' (15 per cent); 'mistreated' (13 per cent); and so on.[9] Such answers were evidence of widespread intellectual empathy with the Aboriginal case and with the High Court's reasoning about past 'injustice'.

In the executive summary, prepared for the Australian Mining Industry Council (AMIC) and the Chamber of Mines and Energy in Western Australia (CMEWA), AMR:Quantum stressed that 'dispossession of their land' was mentioned 'spontaneously' by 'only' 31 per cent of those who agreed that Aborigines had been 'disadvantaged' or by 'only just over 20 per cent of the total population'.[10] But other evidence suggests this was an underestimate. Asked, in this and the subsequent industry survey, whether 'ownership of land is more important, and a more essential part of their feeling of well being for Aborigines than it is for other races', 44 per cent agreed that it was and 46–49 per cent said it was not.[11]

Respondents to these surveys were not asked explicitly if they thought that at least part of the 'disadvantaging' of Aborigines arose from their being dispossessed of their land. However, they were asked: 'In your opinion, should the Government recognise *any* and all claims made by Aboriginals on the basis that the land was theirs prior to European settlement, do you feel that such claims should be totally disregarded or does your opinion lie somewhere in the middle?' Only 17 per cent in the first survey (16 per cent in the second) expressed the view that Aboriginal claims should be 'totally disregarded'. Overwhelmingly, respondents said that their opinions lay 'somewhere in the middle'. Invoking qualifications that we have demonstrated, in previous chapters, to be significant, 72 and 69 per cent respectively said that there should be some recognition—depending, among other things, on whether the claims were to 'genuine tribal lands' (22 to 27 per cent), whether they were to 'proven sacred sites' (21 per cent), or whether they had 'individual merit' (19 per cent).[12]

Pollsters as Critics of 'Native Title'

The High Court's judgment was a bombshell to many of those who had successfully lobbied against the Hawke Government's national land rights policy a few years earlier. Ready, once more, to diminish the land rights cause, their campaign included the commissioning—and publicising—of market research generally hostile to the *Mabo* decision and to the Keating Government's legislative response. In these polls and those commissioned by the press, the contextualisation and wording of questions was more likely to resonate with mining than with Aboriginal interests. More than 60 per cent of the answers that the press paid for, or were invited to report, were sponsored by the mining industry's peak council or produced at the initiative of an organisation with direct mining links. Surveys commissioned by the mining industry (the AMIC in association with the CMEWA) accounted for more than one-third of the questions to which journalists had open access. Polls conducted by the Roy Morgan Research Centre—whose executive chairman was also chairman of a Western Australian mining company—accounted for another quarter. The Morgan Poll, for example, twice posed this question: 'In your opinion, are Aborigines a severely underprivileged section of Australian society or not?' Opinion divided: 40:50 in January 1993, and 39:55 in January 1994, with the balance of opinion against.[13] But in a debate about Indigenous rights, these questions were apposite only if 'rights' were somehow contingent on people being 'severely underprivileged'.

Is 'incompetence' or 'political mischief' the better way to describe the first sampling of opinion to be published on *Mabo*? In January 1993 interviewers for Morgan explained to respondents that the High Court's decision 'determined Aboriginal people may be the traditional owners of various land areas of Australia and entitled to be granted or given those various land areas'.[14] The respondents were from Western Australia—the key state in the ensuing battle—and most (57 per cent) of them declared that prior to the interview they had been unaware of the Court's decision. Nonetheless, 81 per cent of those interviewed gave their opinion: 32 per cent approved the '*Mabo* case decision', 49 per cent disapproved. If we assume that the rest—the 19 per cent who either refused to answer, said they did not know or were undecided—had hitherto been unaware of the case, then about half of those who expressed a definite view (57 less 19 equals 38 per cent, which is just under half of those expressing a view) must have relied on Morgan's account in formulating it. Alternatively, if we assume that all of the 19 per cent were aware of the decision, as seems less likely, that still means that almost one-third (43 less 19 equals 24, almost one-third of 81) of those who expressed a view had to depend on the information about *Mabo* provided by the poll.[15]

It was unfortunate that between one-third and one-half of those expressing an opinion were dependent on the information in Morgan's question, for in three respects it was misleadingly worded. First, the use of the phrase 'may be', suggesting that the High Court itself was uncertain whether Aboriginal Australians were the 'traditional owners of various land areas'. Second, the reference to land as 'granted' or 'given', when the Court was actually recognising a property right. Over the next twelve months, twenty-one Morgan items on native title were published in *Time*: none of them acknowledged the Court's declaration of Aboriginal rights.[16] Third, the failure to spell out any of the conditions attached by the Court to native title; not a word on the requirement that Aboriginal claimants establish a continuing association with the land, that private ownership extinguished native title or that native title rights were more circumscribed than the rights of freehold.

Polls as News

In terms of the number of polling organisations involved, the number of surveys commissioned or the number of questions asked, Australia has never seen an issue quite like the native title debate. In a little over a year, from January 1993 to January 1994, seven market research organisations conducted nineteen surveys, producing and publicising the results to over 160 questions on *Mabo*. No doubt a good deal more was commissioned by some of the political parties (the Liberal Party, in particular) and by a variety of other players (especially in the mining industry) and kept under wraps. Even if we count only those items produced for the press, the number of questions on *Mabo* was not far short of all the questions relating to Aborigines since the start of public opinion polling over fifty years before.[17] Because the *Mabo* judgment and the subsequent debate were big news, the polls became frequent and important news stories in their own right. The latest polls punctuated the continuing debate.

Before we extend our analysis of the 1992–94 poll results, we want to emphasise, again, the part that journalists, sub-editors and editors played in the interpretation of the public opinion research. The newspaper headlines generated by the polls were selective, focusing on only one of the items in any one set. Almost always they were episodic—written without regard to the findings reported by other organisations—and often they were incomplete and partial in their account of the item's meaning. With an issue as complex as 'native title'—and some polling organisations confided that *Mabo* was too difficult an issue on which to poll—it was easy for the headlines to confuse. Compare: 'Mabo a mystery to most of WA' (*West Australian*, 21 May 1993) with 'Poll shows firm grasp of main Mabo issues' (*Age*, 4 August 1993); or 'Community divided on native title ...' (*Australian*, 17 June 1993) with either 'Voters say no to Mabo' (*Australian Financial Review*, 30 August 1993) or 'Aust backs black title' (*Bulletin*, 26 October 1993); or 'People's verdict on Mabo: no worries' (*Sydney Morning Herald*, 4 August 1993) with 'Mabo worries 86% of people: survey' (*Sydney Morning Herald*, 22 November 1993).

It is unlikely that such headlines described dramatic shifts in public sentiment. Not many of the poll questions were repeated and the results generated by those that did do not indicate massive shifts. To be sure, there was a vast increase in the number saying that they were *aware* of the High Court's decision. According to the first national poll, taken in January 1993, only 31 per cent had 'read, seen or heard anything about *Mabo*', while in June, after the widely reported Council of Australian Governments meeting on *Mabo* ended in acrimony, the number 'aware' of the Court's decision had grown to about 80 per cent.[18] Polling in January 1994 suggests that 'awareness' peaked at about that level.[19] Many of those 'aware' of the High Court decision remained imperfectly informed about it. At no stage, however, was there a dramatic change in *attitudes* towards 'native title'.[20]

The polls helped the press promote the 'native title' debate as a drama in which 'the public' was a protagonist. Consider the headline: 'Mabo worries 86% of people: survey'. Here the *Sydney Morning Herald* took its cue from the opening statement on the AMIC's media release: 'MABO DOUBTS REMAIN HIGH'. But the item in the poll to which the headline referred was about the level of concern that *might* be generated if the High Court's decision 'put at risk the existing property titles of other Australians'. What the handout failed to mention, and what the press did not notice, was that no attempt had been made to discover how *likely* respondents thought such a consequence might be.[21]

While those opposed to *Mabo* were the most consistent and important imparters of spin, they were not the only ones. Headlines like 'People's verdict on Mabo: no worries' (*Sydney Morning Herald*, 4 August 1993) and 'Poll shows firm grasp on main Mabo issues' (*Age,* 4 August 1993) also took liberties with the data. Both headlines referred to a poll that invited respondents to choose between the statements: 'Aborigines may be able to claim any land in Australia, including land in our major cities'; and 'Aborigines can only claim land which they can prove they have had a continuous relationship with since white settlement'. The result: 7 per cent chose the former, 88 per cent the latter.[22] But to conclude that most of those interviewed had 'no worries' is to assume that worries about

Aborigines being able to claim land anywhere are the only worries anyone could have. It is to ignore other worries respondents might have had, including worries about compensation, economic development and whether Indigenous Australians were being fairly treated.

Any attempt to go beyond the headlines must evaluate the performance of the polls in terms of the questions asked, the information offered and the interpretations given. That is our task in the rest of this chapter.

Land at Risk

That native title could not threaten their homes was something many people did not understand, at first. Yet the High Court decision upheld existing rights in land, declaring them to be stronger than any assertion of 'native title'.[23] Some polls tried to find out how many people feared that Aboriginal people might take 'my land'. Asked, in June 1993, about what sort of land Aborigines could claim, in a poll conducted in mainland capitals, 35 per cent said 'Crown land used for public purposes'; 20 per cent thought Aborigines might have a claim to 'Crown land leased to companies, farmers, etc.'; only 9 per cent thought 'privately owned land' might be at risk. The poll did not attempt to discover how many respondents were unsure which land might pass into 'native title', but it was able to report that 39 per cent felt they did not 'understand the Mabo decision and the consequences of it' either 'very well' or 'at all well'.[24] In a subsequent poll, in August, 12 per cent agreed (or at least did not disagree) that 'Aborigines may be able to claim any land in Australia, including land in our cities'. In the same poll, 12 per cent of the homeowners interviewed felt that the land their homes were on was 'threatened by the Mabo judgment'.[25]

While not many people thought that their homes were vulnerable to native title, the proportion was large enough to make a difference to the proportion of people supporting native title. Of the three items in national polls that measured support for the High Court's decision, the one that registered greatest support was the item that explained that privately owned land was not affected and that claimants to land would have to pass certain tests (to demonstrate their ongoing association with the land):

> The High Court of Australia recently decided that Aboriginal people own land which they have been continually associated with since before European settlement. This does not affect any privately owned land. How strongly do you agree or disagree with the High Court decision that Aboriginal people should own their traditional land?

Couched in these terms, by AGB McNair, the decision in *Mabo* won majority support: 55 per cent in favour, 24 per cent against.[26] Compare this with the response to Morgan's question: Morgan explained the *Mabo* decision as meaning that 'Aboriginal people may be traditional owners of various land areas of Australia and entitled to be granted or given those various land areas'. This question elicited only 38 per cent approval, with 32 per cent disapproving of the decision.[27] A greater proportion of AGB McNair respondents answered the question (if the 'don't know' figures are anything to go by) and the AGB McNair margin in favour of the decision was not Morgan's 6 percentage points, but an impressive 31.

In a third survey, Newspoll explained to respondents that 'Native title means the right to occupy land but not own and sell it and the High Court has now ruled that native title exists'. Newspoll then asked: 'Are you in favour or against this High Court decision that allows the Aboriginal people to claim native title to government land for which they can establish a claim?'. This account diminished the High Court's judgment by reducing native title from a right of ownership to a right of occupation, did not explicitly exclude privately owned land from the scope of the judgment, and made no reference to the continuing association requirement. The result was a marginally negative balance, 43 in favour and 46 per cent against.[28]

The effect of the question on the pattern of response can be confirmed by looking at the earlier AGB McNair poll, based on mainland capitals, where respondents had been told that 'The *Mabo* decision recognised that native title to land did exist in accordance with the laws and customs of Aboriginal people. In order to claim native title any Aboriginal group will need to be able to demonstrate an ongoing association with the land in question.' Thus described, the decision met with the approval of 45 per cent, while 34 per cent disapproved. In response to the Newspoll question, asked the same weekend and cited above, respondents living in the mainland capitals favoured the decision more narrowly, 46:43.[29]

Equal Rights

'Equal rights' has long been the rallying call of those opposed to such rights.[30] From the start of its national polling, Morgan sought to position 'native title' within a framework of 'equal rights':

> Next about land being claimed by Aborigines. In your opinion should Aborigines have more, the same, or less [sic] rights than other Australians making claims over (the same) land?

Having first asked the question at least ten years earlier, after Labor had put national land rights on its agenda, Morgan could hardly have been surprised by the response: 70 per cent to 80 per cent support for Aborigines having the 'same' rights.[31] In June, AMR:Quantum, on behalf of the mining industry directly, also asked whether 'Aboriginal rights to land should be greater than, lesser than, or equal to other Australians'. The results were virtually identical to Morgan's: 15 per cent supported 'greater' rights, 6 per cent supported 'lesser' rights and 74 per cent supported 'equal' rights. In the same survey, 19 per cent felt that 'Aboriginals should be treated differently from other Australians' and 79 per cent thought that 'Aboriginals should be treated in all respects just the same as other Australians'.[32]

The mining lobby and its political friends hoped that supporters of 'equal rights' would disagree with the High Court's upholding of 'native title'. '*Mabo* creates privilege', said Bill Hassell—a lawyer, and the Western Australian Liberal Party President who, as the State parliamentary leader, had led the opposition to native title rights in the 1980s—'legal privilege based on race'.[33] The mining industry's polling, according to its own gloss, showed that a 'strong belief in equal rights' was a 'major element' of 'community views of the Mabo/native title issue'. It was with 'unequivocal certainty', it insisted, that the public demanded that the 'redressing' of 'Aboriginal disadvantage must be based on equal rights for all'.[34] In full-page advertisements, the industry implied that native title, to which only Indigenous Australians had access, represented 'greater' rights, and thus violated 'equality'.[35] But respondents who supported equal rights did not necessarily disapprove of the *Mabo* decision. In the Morgan poll, the High Court's decision in *Mabo* drew the opposition not of 70 per cent of those interviewed—the proportion seemingly committed to giving people the 'same' rights—but of 32 per cent, less than half that number.[36]

From the perspective of the High Court and of those who approved its decision, the cause of 'equality' was well served by 'native title'.[37] The first Saulwick poll on native title asked which of the following statements came closer to the respondent's view: 'Aborigines should have to pay for any land they want, just as everyone else does'; or 'Aboriginal owner-ship of land they have occupied since white settlement should be acknowledged without any payment'. Half of those interviewed opted for the latter, and just under half (45 per cent) for the former.[38] If we assume that the distribution of opinion on 'equal rights' would have been the same across Saulwick's first national poll as it was across Morgan's, then it is clear that support for 'equal rights' tells us almost nothing about attitudes to land rights.

Again, in the second of the two polls conducted by AMR: Quantum for the mining industry, 78 per cent of the respondents agreed that 'Aboriginals should be treated in all respects just as other Australians'. But in response to another question, 14 per cent agreed that 'due to their historic association to land', Aborigines should 'have rights to land which give them title and permanent ownership of that land', while 37 per cent agreed that Aborigines should have 'rights of access to carry out their traditional land use but without exclusive ownership of the land'.[39] That is, only 42 per cent— not 78 per cent—took the view that Aborigines were 'entitled to the same rights as other Australians'.

Ignoring such details in the polling on native title, some participants in the debate assumed that the responses to 'equality' questions told us unequivocally what the public wanted. Liberal Senator Bronwyn Bishop, whose party wanted to respond to the High Court by extinguishing native title altogether, was confident that a 'dose of democracy' would show public support for that position. She called for a referendum that would ask 'a question related to things like ensuring that all Australians are equal under the law and have the same rights and entitlements'.[40] Had such a referendum recorded widespread support for 'same rights', the contested nature of such rights would have left the miners free to read the result one way and the supporters of native title free to read it in the opposite way. The public would not have been empowered to speak on native title by Bishop's referendum; paradoxically, its views would have been no clearer than if a referendum had not been held at all.

Equality of Outcomes: Should Population Equal Acreage?

In its first national poll on the issue, in January 1993, Morgan tackled the question of equality not only in terms of rights but, more audaciously, in terms of outcomes. 'To the best of your knowledge', respondents were asked, 'what percentage of the Australian population are Aborigines?'. And later: 'In your opinion, about what percentage of Australia's land should Aborigines be granted or given title to?'. The results of these two questions were not released until early June 1993.[41] Not for the first time, the agendas of the mining industry and of the Morgan Gallup Poll coincided. 'Right now', the AMIC was soon to point out in full-page advertisements, 'Aboriginal people constitute 1.5% of Australia's population. And yet they already have title to, or reserves for 14% of Australia's land area.'[42]

If the Morgan organisation anticipated that responses to the questions on population and ownership might be related it was not to be disappointed. Of those who expressed an opinion (87 per cent), the mean estimate for the size of the Aboriginal population was 13 per cent. Of those who expressed an opinion on Aboriginal land entitlements (just 57 per cent), the mean figure was 12 per cent. Whether those who vastly overestimated the number of Aborigines felt that Aborigines were entitled to considerably more land than those whose estimates were closer to the mark, Morgan's report does not allow us to say. All that can be said is that the two averages coincided.

Morgan seemed surprised, even dismayed, not that the figures matched but that both figures were so high. Headed 'Australians Off the Mark on Aborigines', the report to subscribers took on an indignant tone: 'Although Australians are of the opinion that Aboriginal land rights' are 'currently at appropriate levels', they are 'patently unaware' of the size of the Aboriginal community.[43] There was a clear inference that if respondents had known that Aborigines constituted only about 1.5 per cent of the population their estimate of what Aborigines were entitled to be 'granted or given title to' would have been correspondingly modest.

The conclusions drawn from the data, however, do not stand examination. If we accept Morgan's premise that respondents thought Aborigines were entitled to 'be granted or given title to' 10 per cent of the Australian land mass, and if we also accept its inference, from open-ended responses, that 12 per cent was what the non-Aboriginal community thought was appropriate, then we might read this not as endorsing the *status quo* but as a mandate for a significant (20 per cent) increase. An increase of this magnitude would have taken Aboriginal holdings beyond anything likely to be achieved under native title. We can debate Morgan in this way, but to what end? Morgan's entire framework was objectionable—a (leading) question on Aboriginal numbers and a question about Aboriginal entitlement, both couched in the language of proportionality.[44] Would Morgan have used this framework to ask about Australians of, say, Italian or British descent? Or Jews? Or citizens whose surname was Morgan?[45]

Elicited by such questions as Morgan's, public opinion could scarcely be said to exist. The idea that the land rights question might be solved by recourse to the notion of equal outcomes certainly lies beyond the bounds of any legal or legislative discourse. That nearly half (43 per cent) of the respondents in the Morgan poll declined to answer the question suggests that, for most Australians, thinking about land rights in these terms is not only unfamiliar but unintelligible.

The 'Cost' of Native Title

Although the High Court narrowly rejected the argument that 'extinguishment of native title by the Crown by inconsistent grant ... gives rise to a claim for compensatory damages',[46] the existing laws of the Commonwealth made it possible that compensation would be due to some native title holders because the Commonwealth's extinguishment of a property right renders the titleholder eligible for fair compensation. In effect, the High Court was now telling the Government that it must review its land grants in order to assess whether any of those grants had extinguished anyone's native title. This instruction applied only to decisions that extinguished native title after 31 October 1975, for it was not until the *Racial Discrimination Act* came into force, on that day, that it became illegal for the Commonwealth to act in a racially discriminatory way. If, after that day, a government had alienated any land that turned out to be 'native title' land, then the native title holders could demand compensation, just as any other landholder could if the government resumed his or her property. Thus, the principle of 'equal rights' entailed the possibility that the Government might have to use taxpayers' money to pay some Aborigines for their land.

Polling on compensation exposed the superficiality and political opportunism of certain pollsters. When they asked about compensation, they did not frame it as a consequence of the much-vaunted value 'equality', but as a 'cost' of native title that the public might have to bear. Eagerness to pose the issue of 'compensation' in this way led Morgan to ask questions that were misleading. In Morgan's first question on the topic, in January 1993, respondents were informed that it had been 'suggested' that 'Aborigines should be compensated for being dispossessed by European settlement'—phrasing that did not let respondents know that very few Aborigines were likely to be eligible for such treatment. Only 22 per cent endorsed the idea in 1993, and only 26 per cent supported it a year later.[47] Morgan also asked a sample of Victorians whether their Government should 'pay compensation to Aborigines in addition to rights of title or not?'. The question obscured the fact that compensation would be paid only to those whose rights had been unlawfully *extinguished*. Perhaps the level of support for compensation (28 per cent) elicited by the question should be seen not as low but as relatively high.[48] In a further poll, in Sydney and Melbourne, only 12 per cent of respondents agreed that 'if Aborigines were granted land title through Mabo-style land claims' they should 'be paid compensation in addition to the rights of title'.[49]

Questions worded more competently generated a more favourable response towards Aboriginal land rights. In surveys conducted in Western Australia—hardly a safe haven for the land rights cause—between 42 and 47 per cent of those interviewed said they would 'support land rights legislation ... if it meant that some form of compensation was paid to Aboriginals for land used for mining and pastoral purposes'.[50] Here the proportion might have been inflated by respondents thinking that compensation would effectively replace land rights. In the first of the AMR:Quantum polls, 41 per cent (37 per cent in Western Australia) agreed that where 'native title is recognised but the land cannot be handed over because it already has use and title ... Aboriginal people should be compensated'; in the second, conducted in November 1993, the figure was 44 per cent (46 per cent for Western Australia).[51] Similarly, when asked by Newspoll about Aboriginal people being financially compensated for 'mining or farming activity', in areas where native title might be granted, 39 per cent expressed support. While the majority was opposed, those 'strongly' opposed were no more numerous than those 'strongly' in favour.[52]

Had respondents been offered a middle option, one that made judgments about compensation contingent on where the money was to come from, the pattern of response might have changed. When Morgan asked: 'If compensation was to be paid to Aborigines, who should pay the compensation—the federal government, the state government or the mining companies?'—two-thirds of those interviewed thought it was a government responsibility (51 per cent saying it was a Federal responsibility); 33 per cent thought the mining companies should pick up the tab; and 7 per cent named all of the above—though multiple responding was more common than these categories suggest.[53] According to the first of the Newspoll surveys, in June 1993, opinion was more widely spread: 'the government' was mentioned by 42 per cent; miners and farmers by 23 per cent; 'someone else' by 11 per cent (compared to 4 per cent in the Morgan poll under 'other'); 'no one'—not an invited response but mentioned spontaneously—by 14 per cent (5 per cent in the Morgan poll); and 10 per cent 'don't know' (13 per cent in Morgan).[54]

The effect of substituting 'taxpayer' for 'government' in these polls illustrates the way public opinion research is, in part, market research on key political words. Thus, when a sample of Western Australians was asked whether, in the event that Aboriginal title were 'found on land where mining is planned', any compensation to Aborigines should be paid 'by miners or by taxpayers', only 10 per cent favoured payment by taxpayers. Insofar as they had an opinion, most (58 per cent) considered payment the responsibility of the miners; the rest (32 per cent) were 'undecided'.[55] When Morgan, in a Sydney–Melbourne survey conducted in August 1993, suggested that if governments 'were to pay compensation to Aborigines it may be necessary to increase taxes', 71 per cent predictably did not like the idea.[56]

Respondents' distaste for compensation that drew on their taxes was not even-handed. It depended on who was being compensated. Only one poll asked about compensation for mining companies or pastoralists if Aborigines dispossessed them. In the first of the Westpoll surveys on native title, in Western Australia, in May 1993, respondents were asked whether compensation should 'be paid to mining companies or pastoralists if they loose [sic] title of [sic] land' through a land rights challenge. Just under two-thirds (64 per cent) of those interviewed said that one or the other (or both) should be compensated. Asked, whether 'as a taxpayer' they would 'be prepared to share the cost of those compensation payments to companies and pastoralists', just under two-thirds (61 per cent) of those in favour of compensation—that is, 39 per cent of the total sample—said they would.[57]

There were other costs of native title that the public were asked about. Litigation is expensive, so who should pay? Here the data suggest that Western Australians took a non-discriminatory position. Asked, on two occasions, whether 'Aboriginal claims to land in court' should 'be funded by taxpayers', 71 per cent (subsequently 68 per cent) of those interviewed said they should not. Asked whether taxpayers should 'also fund the legal costs of mining companies and pastoralists who now occupy the land in question', 73 per cent (70 per cent) said they should not.[58]

Native title could also be framed as a 'cost' to the 'economy' and to the general wellbeing of Australians. In each of the surveys conducted on behalf of the mining industry, AMR: Quantum asked:

> whether you would be very concerned, somewhat concerned or not at all concerned if the effect of this *Mabo* decision were to:
> - put at risk the existing property titles of other Australians
> - discourage mining investment in Australia
> - delay or prevent economic developments
> - reduce or prevent employment opportunities in Australia
> - result in the control of some publicly owned natural resources by a minority group
> - result in large areas of Australia being claimed by Aboriginal people.

The miners' press releases made much of the level of 'concern' picked up by these questions. Upwards of 80 per cent of those interviewed would be 'concerned' (or at least 'somewhat concerned') if the High Court's judgment adversely impacted on existing property titles, mining investment, economic development or employment opportunities, or if it resulted in large areas being claimed by Aborigines or some natural resources falling to the control of a 'minority group'.[59] What the surveys did not report—indeed, did not attempt to measure—was whether respondents thought any of these outcomes likely. Other surveys, as we have shown, suggested that the number who believed that 'native title' put 'existing property titles' at risk was relatively small. If that is the case, the AMR:Quantum finding that 89 per cent of the electorate 'would be ... concerned' if the property titles of other Australians were 'put at risk' is of little value—except, of course, for purposes of propaganda.

In the 1980s, the mining industry, backed by some State premiers, lobbied hard against allowing Aborigines to veto mining on their land: the cost of the veto to the national economy was their theme. In the Keating Government's proposed native title bill, title holders were not to get a veto over mining, but this did not stop pollsters from canvassing the risk that native title posed to mining. AMR:Quantum reported that over 80 per cent of its respondents would be 'concerned' were *Mabo* to 'discourage mining investment in Australia', while a similar proportion would be 'concerned' were it to result in 'the control of some publicly owned natural resources by a minority group'.[60] Confronted by these figures (the only ones in the media release to touch on the question of a veto) one could be excused for imagining that opposition to the idea of an Aboriginal veto would have been overwhelming. Not so. The same surveys failed to produce figures indicating anything like the same level of opposition to a mining veto. The best they could manage were figures that put the level of concern on a par with the much smaller proportion (roughly half) who said they were *very concerned* about discouraging mining investment or the possibility of 'minority' control of 'publicly owned natural resources'.[61]

But how mighty the labour to produce even this. Respondents were first told that 'Most of Australia's mineral resources are owned by the government on behalf of all Australians, *irrespective of who owns the land itself*; for example, a miner who wants to develop mineral resources pays a royalty to government—that is the people of Australia'. (For the mining industry to equate 'government' with 'the people' was unusual, to say the least.) Just to make sure that they had got the message, respondents were asked whether they had understood the statement or would like it read again. 'Given that most of Australia's mineral resources are owned by the government', they were then told, did they believe 'that Aborigines should be treated differently by being able to claim total ownership of the minerals on their land?'. Just 13 per cent in June 1993 (10 per cent in November) said they should. Then and only then were they asked whether they believed that 'Aborigines should be able to prevent exploration and mining on their land?'. Notwithstanding this protracted softening up, 35 per cent (34 per cent in November) said they should; no more than 49 per cent believed they should not.[62]

We suspect that AMR:Quantum's information about the 'public ownership' of minerals helped to boost support for the miners' position. In a subsequent poll, conducted by Saulwick, respondents were not invited to see minerals as part of the common wealth; instead, they were asked whether they agreed that, 'if Aborigines who gain land as a result of the *Mabo* decision do not want mining on this land, their wishes should be respected'. Those who thought that Aborigines' wishes should be respected prevailed, 51:43—a favourable margin of 8 percentage points rather than the unfavourable margin of 14 (or 15) percentage points in the AMR:Quantum poll. This proportion expressing respect for Aboriginal wishes was all the more remarkable considering that, by a margin of 55 per cent to 33, the same respondents had conceded that *Mabo* was 'likely to damage Australia's economic development'.[63] In an October 1993 poll conducted by AGB McNair, more than twice as many (47 per cent) expected 'the proposed legislative response' to the decision to have a 'negative' impact as expected it to have a 'positive' effect.[64]

Different ways of formulating the issue produced different results. When respondents were asked whether they believed that 'Australia must recognise Aboriginal land claims even at the expense of economic development and investment',

48 per cent of those interviewed in a Western Australian poll in May 1993 said 'yes' (18 per cent) or 'yes, with reservations' (30 per cent).[65] Had the coding frame allowed it, some of the straight 'no' responses might have been recorded as '"no" with reservations'.

We get a fair-minded perspective on these polls about 'cost' when we recall that, from an Indigenous perspective, there was a 'cost' in not having native title. Did the polls ever ask people to ponder the cost—to Indigenous Australians, or to the nation as a whole—of refusing to allow native title? They did not. However, when the polls measured respondents' willingness to pay some economic cost—for litigation, for compensation— or to accept some risk to mining or to general prosperity, they were arguably measuring the public's recognition that native title was a fair thing, a necessity to be paid for. In AGB McNair's October poll, the majority (53 per cent) expected the High Court's decision to have a positive effect on Aborigines. At the same time, there was clearly division over whether the legislation then proposed by the Federal Government would 'help the process of building better relations between Aboriginals and other Australians' (37 per cent said it would) or 'hinder' it (as 34 per cent believed); the rest (29 per cent), almost as numerous as those on either side, either said it would have 'no effect' or ventured no opinion.[66] Other attempts to elicit opinion on the Commonwealth's legislation, either as initially proposed or after it was finally passed, show the same pattern: a more or less even division, with almost as many declining to respond as there were taking one side rather than another. This should hardly surprise: three weeks after the legislation became law, about one-quarter of the respondents in the polls were still oblivious to it and no attempt was made by any of the pollsters to outline the arguments of those in favour of the legislation or the arguments of those against.[67]

Native Title and the Australian Constitution

Because the Keating Government's proposed native title legislation would bind the State governments, the native title debate
was also a debate about the relationship between Commonwealth
and State powers to deal with Indigenous Australians—an issue
the 1967 referendum had opened up rather than settled.
Although empowered by the referendum to override the States,
the Commonwealth had until now shied away from such
confrontations. Keating was the first Prime Minister to coax
and cajole the States to adopt a policy determined in Canberra.
It is not surprising then, that pollsters canvassed native title as
if it were a constitutional issue.

It was Morgan that put 'States' rights' on the polling agenda,
after *Mabo*, and kept it there. In Morgan's first survey, in Western
Australia, respondents were told that:

> Until recently, the Western Australian State Government had the
> sole right to determine Western Australian land title, including
> whether or not Aborigines should be granted title to land. The
> *Mabo* case may mean the Federal Court can override State rights
> and enable Aborigines to claim Western Australian land through
> the Federal Court.

Thus briefed, respondents were asked whether they believed
'the Western Australian State Government should have the sole
right to determine Western Australian land title for all people'
or whether 'the Federal Court should be able to override the
Western Australian State Government in regard to Aboriginal
land claims'. The majority (57 per cent) backed the State
Government; the minority (38 per cent) backed the Federal
Court.[68] Morgan's question misinformed respondents. The
States do not have 'the sole right' to determine land title (the
Commonwealth's defence and external affairs powers apply to
land use). Nor was it a result of *Mabo* that Federal law could
prevail over State law in Aboriginal matters: the 1967 refer-
endum decided that. That the Federal Government had not

previously exercised its power over State land policy was a matter of political will, not of constitutional law. In another question that resonated with the Western Australian Government's strategy of legislating its own version of native title—a question posed on the Government's behalf—Morgan asked a sample of voters, in December 1993, whether they would 'support a request to the High Court to determine which *Mabo* legislation should deal with the *Mabo* problem'.[69] But to pose this question was to sink the shaft into an empty mine: there was no constitutional issue for the Court to decide.

Morgan addressed another question on inconsistent legislation to respondents in Melbourne and Sydney: 'Regardless of whether you approve or disapprove of the rights of Aborigines to make *Mabo*-style claims, do you believe the Federal government should or should not be able to override [Victorian/New South Wales] government legislation on this issue?'. The following statement prefaced the question: 'The federal government maintains that they can override the [Victorian/New South Wales] government so that Aboriginal people can make *Mabo*-style land claims'. The question spuriously implied doubt about the Federal Government's powers. It also mentioned '*Mabo*-style claims' while asking respondents not to think of them as a context for the (ostensibly) constitutional issue. The States' resistance to Canberra's 'override' was supported by 55 per cent, almost identical to the proportion of Western Australian respondents in favour of the 'rights' of States.[70]

The highest level of support for the States against the Commonwealth was recorded in response to a question asked on behalf of the mining industry. 'Under the Australian Constitution', respondents were told by AMR:Quantum:

> State governments have responsibility for land management. The Prime Minister is proposing to override this so that he can implement his *Mabo* plan. In your view should land management

continue to be controlled by the state government or should it
be controlled by Canberra?

Wrongly describing the constitution, the question implied
'override' to be a violation of it. Note also that the question
was framed so that the legislation was no longer the Parliament's
or the Government's but the Prime Minister's, and that
'Canberra' (not the Commonwealth) was to control land
management. Such wording was likely to arouse Liberal–
National Party voters, and voters, especially in the west, loyal to
the idea of 'State rights'. Respondents were being asked to
judge an unconstitutional power grab by a dangerous man
leading a distant and uncaring government. Their verdict was
hardly remarkable. Nearly two-thirds (64 per cent) of those
polled, including 77 per cent in Western Australia, wanted
control by the States.[71]

In addition to being addressed directly, the question of
'State rights' was addressed indirectly. Thus, Morgan asked:
whether the Victorian Government was 'right to legislate to
protect existing title from Aboriginal land claims or not?';
whether 'the [Victorian/New South Wales] government
should legislate to protect all existing titles ... from *Mabo*-style
land claims'; and, in Western Australia, whether respondents
approved or disapproved of the State's '*Mabo* legislation'.[72] In
Western Australia respondents also were asked whether the
State Government 'should legislate to try to guarantee security
of access for miners and pastoralists'.[73] On each occasion the
idea of State legislation received majority backing. And, if we
may generalise from one of the Western Australian polls,
support for State initiatives went hand in glove with opposition
to the Commonwealth's moves.[74]

Beyond this, nothing was said about the content of the
States' legislation or where it differed from the Commonwealth's. In the absence of any attempt by Morgan to establish
what, if anything, respondents knew about each legislative

package, these answers might have been recording general attitudes to federalism, to the Federal Government and the respective State Governments, to the Prime Minister and to the various premiers, rather than attitudes to the legislation. Perhaps it was indicative that in Western Australia, where 29 per cent of those interviewed by Morgan conceded that they had not heard of the Federal Government's legislation (even though it had passed through the House of Representatives) and (a partly different?) 21 per cent admitted to being unaware of the fact that Western Australia had passed its own legislation, only 15 per cent declined to give an opinion as to whether the High Court should rule in favour of the Federal Government's legislation or of Western Australia's.[75] Answers to the latter question were virtually identical to the answers given to the question about which form of legislation respondents would prefer—the Western Australian (Court's) or the Federal (Keating's).

Among those opposed to native title were critics who thought the High Court's approach to the common law reckless. 'Regardless of whether you approve or disapprove of the decision', Morgan asked respondents, 'in your opinion did the High Court go beyond its constitutional power in the *Mabo* decision, or not?'[76] Although most respondents (84 per cent by Morgan's reckoning) were aware of the decision— Commonwealth legislation had passed through the Parliament only weeks before—few would have had any sort of handle on constitutional law (assuming they knew the Constitution existed) or given such arcane matters much thought. In any event, *Mabo,* as we have noted, was not a constitutional case, and even if it had been it could make no legal sense to say the High Court acted unconstitutionally because the High Court itself is the final arbiter of what is or is not constitutional.

Most respondents would have faced two very different choices to those actually written into Morgan's script: admit to being completely out of their depth; or enter a judgment on the basis of extraneous considerations, most obviously their feelings about the substance of the decision. That this is indeed what happened is suggested by the result. No fewer than 30 per cent of those interviewed declined to enter a judgment at all; of the rest, how many came down either in favour of the High Court (39 per cent) or against (31 per cent) simply by taking a punt is anyone's guess. And in which state was contempt for the High Court's grasp of constitutional law greatest? Western Australia—not, surely, because legal training was more widespread there but because in Western Australia disapproval of the decision (and of the High Court for handing it down) was more marked.[77] Notwithstanding Morgan's instruction that respondents put to one side their feelings about the outcome of the case, the pattern of response across the states to the High Court's exercise of power was remarkably similar to the pattern of response to the substantive decision—allowing, of course, for differences in the numbers 'undecided'.[78]

Native Title and Reconciliation

How did the irruption of 'native title' into the intended consensus of 'reconciliation' affect the approach of the Council for Aboriginal Reconciliation when promoting that ideal? From 1991, well before *Mabo*, until 1995, when some of the dust from the legislative response to *Mabo* had settled, Donovan asked respondents nationwide what they thought reconciliation meant and what they thought the Government meant by the term. The results, reported in Table 3.1, are consistent with what one would expect: that the debate on native title (beginning in the second half of 1992) made more people think that reconciliation must have something to do with dealing with the issues of land and native title.

These data do not tell us whether the respondents were for or against reconciliation and native title; they tell us only that the proportion that saw the two issues as linked peaked during

Table 3.1 What 'reconciliation' means (medium type) and what it means to the government (bold type), 1991–95 (percentages)

Questions

'What thoughts, pictures or feelings do you have when you think of the words "Aboriginal Reconciliation"? What else?' [Probe fully for first, second and other mentions].

'The federal government has set up an organisation called the Council for Aboriginal Reconciliation to assist in the process of aboriginal reconciliation. What do you think the government means by "Aboriginal Reconciliation"? What else? [Probe fully]

	1991 Nov.		1993 Feb.		1993 Sept.		1994 Mar.		1994 Aug.		1995 May
Fairness/make up	25	**15**	23	**17**	27	**24**	25	**23**	26	**22**	26
Better relationships	12	**10**	21	**11**	21	**11**	18	**12**	14	**10**	15
Return land/ *Mabo*	9	**9**	12	**12**	19	**19**	14	**16**	19	**17**	12
More facilities, etc	11	**10**	7	**9**	7	**6**	11	**12**	10	**12**	10
More spending	11	**1**	6	**2**	11	**1**	9	**3**	13	**3**	15
Other											
Nothing/Don't know	22	**37**	19	**34**	15	**28**	19	**32**	16	**35**	27

n = 1300 in each survey

Source: Donovan Research, 'Aboriginal Reconciliation Tracking Study August 1994', for the questions; 'Research Report: Aboriginal Reconciliation Tracking Research', pp. 8–10, for the data.

the native title debate. Whether this was a public relations setback for the Council is open to doubt. For a start, the proportions that linked land or '*Mabo* issues' to reconciliation never climbed above one in five. As well, the Council was ambivalent about giving 'reconciliation' definite meanings: the term's popularity might depend on the fact that it meant different things to different people. But sooner or later the idea had to be given some specificity. In May 1995, Donovan advised the Council that 'Communication tactics since 1993' had 'not resulted in any overall increase in awareness for [sic] the Reconciliation Process'. After analysing data elicited by the open-ended question 'What thoughts, pictures, or feelings do you have, when you think of the words "Aboriginal Reconciliation"?', Donovan reported that 'there is *still no major single concept in the minds of the general public as to the nature of the Aboriginal Reconciliation process*'.[79] And, as Table 3.1 shows, the number of respondents who, in response to this question, could say nothing had jumped from less than one in five (15 to 19 per cent) in 1993–94 to one in four (27 per cent) in 1995.

Conclusion

The polls on native title reveal public opinion around Aboriginal issues—not for the first time—in a highly equivocal state. There was agreement with the principle of 'equality', but not necessarily with the application of the principle to the issues raised by 'native title'. On these issues, opinion was often evenly divided. As we have pointed out many times, what the polls revealed was affected by how the questions were framed and by the information provided by the pollsters. Where the decision of the High Court was accurately represented, support for native title was likely to be greater than when it was represented in less accurate and more threatening ways. In the native title debate, more than in any other discussion about Indigenous issues, the polling was tendentious: background information provided by the pollsters was mistaken or misleading; and respondents were asked to make judgments about matters that (considering the high proportion of 'don't knows') many felt ill-prepared to make.

The Council for Aboriginal Reconciliation responded to the native title debate by building 'native title' into its strategy for promoting 'reconciliation'. In August 1992, it greeted the High Court's rejection of the doctrine of *terra nullius* as 'a new impetus for reconciliation'.[80] Quoting data that we will return to in the next chapter, Donovan advised the Council in April 1994 that

> With respect to communications dealing with Mabo, it should be noted again that the vast majority of the general public (75%) are prepared to accept that '*Aboriginal and Torres Strait Islander peoples were the original inhabitants of Australia*' as part of the process of Reconciliation. This suggests that most people would accept the Mabo decision, at least in principle, and *provides an entry point for acceptance of a treaty and the land rights implications of Mabo*.[81]

However, as the Council acknowledged, the native title debate 'presented a major challenge ... The Council had members representing many political, cultural and economic perspectives of the debate.' Consequently, it did not try to contribute to 'the everyday detail of the debate'. Rather, it promoted principles and procedures it hoped would bring about legislation and institutions that would reconcile 'governments, industry, the wider community and the Aboriginal and Torres Strait Islander communities'.[82]

4
Reconciliation and Responsibility

On 27 May 2000, at the Corroboree 2000 ceremony in the Sydney Opera House, the Council for Aboriginal Reconciliation formally presented to Australia's political leaders two 'Documents of Reconciliation': the 'Australian Declaration Towards Reconciliation' and the 'Roadmap for Reconciliation'.[1] The documents were a 'synthesis of the wisdom of the people of Australia', for they had resulted from what Council Chair Dr Evelyn Scott later described as 'arguably the most extensive consultation process ever undertaken in Australia on a matter of public policy'.[2]

Since its inception in 1991, the Council had used survey research to gauge the public's understanding of and commitment to 'reconciliation'. From 1991 to 1995, Donovan Research had produced six reports for the Council based on surveys undertaken by Newspoll in November–December 1991 (the benchmark), February and September 1993, March and August 1994, and May 1995.[3] Donovan also produced a report based on focus groups conducted in June 1995 in New South Wales, Queensland and Western Australia.[4] Subsequently the Council

had engaged Brian Sweeney to assist 'the Council's communications and public awareness program for the 1995–98 triennium,
including … issues arising from the Council's social justice
submission to the Commonwealth Government'. Sweeney
reported focus group research conducted in December
1995 in each of the States and the Northern Territory; he
later added reports on focus group and survey research, both
conducted in May 1996.[5]

The Council had not publicised these studies. However, in
1999 and 2000, as the Council approached Reconciliation's
climactic ceremony and the presentation of the National
Reconciliation Documents, the Council decided that, when
presenting the Documents, it would not be enough to refer to
its 'extensive public consultation meetings' with over ten
thousand Indigenous and non-Indigenous Australians from
July to November 1999.[6] As well, data from a representative
national sample would be required to demonstrate that the
Council had obtained the views of the whole community.
When Hawke had contemplated a treaty, as an instrument of
reconciliation, one of the conditions he laid down was that it
must be 'acceptable to the majority of Australians'.[7] In signing
up to any other document of reconciliation, the Howard
Government was unlikely to demand anything less.

The design and strategic decision-making of the Council's
surveys in 1999–2000 was primarily in the hands of staff of the
Department of Prime Minister and Cabinet, who made up
the Council's secretariat, and of some members of the Prime
Minister's Office.[8] They commissioned three final studies of
Australian attitudes to reconciliation: focus groups, conducted
from early December 1999 to mid-January 2000 by Irving
Saulwick and Dennis Muller (the Saulwick Report); a survey,
conducted in late January by Newspoll, on a document of
Aboriginal reconciliation; and further focus groups, conducted
by Saulwick and Muller in March and April 2000, on the
Council's *Draft Document for Reconciliation* (which consisted of

both the Declaration and the Roadmap), this time with Aboriginal participants only.[9]

In this chapter we begin by describing some interpretations of the first Saulwick focus group study (widely reported as representative of non-Indigenous views). We then move on to the interpretations of the Newspoll study. We note two features of these interpretations: dismay and disappointment about the continuing public indifference or hostility to Indigenous grievances; and a tendency to reduce attitudes to reconciliation to views about whether the Prime Minister should apologise to the 'Stolen Generations'. As an alternative to the focus on an apology, we read the Newspoll results in the context of the earlier studies by Donovan Research and Sweeney. The single most important theme to emerge from all these studies, we argue, is the theme of 'responsibility'. But 'responsibility', like 'reconciliation', has been open to conflicting understandings— understandings that in the thinking of many Australians co-exist.

What the Press Made of the Council's Research

The first of the Saulwick focus group reports was presented to the Council in February. By Friday 25 February 2000, or perhaps as early as Tuesday 22 February, the Prime Minister knew the results.[10] By the beginning of the following week Saulwick's report, in whole or in part, had been leaked to the press. A week later, the press was also covering Newspoll's quantitative research. While 'the public' was now a news story, the press was not uniformly attentive. The country's best-selling paper, the Melbourne *Herald Sun,* referred to the research only once; the Brisbane *Courier-Mail,* the Adelaide *Advertiser,* the *West Australian*, the Hobart *Mercury* and Sydney's best-selling paper, the *Daily Telegraph*, referred to it not at all.[11] The papers excited by the Council's research were the Sydney, Melbourne and Canberra broadsheets,[12] papers that address a constituency skewed towards the university-educated, professional and managerial middle class.[13] Such readers do not rate Aboriginal issues as such very highly, but they appear more likely than others to regard reconciliation as important.[14] Journalists working for these papers also regard reconciliation as important, and it seems that many expected the Council's research to show a higher proportion of the public to be engaged with the issue. Saulwick's summary of the focus groups' opinions struck them, on the whole, as bad news.

Before we retell what the journalists said, we pause to summarise Saulwick's account of the group discussions that he convened. On the 'positive' side, the report noted 'a widespread feeling' evident 'throughout Australia' that Aborigines had been 'badly treated'. According to Saulwick it was agreed 'universally' that 'the position of Aborigines' was 'a tragedy'. Saulwick also found that there was 'little overt prejudice directed towards Aborigines … on the basis of race alone'. Most supported 'the concept of a safety net' and 'tolerance' of difference—or at least of 'the IDEA of difference'. On the 'negative' side, the list was much longer. While most recognised that Aborigines had been treated badly in the past, there was 'little recognition' of the impact this might have had on Aborigines today.[15] Aborigines needed to do two things they seemed not to be doing: 'make some attempt to "be like us"', and 'be prepared to help themselves and not rely on handouts'. Many of the respondents blamed 'white society for what they saw as the development of a handout mentality among Aborigines'.[16] The 'bulk of our respondents' believed that 'formal reconciliation would be a process in which the white community was once again lacerated for past misdeeds, and milked for further money which would be squandered in exactly the same way as the billions which were perceived to have been spent ineffectually on Aborigines already'. For these respondents 'formal recognition' was 'a divisive, rather than a unifying, influence'.[17]

Reporting these results in the *Sydney Morning Herald*, Michelle Grattan, the editor that year of a book called

Reconciliation, described Saulwick's focus group study as 'depressing, troubling and salutary'—Australians didn't want to 'own' the past because they thought it would mean accepting blame for the past.[18] Michael Gordon, in the *Age*, believed 'the bleak take-out from the most recent survey [sic] material is that mainstream sympathy for the indigenous cause may have even taken a step or two back in the past four years'; that is, in the years since the election of the Howard Government.[19] In the *Australian*, Paul Kelly concluded that the 'main impression left by the document' was 'that the exchange between Australians and Aboriginal Australians is a dialogue of the deaf'. Australians wanted Aborigines 'to conform to "our" values', were 'uncomprehending of land rights' and felt 'no need for any formal apology for past injustice'. They were 'largely disengaged from the notion of Aboriginal reconciliation'.[20] The *Canberra Times* quoted Jackie Huggins, a member of the Council for Aboriginal Reconciliation Executive from 1994 to 2000, lamenting that Australia was 'a country in denial about its history, about the racism'. As an editorial in the paper put it, if the research results were 'anything to go by, we're not even trying'.[21]

Much of the coverage reported what the focus group participants said about whether the Prime Minister should apologise formally to the 'Stolen Generations'. This gesture, the *Sydney Morning Herald* insisted, was the 'centrepiece' of reconciliation.[22] In the introduction to this book, we have shown that the polls on the apology in 1997 varied greatly in their representation of public opinion, depending on the different ways that they posed their questions. In 2000, journalists concerned about public support for the apology paid a lot of attention to Saulwick's focus group research. The 'as-yet-undisclosed' Saulwick document, Aban Contractor told readers of the *Canberra Times*, 'shows Australians are overwhelmingly opposed to an apology'.[23] The research, said Debra Jopson in the *Sydney Morning Herald*, 'is believed to have found the apology calls are a "turn-off" factor in the quest for reconciliation'.[24] Australians, fearing that an apology could lead to compensation claims, were 'strongly against' apologising, Grattan and Margo Kingston told their readers, adding that this was 'one of a number of very negative attitudes'; other 'negatives' included a failure to recognise how the past treatment of Aborigines affected their present attitudes, and the idea that Aborigines benefited unfairly from 'special treatment'.[25]

Nor did the 'negatives' stop there. Attitudes to 'key parts' of what Grattan and Kingston referred to as the Council's draft Reconciliation Document (a conflation, in these news reports, of both the Declaration and Roadmap) were 'very negative' and thus 'a blow to reconciliation'.[26] While 'a few liked [the document] in its entirety', Kelly reported, quoting from Saulwick's focus group study, 'most did not'.[27] Grattan and Kingston, quoting from Saulwick, highlighted respondents' views that the document was 'divisive, backward-looking, based only on the Aboriginal perspective'. The document required 'a series of concessions from non-Aboriginal Australians without any corresponding "give" by Aboriginal people'. It was 'a high-risk document which would probably be used as the basis for claims for land and monetary compensation'.[28] Contractor picked out words such as 'divisive', 'backward-looking', 'high-risk'; she noted the complaint that the document was based only 'on the Aboriginal perspective'.[29]

The journalists did not report Saulwick's focus group participants as wholly negative. Grattan noted a number of 'bright spots': participants recognised that Aborigines had been badly treated in the past, and they appeared interested in 'the practicalities of reconciliation'.[30] The leader writer in the *Sydney Morning Herald* detected a 'consensus' in 'mainstream politics' over 'the need for reconciliation in the sense of working to end the obvious disadvantage of Aboriginal Australians' and was reassured that the study had done nothing to 'shake that consensus'.[31] Kingston and Amanda Vaughan, steering clear of the word 'consensus', implied that if '40 per cent of Australians, and a big majority of women, support reconciliation', as 'leaked council research shows', this represented a movement in the right direction.[32] Kelly noted that that the report on Saulwick's focus groups revealed 'little overt prejudice directed at Aborigines ... on the basis of race alone', a point underlined by P. P. McGuinness. He also observed that the report was 'far more optimistic on attitudes of police, local government and industry towards Aborigines', a point about 'community leaders' made by Grattan and Kingston as well.[33]

These journalists did very little to explain to readers the limitations of focus group studies. They tended to imply that Saulwick's participants were representative of the Australian population. However, Saulwick had merely convened fourteen group discussions—six in the mainland capitals (two in different parts of Sydney and one each in Melbourne, Brisbane, Adelaide and Perth), the other eight in Moree, New South Wales; Ballarat, Victoria; Townsville and Mt Isa in Queensland; Mt Gambier in South Australia; Kalgoorlie in Western Australia; and Katherine and Darwin in the Northern Territory. The groups, each consisting of men and women, were made up of people from either 'white collar' occupations (seven groups) or 'blue collar' occupations (seven groups), aged either under thirty-five (seven groups) or thirty-five and older (seven groups). In addition there were 'in-depth' interviews with twenty men and three women described as 'community leaders' or 'leading citizens' (the mayor or deputy mayor, the presidents or vice-president of the local Chamber of Commerce, senior police or military men, management representatives—but no union leaders—from different industries, including the press, plus an academic) that came from all but two (Ballarat and Mt Gambier) of the regional centres. Saulwick did not explain how people were recruited to these discussion groups, but the study did acknowledge that none were Indigenous.[34] Academic social scientists were quick to comment on the limitations of focus group research.[35] But it is unlikely that this did much to undermine the journalists' presentation of 'the public'.

The Council for Aboriginal Reconciliation regarded the Saulwick results, Paul Kelly reported, as 'a pessimistic and misleading overview of Australian attitudes'.[36] The Canadian researcher Rick Ponting, who interviewed many of the government and Council personnel who had handled the Council's surveys, says that the Council was shocked when first briefed on Saulwick's results and outraged when the results were leaked.[37] As soon as the Saulwick study was made public, Evelyn Scott, the Council's Chair, warned that any 'reference to the research at this stage' would be 'premature and misleading', a warning also issued by Jackie Huggins. People should wait, Scott pleaded, for the 'release of the complete results of the qualitative and quantitative social research before jumping to any conclusions'.[38] The Newspoll results were not released 'about two weeks' later, as Scott had estimated; with more urgency, they were released about a week later.[39]

Newspoll proved a much better source than Saulwick for the views of the Australian public. In Stage I of its research, Newspoll conducted a national telephone survey. Half those interviewed were asked whether they would read the Draft Declaration and answer further questions; of these, less than half (280 or 43 per cent of those approached) agreed and were re-interviewed. Not only was the sub-sample relatively small, but it was also less representative of the adult population than the original survey; in particular, it over-represented people aged thirty-five or more and respondents who believed Aboriginal people were 'a lot worse off' than other Australians. To compensate, the results were post-weighted by age and by attitudes to Aboriginal disadvantage.[40] Later in this chapter we will analyse some of Newspoll's findings. Here, what interests us is how the newspapers covered Newspoll's research.

Newspoll's coverage was more 'positive' than Saulwick's. Under the heading 'We Want to Get it Right on Race', Paul Kelly's front page story in the *Australian* started by noting that '81 per cent of people' in the survey believed 'the process of Aboriginal reconciliation' to be 'quite or very important' and that '74 per cent' supported 'all or most of the draft national reconciliation document'; on an inside page, responses to the eleven propositions in the draft document from an earlier test indicated majority support for seven but majority opposition to none.[41] Kelly went on to argue that by supporting a shift in focus 'from government welfare to economic independence', respondents showed how to resolve the 'disconnection between past and present'. The headline in the *Canberra Times*— 'Majority Support Aborigines in Survey'—was even more upbeat, with the article in the paper reporting that the 'majority of Australians' had 'given reconciliation the thumbs up'.[42]

Nonetheleless, journalists interpreted the Newspoll results as worrying for the Council. Kelly, who believed that the findings gave 'a degree of support to the Council', also described the findings as 'mixed, complex' and apparently 'contradictory'.[43] The *Age* headlined its front page report: 'Nation Divides Over Reconciliation Issue'. In his opening sentence, setting out Newspoll's 'key findings', Michael Gordon described Australia as 'a nation divided, confused and living in denial, with half the community believing Aborigines are not disadvantaged and most considering they receive too much government help and are not entitled to "special rights"'. Moreover, while the majority accepted that Aborigines 'were treated harshly in the past', they opposed 'a formal apology'. Though Gordon went on to outline 'more positive findings'— widespread support for recognising Aboriginal people as 'the original owners of the land', for 'the reconciliation process', and for 'a reconciliation document'—the emphasis of his story lay elsewhere.[44] Writing in the *Sydney Morning Herald*, Grattan also emphasised the 'strong opposition to an apology'.[45]

The Prime Minister's Leadership

The Prime Minister was the first person to offer an interpretation of the polls to the public, and his reading seems to have influenced how others interpreted their significance. On Monday 28 February 2000, the Political Editor of the *Australian*, Dennis Shanahan, reported that the 'stumbling block' (Shanahan's phrase) to reconciliation, for the Prime Minister, was 'the continuing difference over an apology to Aborigines and Torres Strait Islanders for the wrongs of previous generations'. In his exclusive interview with Shanahan, the Prime Minister 'announced that Aboriginal reconciliation' would 'not be achieved by the December 31 [2000] deadline and that real reconciliation will take years'. This announcement came two weeks after Howard had declared that the process of reconciliation should not be 'time sensitive'. Shanahan also noted that the Government was 'aware of the results of a survey conducted by the Reconciliation Council' and that this was 'understood to show community opposition to an apology to Aborigines for appalling treatment by past generations'.[46]

In refusing the idea that reconciliation could be encapsulated in the apology and governed by a deadline, Howard was presented by Shanahan as both disappointing his critics and following the public. In his 1998 victory speech, as Shanahan reminded readers, Howard had committed himself 'very genuinely to the cause of true reconciliation with the Aboriginal people by the centenary of Federation', 1 January 2001. And the Council of Aboriginal Reconciliation was hoping to present the Document of Reconciliation (that is, the Declaration and the Roadmap) for the Prime Minister's signature on 27 May, the anniversary of the 1967 referendum. Now, Howard was saying that setting a deadline had been 'a big mistake' and that had he been Prime Minister in 1991 'he would not have agreed to a formal deadline for reconciliation'. It would be a mistake 'to feel that unless we resolve all this by May or December, it's all been wasted'. Far from having wasted its efforts, his Government, in Shanahan's words, was 'beginning to emphasise improving services to Aboriginal communities' and, in the Prime Minister's words, 'progress was being made'.[47]

Because Shanahan presented Howard as knowing the results of the public opinion research before he made his position clear, the Prime Minister was open to the accusation that he was simply a poll follower who had failed to lead on 'true reconciliation'. Central to these criticisms was the charge that his refusal to apologise to the 'Stolen Generations' was poll-driven. On the day Shanahan's story appeared, the *Australian* described Howard's position as 'predictable', another case of 'putting populism ahead of principle'. The Prime Minister, it argued, had 'again reacted to the touchstone of public opinion—this time on the question of a formal apology for the stolen generation. He has decided that if the people surveyed do not think it relevant then he does not have to do it.'[48] The following day, the *Age* quoted Huggins' linking Howard's position to 'an unreleased Council survey that found community opposition to an apology to the "stolen generation"'. The *Age* went on to report that Howard himself had 'cited widespread community support for his opposition to a full apology to indigenous people'.[49] 'The Prime Minister appears to believe that his new position on reconciliation accords with popular sentiment', it noted. Admonishment followed: 'If ever there was an issue that a government should not tie to the results of opinion polling, it is this'.[50] In the *Sydney Morning Herald* it was claimed that polls had 'helped' Howard 'abandon his deadline' and that he was 'partly relying on leaked Council research which shows that most Australians do not support an apology to the stolen generation'.[51] The *Canberra Times* said that Howard's knowledge that Australians were 'overwhelmingly opposed to an apology to Aborigines' added 'weight to accusations' that his 'recent comments on reconciliation were poll-driven', and that Howard was a poll-driven politician who had 'elevated poll watching ... to an art form.'[52]

Not everyone thought that Howard was influenced by the research, much less driven by it. Some suggested that Howard was simply comforted to discover that his outlook and that of 'most Australians' had a lot in common.[53] After it emerged that Peter Vaughan, head of the Prime Minister's policy unit, had written one of the questions in the Newspoll survey, it was also remarked that the research had 'found pretty much what the government wanted'.[54] Grattan implied that, while Howard's 'own narrow view of what is important in Aboriginal affairs and where he thinks public opinion stands' might line up together in 'a nation full of John Howards', his 'desire to make some progress' might put him at odds with public opinion.[55]

However, even if these readings of Howard's approach to leadership were different, they rested on the same unquestioning reading of public opinion: that the surveys showed a public unsympathetic to a prime ministerial apology and thus to reconciliation. Whatever they wrote about Howard's use of the polls, the journalists who debated his 'populism' helped to establish, as a by-product of their discussion, the credibility of a certain reading of the Council's research—before the surveys became available for more careful scrutiny.

When Howard admitted to being a poll reader, he was taking a calculated risk. Why would any political figure cite public opinion research? We see two reasons. First, by citing such research, a political leader implies that what the public thinks really matters to policy formation. A policy's popularity becomes a measure of its worth. Yet political figures are not obliged to propose such a test. They can justify or reject a policy on other grounds: morality, the necessities of an international treaty, and so on. Australian political leaders can choose the issues on which to declare that 'public opinion' is important. Howard judged that reconciliation, the apology, and the reconciliation documents were such issues. Curiously, none of those in favour of the draft Document of Reconciliation, and who sought public approval for it, spelt out why such approval was needed. Frank Devine, a critic of the Document, insisted—without explaining why—that reconciliation could not 'be sustained without clear, not to say enthusiastic, public approval'. Devine's insistence that the public first needed to accept the document, which it 'refuses' to do, suited his immediate position perfectly even as it created problems for his broader view that there was 'an unanswerable argument in favour of [Aborigines] receiving special treatment'.[56]

The second, and related, reason for political leaders to cite public opinion research is that it gives them a chance to interpret the research—a powerful political act in itself. Howard offered his own summary of the Council findings. They were, he said, 'fairly commonsense'. He elaborated: 'People are generally sympathetic to Aborigines, recognise that they've had a hard time in the past, acknowledge that there are gaps to be narrowed, but want it done in an all-Australian atmosphere'. Of the Council's draft Document of Reconciliation he commented: 'You can have a document, but that doesn't give you reconciliation. All it gives you is agreement on a document and I can tell you, that is what the average Australian is saying … and the average Australian is right.'[57] He had favoured dumping the reconciliation deadline, he said, 'well before' he had seen the research. Nonetheless, some aspects of public opinion, whatever their 'commonsense', were in conflict with his views. For example, research suggested that most respondents did not consider Aborigines to be disadvantaged; this was not Howard's view.[58]

Reconciliation and Responsibility— A Longer View

We think it unfortunate that, in February and March 2000, 'reconciliation'—a word difficult to pin down—came to be defined (though not by the Prime Minister) largely in terms of the Prime Minister's willingness to apologise.[59] The 'Stolen Generations' are owed that apology—and still are, whatever the polls say.[60] But the focus on the apology was an unhelpful simplification of the issues presented by Australia's discussion of reconciliation. In the rest of this chapter we will examine all of the Council's survey research on public opinion in order to offer our interpretation of the deeper structures of public understandings of reconciliation.

In 1992, the Council was advised by Donovan Research that the expectations of 'many Aboriginals' (a term intended to include Torres Strait Islanders) 'are clearly inconsistent with what many non-Aboriginals favour as part of a Reconciliation Process'. While Donovan was not sure what Aborigines wanted—'Aboriginals' desires', he argued, needed to 'be assessed prior to the [Reconciliation] process'—he was confident that Aboriginal wants would include: 'Health, education, employment'; 'Recognition of past and present racism'; and '"Something up front": especially land rights'.[61] Was Donovan justified in his claim that 'many' non-Aboriginal Australians would resist such demands and desires? 'Many' is a suggestive, but imprecise, word.

In March 1992, prompted by a clear incident of police racism, the *Sydney Morning Herald* commissioned Saulwick to pose a number of questions to Australians about the justice or injustice of Aborigines' situation. Two-thirds of respondents answered 'no' when asked: 'Do Aborigines have social equality?' and slightly fewer (60 per cent) answered 'no' when asked 'Do Aborigines have economic equality'?[62] Given the value that Australians have always placed on 'equality', these figures would seem to indicate a widespread acknowledgment that Aborigines had a grievance that governments must address. Such an interpretation is strengthened by the responses to Saulwick's questions about a treaty: of those who were asked 'Do you support or oppose a treaty or compact?' 65 per cent expressed support. However, asked about possible contents of the treaty, a smaller proportion was sympathetic to Indigenous wishes. Respondents were evenly divided (46 per cent 'yes', 45 per cent 'no') about whether a treaty or compact should 'say the land was taken from the Aborigines', and they were divided (though less evenly) about whether it should offer further land ownership (43 per cent 'yes', 49 per cent 'no'). Only one-quarter (27 per cent) of all respondents wanted a treaty or compact to provide for 'compensation or reparation', but twice that proportion (51 per cent) was willing for it to 'provide money for Aborigines to spend on education, health and welfare'.[63]

Using this evidence to evaluate Donovan's description of non-Aborigines' sympathies in 1991–92, we suggest that Donovan could have advised the Council that non-Aborigines were divided in their response to Aboriginal claims. That is, any generalisation about the 'non-Aboriginal' perspective—implied by the use of 'many'—was untenable. Responses to questions about 'land rights' at this time could be interpreted in more than one way. As the reader will now realise, a lot depended on how the questions were framed. In the 1990 Australian Electoral Survey (AES), 54 per cent of the respondents thought that the 'transfer of land rights to Aborigines' had gone 'too far' or 'much too far'. Yet, in the 1991 Rights in Australia survey 58 per cent thought 'the government has a responsibility to grant land rights to Aborigines, so that they can pursue their traditional culture', and 58 per cent thought that 'land claims settlements with Aboriginal people should be reached before using their land for economic purposes'.[64]

At the same time, Donovan could have pointed to some research that supported his characterisation of non-Aboriginal opinion as largely hostile to Indigenous grievances. In the discussions following the Royal Commission into Aboriginal Deaths in Custody (1988–91), Aboriginal criticism of the justice system had never been more intense, yet only one-quarter (25 per cent) of Saulwick's respondents agreed with the proposition that 'the law treats Aborigines more harshly than non-Aborigines'.[65] And there was evidence that the public was hostile to governments spending more money on Aborigines (as the Royal Commission argued it must be prepared to do). Saulwick's finding that one in two respondents welcomed a treaty commitment to 'provide money for Aborigines to spend on education, health and welfare' revealed an unusually large proportion for those times. From the late 1980s to the mid-1990s, the National Social Science Survey (NSSS) asked respondents whether 'We should spend more to improve conditions for Aborigines'. In 1988–89, 20 per cent wanted more spending; in 1993, 34 per cent said spend more, and in 1994 the proportion agreeing with more spending was 40 per cent.[66] The AES, in 1990, found that only 14 per cent agreed that Aborigines were getting 'too little' government help. In 1991, the Rights in Australia survey found that only 17 per cent agreed that Aborigines were getting 'too little help from the government'. The AES survey in 1993 found that only 24 per cent thought that 'government help for Aborigines' had not gone far enough.[67]

To sum up, when the Council was first considering how to promote 'reconciliation', research showed non-Indigenous Australians to be divided about some Aboriginal grievances; and on those aspects of the Aboriginal agenda that required reform to law and order and the greater expenditure of money, Aboriginal sympathisers were clearly in the minority. This did not justify as bleak a generalisation as Donovan offered the Council—the use of 'many' begged the question of the proportion who *favoured* Aboriginal demands—but there were certainly grounds for Donovan to advise caution. There were tendencies supporting the Indigenous agenda, but there were tendencies to the contrary as well.

Donovan's initial approach, however, did not ask: how can the Council for Aboriginal Reconciliation build up further support for what Indigenous Australians want? His question was: how can the Council win widespread acceptance of 'reconciliation'? His answer: identify 'reconciliation' with propositions widely supported by the public already. To identify these propositions was, in large part, what his surveys were about.

Donovan's most impressive statistic was that 95 per cent of his respondents supported the proposition that 'reconciliation' should include 'Aboriginals becoming more responsible for their own lives'.[68] Donovan understood the phrase to mean that Indigenous Australians would be more 'responsible' to the extent that they were less in need of government funding. In 1993 his qualitative research pointed 'to the importance of Aboriginal people *being seen* to assume responsibility for solving many of the problems associated with "the Aboriginal situation"'.[69] By then Donovan had told the Council that, as the 'eventual goal' of reconciliation, it should declare 'Aboriginals to be self-supporting—economically and socially—and hence obviating the need for "*massive*" government funding ("*taxpayer's money*")'. In addition, 'the *first phase of the Reconciliation process and communication/education process* [should] *include … improving the "public image" of Aboriginals with respect to their perceived genuineness in attempting to deal with their situation*'.[70]

What was the 'public image' of Aborigines' genuineness? To measure perceptions of their good faith, Donovan asked: 'How would you rate Aboriginals' efforts to genuinely deal with their situation rather than just accept government money? Would you say that Aboriginals' efforts are genuine or not genuine?' Asked on five occasions, from 1991 to 1994, this question prompted respondents to entertain the thought that to 'accept government money' was a sign that one was not 'genuine' about 'reconciliation'. Donovan's phrasing thus appealed to the view, evidently held by about half of those polled in the 1990 AES and in the 1991 Rights in Australia survey, that Aborigines were already getting too much help from the government.[71] To the extent that a respondent agreed with this view, the wording of Donovan's question suggested a tough criterion of Aboriginal 'genuineness'. Notwithstanding that test, about one-third (36 per cent) of his respondents on average perceived Aborigines as 'definitely' genuine (10 per cent) or 'probably genuine' (26 per cent) in their efforts to 'deal with their situation'.[72]

However, this level of doubt about Aborigines' genuineness might have reflected a general cynicism about 'reconciliation', rather than a low opinion of Indigenous Australians. Thus, when Donovan asked: 'How would you rate Australian people's efforts in general to deal with the Aboriginal situation?', less than half (46 per cent on average) of his respondents said 'the efforts of the Australian people in general were 'definitely' (12 per cent) or 'probably' (33 per cent) 'genuine'.[73] Note that this question did not prompt the respondent to apply any test of genuineness; for the 'non-Aboriginal Australian' there was no moral equivalent to 'just accept government money'. There was no widespread action by 'the Australian people' that was implied to vitiate their 'genuineness'. Without that unfavourable inference built into the question, 'all Australians' scored a higher rate of attributed genuineness than 'Aboriginals'; but the difference, on average, was just 10 percentage points.

'Mabo' as an Opportunity to Define 'Reconciliation'

One possible reason for such cynicism was that 'reconciliation' remained too vague an idea to be judged worthy of genuine commitment. The cost of being cautious about defining 'reconciliation' was that the term meant too many things, and thus not much at all. In the Australian Parliament, too, members had given 'reconciliation' many meanings, but under the pressure of events some meanings were beginning to acquire prominence. During the intense debate over 'native title', from September to December 1993, one meaning came to the fore:

in thirty-five speeches, Angela Pratt reports, 'reconciliation' was used to refer to the 'recognition of indigenous-specific rights'. Other meanings were also in play: reconciliation 'as practical improvement to Indigenous life chances' figured in eight speeches, as did reconciliation 'as relational and/or attitudinal' and reconciliation 'as a general sense of goodwill, including national unity'. In a smaller number of speeches three other meanings were deployed: reconciliation as 'not recognising Indigenous rights', reconciliation as not needing to be guilty 'for past wrongs' and reconciliation as 'recognition of Indigenous history, culture, heritage'. However, even in that period there were forty-six speeches (thirty-three by Coalition members) where the uses of 'reconciliation' were 'ambiguous, undefinable or unstated'.[74]

In Donovan's surveys the proportion of respondents who said they did not know what the Government meant by the 'Aboriginal Reconciliation Process' remained high: 37 per cent in November–December 1991, 35 per cent in August 1994, and an average over five surveys of 33 per cent.[75] Faced not only by a high proportion of 'don't knows' but also by a proportion that was not shrinking by very much, Donovan called for 'a clear statement of what was meant' by the Aboriginal reconciliation process.[76]

What might that 'clear statement' have said? The Council for Aboriginal Reconciliation faced a choice. One option was to emphasise those senses of 'reconciliation' that they knew, from Donovan's surveys, were popular. Each of the meanings below, suggested by Donovan, were approved by more than 60 per cent on average in the five surveys conducted between the end of 1991 and the end of 1994.[77]

- 'Aboriginals and Torres Strait Islander peoples maintaining their cultures' (90 per cent)
- 'Better personal relations between Aboriginals and other Australians' (90 per cent)

- 'Increased education of society in general about Aboriginal culture' (83 per cent)
- 'Recognising that Aboriginal and Torres Strait Islander peoples were the original inhabitants of Australia' (76 per cent)
- 'Increased protection for Aboriginal sacred sites' (66 per cent)
- 'Special health, housing, education and employment programs for Aboriginal people where it is demonstrated that they are worse off than other Australians' (62 per cent)[78]

The other option was for the Council to define 'reconciliation' as it thought best and then to advocate policies consistent with that definition, even if this jeopardised the Council's (and the word's) bipartisan status. Donovan advised the Council that this risk might be worth taking. Having continued to find that the public held a range of opinions about what a government committed to 'reconciliation' would actually do, he warned: 'There is a clear need for Reconciliation publicly to focus on one single major feature, or one single set of related features before these fragmented beliefs and "don't knows" become negative'.[79] Later he ventured that '*If the "treaty" component is considered a high priority, then it is recommended that action be taken now while a substantial proportion of the population* [50 per cent, on average, across his five surveys] *remains in favour of such a document* [no more than 27 per cent were against]. *This would serve to pre-empt potential negative publicity in this area*.' And: 'With respect to communications dealing with Mabo, it should be noted again that the vast majority of the general public (75%) are prepared to accept that "*Aboriginal and Torres Strait Islander peoples were the original inhabitants of Australia*" as part of the process of Reconciliation. This suggests that most people would accept the Mabo decision, at least in principle, and *provides an entry point for acceptance of a treaty and the land rights implications of Mabo*'.[80] In short, Donovan advised that the native title debate had made it possible for the Council to define reconciliation in terms of the Indigenous rights agenda.

In 1994–95, the Council committed itself to a vision of reconciliation as 'social justice'. The Keating Government had acknowledged during the debate on its 'native title' legislation that because many Indigenous Australians would not be eligible for land under native title an additional 'social justice package' was needed. Accordingly, in January 1994, the Deputy Prime Minister, Brian Howe, invited the Council to articulate a social justice policy. By March 1995, the Council had produced *Going Forward: Social Justice for the First Australians*. The Council spoke the language of rights in this document— both citizenship rights (securing services in health, education, and housing, for example) and Indigenous rights (title to their lands, protection of their culture). Council Chair Patrick Dodson declared Indigenous Australians no longer to be 'the beggars of Australia's welfare system'.[81]

The Keating Government had already introduced legislation consistent with the Council's dual 'rights' approach. To devote substantial public funds to the purchase of land for Aborigines was central to both the Government's and the Council's notions of reconciliation as social justice. However, the Liberal and National parties continued to be critical of the doctrine of Indigenous rights, preferring to see Indigenous Australians merely as especially needy citizens, no different in kind from other especially needy citizens. When the Government introduced the ATSIC Amendment (Indigenous Land Corporation and Land Fund) Bill in June 1994, the Opposition argued that money from the land fund should also be spent on health, education and housing programs. When the Government, insisting that land was an Indigenous priority, rejected the Opposition's amendments, the leader of the Liberal Party, Alexander Downer, accused the Keating Government of not being seriously committed to 'reconciliation'. Pratt's research on the use of the word 'reconciliation' in the parliamentary debates on the Indigenous Land Fund (June 1994 to March 1995) shows that, when

Coalition speakers' use of that word was not 'ambiguous, undefinable or unstated', they were using it in the sense of 'practical improvements to Indigenous life chances' or to denote 'a general sense of goodwill, including national unity'. Opposition leaders consistently avoided using 'reconciliation' as 'Indigenous-specific rights'—the sense deployed by Labor, the one Indigenous MP (Aden Ridgeway) and the Greens.[82]

Thus, from 1993 to 1995, the Council adopted a position on 'reconciliation' to which the Government was sympathetic and the Opposition hostile. What would the Council do if the Liberal and National parties came to power?

Whatever else divided them, both sides of politics agreed that Indigenous Australians were a disadvantaged minority with a strong claim on public assistance. However, according to some of the Council's research, this belief was not widely supported by the Australian public. Certainly the public knew something was wrong and that 'reconciliation' was needed. In its first, 1991, survey Donovan Research asked: 'Do you think there needs to be an improvement in the way that Aboriginals and other Australians get on with each other, or do you think that relations are OK?' While 9 per cent thought relations were 'OK', half (50 per cent) of the sample thought 'a lot' of improvement was needed.[83] However, despite the Council's campaign to define 'reconciliation' as the correction of social injustice, many Australians did not see socio-economic inequality as the problem to be fixed. Indeed, during the 1990s the proportion of respondents that thought that the living conditions of Indigenous Australians were worse than those of non-Indigenous Australians might have declined. In 1991, when Donovan asked respondents to think 'of overall living conditions such as employment, housing, health, nutrition and education', and whether 'most Aboriginals' were 'better off, the same, or worse off than most other Australians', about one-third (36 per cent) saw 'most Aboriginals' as 'the same' (20 per cent) as 'most other Australians' or 'better off' (16 per cent);

57 per cent saw them as 'worse off'.[84] By 2000, when Newspoll asked a very similar question about whether 'Aboriginal people' were 'better off, worse off, or about the same as other Australians in terms of living conditions', the proportion that thought Aborigines 'about the same' (32 per cent) or 'better off' (9 per cent) was higher (41 per cent) and the proportion for whom Aborigines were 'worse off' (52 per cent) was lower. Indeed, when respondents were asked in 2000 to compare 'Aboriginal people as a group in the community' with 'other groups', the proportion for whom they were 'disadvantaged' (41 per cent) was smaller than the proportion for whom they were 'not disadvantaged' (52 per cent).[85] In short, by insisting that the principal task of reconciliation was to overcome Indigenous disadvantage, the Coalition—certainly the Prime Minister[86]—was at odds with the commonsense of many Australians who thought that Indigenous Australians were doing well or at least not doing badly.

If reconciliation was not, for a large minority of Australians, about correcting inequality between Indigenous and non-Indigenous Australians, what was it about? Our examination of the data suggests that for Australians reconciliation was largely about non-Aboriginal Australians acknowledging the past and about Aboriginal Australians taking responsibility for their future.

The Relevance of History

Historical scholarship since the 1970s has persuaded many Australians that the story of Indigenous suffering must be added to other stories of nation building, such as those about soldiers' bravery and about immigrants' success. The Indigenous intervention into the 1988 Bicentenary might have helped to consolidate, in wider public understanding, what academic research—building on a long tradition[87]—had established in the 1970s and 1980s.

Donovan attempted to understand the relevance of this new national history to reconciliation by asking: 'To what extent do you feel that the early settlers' poor treatment of Aboriginals makes it hard for Aboriginals to adjust in society today?' This way of exploring the connection between views of the past and assessments of the present wasn't very helpful.[88] What did the strange phrase 'adjust in society' mean to those polled? We see a double implication: that Aborigines must 'adjust', and that they may not be able to adjust (and so remain 'maladjusted'?). Sympathy for Indigenous people as victims in a revisionist national history was, in this question, laced with pity and with implied doubts about their capacity to recover. Alternatively, 'adjust in society' may have been understood to mean an end to Aborigines' aggrieved talk. Certainly, Donovan's first survey had shown a popular desire for 'adjustment' in this sense: four out of five (80 per cent) of the respondents had said that they would support 'reconciliation' if it were defined as 'Aboriginals accepting what has happened in the past and letting bygones be bygones'.[89]

Whatever was understood by 'adjust', less than half the respondents felt that 'the early settlers' poor treatment of Aboriginals' had made it 'hard for Aboriginals to adjust in society today', and after February 1993 the proportion feeling that the treatment had made it 'very hard' or 'quite hard' appeared to have diminished while those saying 'not hard at all' had increased (Table 4.1), implying either that Aborigines were 'adjusting' or that their failure to adjust had other causes.

In naming 'early settlers' as the culprits, Donovan did not prompt respondents to think about more recent actions towards Indigenous Australians. But in his August 1994 poll, Donovan changed the question so that the mistreatments were particular, rather than abstract, and not delimited by the adjective 'early': 'To what extent do you feel that the loss of land, forced breakdown of culture and forced removal of children makes it hard for Aborigines to adjust in society today?' The problem to be fixed remained the same— Aborigines 'adjusting' (or not)—but the impact of colonial and post-colonial history was spelled out in terms likely to arouse a feeling that Aborigines had been grossly wronged. These changes yielded a much higher percentage of respondents (58 per cent) who conceded that history was relevant to understanding Aborigines' difficulties in 'adjustment'.[90] However, the meaning of 'adjust in society today' remained open to interpretation. From the Council for Aboriginal Reconciliation's point of view, the persistence of this phrase in their survey research was a problem. By 1994–95, the Council was seeking not Aborigines' 'adjustment' but a more just ordering of Australian society.[91]

Table 4.1 How hard do colonial (1991–94) and post-colonial (1994) experiences make it for Aborigines to adjust?

Questions

'To what extent do you feel that the early settlers' poor treatment of Aboriginals makes it hard for Aboriginals to adjust in society today? Would you say very hard, quite hard, a little hard or not hard at all?' (November/December 1991–March 1994)

'To what extent do you feel that the loss of land, forced breakdown of culture and forced removal of children makes it hard for Aboriginals to adjust in society today? Would you say very hard, quite hard, a little hard or not hard at all?' (August 1994)

	1991 Nov./Dec.	1993 Feb.	1993 Sept.	1994 Mar.	1994 Aug.
Very hard/ quite hard	21/21 (43)	26/21 (47)	20/19 (39)	20/20 (40)	32/25 (58)
A little/Not hard at all	24/27 (51)	21/27 (48)	23/30 (53)	20/34 (54)	22/14 (36)
None/Don't know	7	5	8	7	6
n	(1300)	(1300)	(1300)	(1300)	(1300)

n = number of respondents

All percentages rounded

Source: Donovan, 'Aboriginal Reconciliation Study November/December 1991', Table 55; 'Aboriginal Reconciliation Study February 1993', Table 43; 'Aboriginal Reconciliation Study September 1993', Table 43; 'Aboriginal Reconciliation Study March 1994', Table 43; 'Aboriginal Reconciliation Tracking Study August 1994', Table 42.

In 1995 the Council appointed a new consultant to advise on public opinion, and the following year Sweeney asked whether respondents agreed or disagreed with this statement: 'Many of the problems seen in Aboriginal communities stem from past mistreatment'. With this statement, the proportion that agreed either 'strongly' (44 per cent) or 'a little' (28 per cent) was high (72 per cent).[92] And in 2000, Newspoll found not only wide agreement (84 per cent) that 'in the past Aboriginal people were treated harshly and unfairly', but also majority support for the view that 'the nation should formally acknowledge Aboriginal people as the original owners of traditional lands and waters' (62 per cent) and for the idea that 'the nation should formally acknowledge that Australia was occupied without the consent of Aboriginal people' (64 per cent).[93]

We should note, however, that none of these items—Donovan's, Sweeney's or Newspoll's—were written in ways that invited respondents to ponder alternative accounts of the past. All of the items encouraged an acquiescent response. And the acquiescence was of the same kind—sympathetic to an understanding of the past that was likely to be particularly welcome to Indigenous Australians.

What is at stake? When Howard attacked the 'black armband' view of Australian history he was not doubting what he described as 'the appalling way in which members of the Aboriginal community have been treated in the past' or denying that 'Aborigines and Torres Strait Islander people are the most profoundly disadvantaged within our midst'.[94] His point was a different one: that Australian history, on balance, is a story of achievement. That most Australians shared Howard's view about the 'balance' of Australian history there can be little doubt.[95]

Historians engaged in the 'history wars' have sometimes imagined the public in ways that the poll evidence does not support. Puzzling over why it is that 'Aboriginal rights', in their view, find 'no place within the mainstream [sic] of Australian politics or culture', Attwood and Markus suggest that 'the main reason for this probably lies in the fact that most white Australians are unable to view the history of this country from an Aboriginal perspective.'[96] In fact, the poll evidence shows that most Australians concede the accuracy of the Aboriginal view that they were treated very badly by the process of colonisation. And the poll evidence has often shown that majorities and large minorities support propositions asserting Indigenous rights. Attwood and Markus have imagined themselves to be more marginal to public debate than they really are. Raimond Gaita and Robert Manne, on the other hand, are more marginal to Australian public opinion than they imagine. They say Australians should not feel 'collective guilt' but should feel a sense of 'historical shame'.[97] Contrary to Manne, who insists that the Prime Minister's claim 'that Australians are simply not interested in dwelling on the past ... was profoundly and dispiritingly wrong', for most Australians the past—including the difference between a sense of guilt and a sense of shame—is of no significance when thinking about what policies would be best for Indigenous Australians now and in the future.

In one early piece of advice to the Council for Aboriginal Reconciliation, Donovan suggested that in presenting the past 'care must be taken ... to avoid connotations of guilt and responsibility'.[98] It is easy to imagine Prime Minister Howard, himself, giving that advice.[99] It was one thing to be able to agree about 'what was done' to Indigenous Australians in the past, but the more pressing question was what was to be done now. What did it mean that four out of five people polled by Donovan in 1991 wanted Aborigines to 'let bygones be bygones' or that in 2000 roughly the same proportion (77 per cent) agreed that 'everyone should stop talking about the way that Aboriginal people were treated in the past, and just get on with the future'?[100]

Responsibility: The Emerging Concept from the Decade of Reconciliation

During the reconciliation decade, the 1990s, the notion of 'responsibility' became increasingly important. What 'many non-Aboriginals' wanted, Donovan told the Council for Aboriginal Reconciliation in 1992, was for Aborigines to become 'self-supporting—economically and socially—and hence obviating the need for *"massive"* government funding (*"taxpayer's money"*)'.[101] In response to a question Donovan asked only once, respondents overwhelmingly (95 per cent) supported the proposition that 'reconciliation' should include 'Aboriginals becoming more responsible for their own lives'. But like 'reconciliation', 'responsibility' can be understood in different ways. Applied to Aborigines, it can be both a virtue that they should strive to embody by working harder and living cleaner, and an entitlement that governments should not deny them. This dual sense of 'responsible', we suspect, accounts for its being endorsed all but unanimously.

As the Council's research shows, both ways of spelling out 'responsible' have been popular. In 2000, although 47 per cent of Newspoll's respondents agreed that 'Aboriginal people have mainly themselves to blame for their current disadvantage', other questions showed that respondents did not want to relieve governments of responsibility for reducing 'Aboriginal disadvantage'. Asked whether 'there is a need for government programs to help reduce disadvantage among Aboriginal people', 72 per cent said there was.[102]

It was not difficult to word questions so that they elicited majorities seemingly opposed to governments taking such actions. In the same survey, most respondents (66 per cent) disagreed that 'not enough is being done by the government to help Aboriginal people'. Most (60 per cent) agreed that 'compared with other Australians, Aboriginal people get too much special assistance from the government'. And a huge majority (79 per cent) agreed that 'although a lot of money and effort has gone into helping Aboriginal people, it doesn't seem to have achieved much'.[103]

So what did Newspoll's respondents in 2000 think that governments should be doing? Three-quarters (77 per cent) of them agreed that 'the nation should be trying to help Aboriginal people become more financially independent and self-reliant'.[104] This is one way to imagine Aborigines 'becoming more responsible for their own lives'. It evokes individual and family diligence, manifested in things such as trying hard at school, securing a job, sustaining a business. Asked to reflect on the 'practical significance' of the surveys, Peter Vaughan, First Assistant Secretary in the Department of Prime Minister and Cabinet's Office of Indigenous Policy, replied that 'the most dramatic revelation in the [Newspoll] survey was that the general public does not buy the notion that the situation of the Aboriginal people today is a result of history rather than *individual* responsibility'.[105] If Brett and Moran are right, in their account of *Ordinary People's Politics*,[106] the aspirations Newspoll's respondents set for Aborigines were precisely the sorts of aspirations they would have set for themselves. In that sense, the demands these respondents were making can be seen as recognising Aboriginal capacity to 'assimilate'. However, as well as demonstrating that many Australians wished Aborigines to be more 'responsible' as individuals, the Council's pollsters found public support for Indigenous people being conceded collective 'responsibilities'.

In the Rights in Australia survey, conducted in 1991, respondents were asked whether they agreed that 'Aborigines should be able to decide for themselves their way of life'. The question left it open as to who the putative decision-makers were intended to be—the individual, the household, the community, the entire Indigenous population, or all of the above.[107] In the event, almost three out of four respondents (72 per cent) agreed. When the survey specified one mechanism—the Constitution—by which Aborigines might 'decide for themselves', support fell away. Only 19 per cent agreed that 'The constitution should recognize the right of Aborigines to self-government'. The idea of a treaty got a better response. More than twice as many (42 per cent) supported the idea of 'a treaty with Australia's Aboriginal peoples, which would recognise their unique rights as the original people of Australia'. Only one-quarter (25 per cent) of those interviewed opposed the idea. Of the rest, most took advantage of the invitation to say that it didn't matter to them.[108]

Donovan tested whether the public might understand 'responsibility' as a change in the forms of government under which Aborigines lived. Again we see how sensitive responses can be to variations in the wording of questions. When respondents were asked whether 'reconciliation' should include 'some form of self-government or autonomy for Aboriginal people', support was limited: 43 per cent approved in February 1993, 34 per cent in October 1993, and 37 per cent in April 1994. However, in August 1994, when Donovan rewrote the possibility as 'greater opportunities for Aboriginal and Torres Strait Islander people to control their own affairs', support jumped to 70 per cent.[109] Was it the word 'opportunities' that triggered a more positive response? Or did the removal of the words 'self-government' and 'autonomy' neutralise the fear of a nation divided?

Another idea—that Indigenous and non-Indigenous Australians might express their responsibilities towards each other in formal agreements—also won wide support. In 1996, when Sweeney asked whether 'the process of reconciliation would be enhanced by some form of *agreement* between indigenous people and the wider Australian community [that] could take various forms, from a national through to a local level' most respondents (73 per cent) agreed that it would. Turning to specifics: 75 per cent favoured 'An agreement at a national level which acknowledges that Aboriginal people were here before European settlement'; 69 per cent favoured 'Regional agreements between people such as farmers and miners and indigenous communities'; and 80 per cent favoured 'Local agreements with indigenous communities about delivery of services such as health, housing and education'.[110]

In 2000, the Council asked Newspoll to test the content and uses of a Declaration of Reconciliation. The draft included the 'Strategy to Promote Recognition of Aboriginal and Torres Strait Islander Rights'. Newspoll found that 31 per cent supported 'all the contents of the strategy'; 41 per cent supported 'most of the contents' but had 'some reservations or concerns'; 20 per cent said that they tended 'not to support most of it', though they were 'happy with some parts'; while only 7 per cent said they could 'support none of the strategy'. However, when Newspoll asked respondents to specify what they liked or felt 'positive about' and what they disliked or had 'concerns about', the results were difficult to interpret. Now only 5 per cent volunteered that 'they liked all of it'. Among the particular ideas that the strategy endorsed, the idea 'that all Australians share equal rights' stood out; 32 per cent said they liked it. In addition, 19 per cent felt 'positive' about the reference to 'responsibilities'; 15 per cent liked what they thought was the document's reference to Aborigines' being 'more involved', participating in 'decision-making', even 'self-management'; and 10 per cent appreciated the reference to 'all Australians' sharing 'opportunities and responsibilities according to their aspirations'. However, 38 per cent didn't respond. Asked to state what they disliked about the document, 10 per cent expressed concern that it might violate the 'equal rights' principle. Of the rest, 48 per cent did not say anything.[111]

Were respondents divided about whether to see 'responsibility' in an individual 'virtue' sense or in a collective 'rights' sense? They were, but this was not a division between two sets of respondents—one hoping that Indigenous Australians would lift themselves up by their own individual efforts, the other urging governments to recognise Indigenous collective rights and capacities for self-government. Rather, the evidence points to the likelihood that majorities of the public endorse both understandings of what it means to be 'responsible'. And why wouldn't they? Australians who take any interest in Indigenous affairs are aware of outstanding individuals whose efforts bring them rewards, just as they are aware of Indigenous organisations that—as a result of public policies and laws—control assets, including land, and exercise devolved powers, sometimes by signing agreements. No doubt, Australians' opinions vary over time about which of these senses of 'responsibility' should be most prominent in this or that public policy. But we do not see a nation made of entrenched, philosophically opposed constituencies. Rather the survey data reveal that a continuum of meanings of 'responsible'—from individual virtue to collective right—is powerfully condensed within this keyword. The numbers show that there were majorities both for the 'virtue/responsibility' propositions and for the 'rights/responsibility' propositions. Newspoll in 2000 showed a nation not divided into opposed camps, but respondents enabled by pollsters' questions to frame the issue of responsibility in more than one way.

Conclusion

In 2000, through the leaking of the Council for Aboriginal Reconciliation's public opinion research, the 'public' became an actor in the drama of 'reconciliation'. Public interpretations of the research—by the Prime Minister and by journalists who commented on his leadership—tended to emphasise the extent of persisting public indifference and hostility to Indigenous grievances. These interpretations also stated or implied that public opinion about whether the Prime Minister should issue an apology defined public attitudes to reconciliation. We have tried to distance ourselves from this view of public opinion by reading the Newspoll 2000 survey results in the context of the earlier studies made for the Council by Donovan (1991–95) and by Sweeney (1995–96). The research commissioned by the Council for Aboriginal Reconciliation showed opinion to be divided on issues of Indigenous rights, with large minorities (and sometimes majorities) in favour of such elements of the Indigenous agenda as a treaty, or agreements setting out in-digenous entitlements including land rights. The research also pointed to the difficulty of deciding the meaning of the acknowledged facts of Australia's colonial history. The 'history wars' have been part of a cultural war in which the realities of colonial conquest are less in dispute than are the moral and political implications. In the court of public opinion the reality of past ill treatment is not significantly disputed. But what does this history mean for Australians? In particular, what does it mean for Indigenous Australians to emerge from this terrible past to become 'more responsible'? 'Responsibility' was the single most important theme to emerge from the Council's survey research over the decade. 'Responsibility'—like 'recon-ciliation'—has been open to conflicting understandings, and in the thinking of many Australians these conflicting understand-ings co-exist.

Conclusion

Who judges the relevance of 'the public'? How important is public opinion in deciding Indigenous policy? And, if Australia is a 'divided' society, along what lines is it divided?

In our view, assertions about the public and about whether the public is relevant are part of the political process itself; they are claims made in order to secure advantage, block opponents, win time, discredit ideas, or commend ideas. 'The public' is a kind of political currency, a stick to wave, a key word in the idiom of democratic politics, an imagined figure—sometimes central, at other times ignored.

Politicians and the press are not bound to mention 'the public' as either a political agent or a stakeholder that must be addressed. Not all newspapers paid attention to 'the public' as Saulwick and Newspoll represented it to the Council for Aboriginal Reconciliation in 2000; only the broadsheets did so, the papers most likely to inscribe 'the public' in polls of their own. When the broadsheets treated 'the public' as an essential stakeholder in reconciliation, they were in agreement—at least in this respect—with a Prime Minister who also invoked 'the public'. Howard explicitly argued (however selectively) his alignment with that public; he thus implied that the demands made on government in the name of reconciliation—the apology in particular—were a legitimate object of popular arbitration.

Nonetheless, Howard, like other prime ministers, has not always dealt with contentious issues by acknowledging the importance of 'the public'. On some matters he has chosen to present himself as a leader actuated primarily by principles of other kinds. For instance, euthanasia has been overwhelmingly supported by the polls; the Prime Minister, as a matter of principle, does not support the public on euthanasia. Surveys show majority support for increasing the ABC's funding, but the Howard Government has chosen to ignore this largely and to act as if a cultural principle—'balance' in current affairs coverage—were the primary consideration of its ABC policy, notwithstanding polls that point to limited public concern about the state of any 'balance'. In 1993, by refusing to sack the then Governor-General, Peter Hollingworth, the Prime Minister implied that public opinion (unfavourable to Hollingworth) was not the proper basis for deciding vice-regal tenure. The privatisation of Telstra and the introduction of the GST were such important economic reforms in the opinion of the Howard Government that their demonstrated unpopularity had to be taken on as a political risk. The Prime Minister, who would not apologise to the Stolen Generations for lack of a popular mandate, went to war in Iraq without seeking one. In Howard's term as Prime Minister we thus see an excellent example of the political leader making choices about when 'public opinion' is relevant to political justification.[1]

The Power of Polls in Indigenous Affairs

What makes 'respondent opinion' a relevant factor in Indigenous affairs? Certainly not just the controversial nature of Indigenous affairs; euthanasia, the introduction of the GST and the privatisation of Telstra have also been controversial. We see three factors that have made it tempting for political actors in Indigenous affairs to conduct public opinion research and to disclose the findings.

First, in the years since the 1967 referendum opinion polls have come to be accepted in the Australia media as one of the forms in which 'public opinion' is best expressed. In a survey of Australian news journalists conducted in 1992, Julianne Schultz asked her respondents to rate a number of sources and institutions for their 'expression of public opinion'. Top of the list, and a long way ahead of anything else, came 'Election results', rated 'excellent' or at least 'good' by almost all (81 per cent) of her 245 respondents; referendums, had they been included, might have been up there as well. The irony should be noted: as we have tried to make clear, referendums (like elections) are among the more opaque forms of public opinion. Bunched around the middle of the list came: 'Letters to the editor' (53 per cent); 'News reports' (50 per cent); 'Judgment of well-informed people' (48 per cent); 'Protest demonstrations' (46 per cent); and, the form of public opinion on which we have focused, 'Poll results' (44 per cent). At the bottom came: 'Pressure group activity' (26 per cent), the form of 'mobilised opinion' that Elkin and Stanner equated with public opinion; 'Parliamentary debate' (14 per cent); and 'Editorials' (13 per cent).[2] The list might have included things such as the feedback MPs get from their constituents directly. In addition, any update of Schultz's study would have to reckon with newer forms of 'public opinion', like those gleaned from talkback radio, dial-in polls, and the use of email. Nor was the survey designed to reveal what journalists saw as trends. But the ranking of the polls far above pressure groups—and the near equal ranking of polls and demonstrations (the walks for reconciliation, the sea of hands, and so on)—is clear.

As journalists' news values have come to include revelations of what the public thinks in the form of 'respondent opinion', political actors in Indigenous affairs have come to anticipate the need to justify their positions at least partly in the same terms—by referring to evidence of what the public, as survey or focus group respondents, seems to think or appears to want. If the public is 'divided' (as so often it is) about a change in law or policy then to journalists, among others, this can weaken the case for change—as it did in 2000, when the Council for Aboriginal Reconciliation found its survey research in the hands of the media.

Second, once one of the groups battling for the ear of the Government commissions polls, there is pressure on other groups to commission polls. The political use of 'respondent opinion' thus stimulates the further production of 'respondent opinion'. In the 1970s and 1980s, one Indigenous issue aroused the fears of an interest group wealthy enough to commission polls: the mining industry. The Chamber of Mines of Western Australia (CMWA) and the Australian Mining Industry Council saw the 'mining veto' (in the land rights model of the Woodward Report) as a threat and used public opinion research to persuade the WA Government that its voters would reject a government that legislated an Aboriginal veto over mining. Importantly, Labor in Western Australia also polled on this issue to check what might otherwise have been discounted as a lobbyist's self-interested claims. After hearing Burke's account of Western Australian 'public opinion', the Hawke Government then commissioned its own public opinion research. This put it in a position where it could either find a way of fighting back or acquire a rationale for capitulating.

The third reason for 'respondent opinion' to be given such weight in Indigenous affairs is that race relations has been seen as a matter not only of public policy but also of 'community' attitudes and behaviour. What is required to improve relations between Indigenous Australians and other Australians, so this argument goes, is not up to governments but up to individuals and groups. This emphasis on 'grass roots' processes has been especially marked since the inception of the 'reconciliation' project in 1991. The Shadow Minister for Aboriginal Affairs, Michael Wooldridge, spoke of how 'the Opposition [was] particularly pleased … that the Council [would] focus its work mainly on a process of reconciliation at a community level'. Labor Senator Margaret Reynolds (Queensland) insisted that 'we will never get adequate reconciliation without the support of local communities'. And Liberal Senator Michael Baume (NSW) argued that 'Where things have worked well in the past, they have done so because people at a community level have made the effort to get along in solving their own problems. In the past, at the community level, many things worked in spite of governments, not because of them … We are overjoyed to see that the concentration of this council will be at the community level.'[3]

The idea that governments' powers to affect relationships are restricted and that the relationship between Indigenous and non-Indigenous Australians is more the responsibility of 'the community' is not new. Elkin celebrated 'local action', and Paul Hasluck, Minister for Territories from 1951 to 1963, also said this about 'assimilation'.[4] Rowley—notwithstanding his firm support for new actions by governments—was moved to warn that Australians were inclined to blame the government for bad race relations rather than examine critically their own behaviour and attitudes.[5] While we agree that Indigenous and non-Indigenous Australians need to deal respectfully with one another as citizens and neighbours, we see this idea helping to promote the significance of 'the public' as an actor in Indigenous affairs.

Leaders, Public Opinion and the Community

In considering the cultivation of democracy, it is difficult to generalise about the relative importance of actions by governments and political leaders and 'community' action and

opinions. Hugh Mackay, commenting in 2000 on the reconciliation debate, found

> good reasons to be grateful for the tension that often exists
> between public opinion and political leadership. Indeed, were
> public policy the mere puppet of public opinion, we would
> pay unrealistically low taxes, treat the poor and disadvantaged
> even more harshly than we do now, be hidebound by draconian
> legislation that responded to every new wave of community
> concern, and, quite possibly, still be administering the death
> penalty. Public opinion is a lumbering, cumbersome creature
> that needs to be twitched into life by the energy of men and
> women of vision.[6]

But Mackay chose his examples carefully. Like most people,
he has not always been grateful for 'the tension that often exists
between public opinion and political leadership'. When the
Prime Minister failed to ignore public opinion on whether he
should apologise to the Stolen Generations, Mackay was
dismayed at the state of 'political leadership'.[7] While the plea for
'men and women of vision' can seem appealing, someone else's
'vision' is not necessarily the same as one's own. One alternative
to endorsing public opinion is to ignore it. This, too, is
tempting—not least when the 'lumbering, cumbersome creature'
is on the nose. The Prime Minister has proved a past master at
this, too. But, again, what the Prime Minister chooses to ignore,
others may wish he had endorsed. When a different poll pointed
to public support for a parliamentary apology Mackay was quick
to criticise the Prime Minister for ignoring it.[8]

While the Prime Minister's position on the question of an
apology was consistent—and consistently conservative—it is
not clear that his insistence from 1997 that 'reconciliation' be
equated by the Government with 'practical reconciliation' was
poll driven. The poll evidence on 'practical reconciliation' was
as equivocal as that on the apology. On the one hand, the
Donovan research showed that two-thirds (65 per cent) of all

respondents endorsed the idea that 'aboriginal reconciliation' should include 'special health, housing, education· and employment programs for Aboriginal people where it is demonstrated that they are worse off than other Australians'; only one-quarter (24 per cent) were against this way of enacting reconciliation.[9] On the other hand most respondents in the late 1990s, as we have noted in Chapter 4, did not think Aboriginal Australians particularly disadvantaged and did not think governments should be spending more money on them.

Many of the Prime Minister's critics have derided his commitment to 'practical reconciliation'.[10] While we agree that 'practical reconciliation' is not enough, we should give some credit to Howard for upholding—as his preferred understanding of reconciliation—the importance of government assistance in relation to health, housing, education and employment. What have been the political effects of Howard's insistence from 1997 to 2005 that the government commitment to reconciliation be confined to 'practical' measures? It is possible that the inclusion of 'practical reconciliation' in the Howard agenda, however limited, does more to strengthen support for 'reconciliation' than to weaken it. However, Howard's terminology has created a problem for any party that focuses on some of the 'non-practical' aspects of 'reconciliation'—a treaty, compensation, even land rights. Politicians supporting these causes must now weigh up whether they will be punished at the polls. On one view, all politicians who sympathetically consider Aboriginal interests—however they are defined—are taking a risk. Parties that concentrate on the marginal seats and are beholden to their focus groups have been advised, on occasion, that they would benefit from repudiating the interests of Indigenous Australians.[11] When the electorate is understood in this de-fensive way, it may not matter whether Indigenous interests are defined in Howard's terms (meeting their 'practical', but not their 'symbolic' demands) or in more radical terms (honouring their Indigenous rights as well as their citizens' entitlements to education, housing, health services etc.).

Since most Liberals as well as Labor activists support 'reconciliation', while differing in their understandings of that word's public policy implications, the idea of reconciliation cannot be dismissed as one of those 'symbolic left-wing issues'.[12] Among the population at large support for 'reconciliation' heavily outweighs opposition. Asked, from what they 'expect, know or have heard', whether they were 'in favour of, or against, or have no feelings either way about a process for Aboriginal reconciliation', roughly half (49 per cent) of those interviewed in Donovan's last tracking study, conducted in May 1995, were in favour; few (8 per cent) were against.[13] The task for political leaders who want to 'twitch into life' the 'lumbering cumbersome creature' is to take words of established popularity such as 'reconciliation' and 'responsibility' and to give them content. However, as will now be clear to the reader, we think that much good can be done by governments without such crusading, taking advantage of the persistently low salience of Indigenous affairs issues in the public's political awareness. As Donovan's figures suggest, a very large proportion of respondents cared too little about reconciliation to express a view on it.

Divided Australia?

In writing and speaking of Australian society, it is almost irresistibly tempting to use language that labels types of Australian. Phrases such as 'battlers', 'aspirationals', 'doctors' wives', for example, persist because they evoke social diversity by pointing to something tangible and—to the extent that the labels persist in the language of social commentary—recognisable. Judith Brett and Anthony Moran have recently added vividly to the tangibility of this cast of social types by interviewing, at length, individuals whom they see as examples of such categories as 'young mums', 'old Labor' and the 'old Melbourne middle

class'. In their analysis of these interviews they seek to charac-
terise both the person and the social category. Brett and Moran
convey the allure and the limitations of such categories when
they express the hope that the individuals whom they have
profiled in *Ordinary People's Politics* 'are representative by being
recognizable'. In doing so, the authors make a calculated appeal
to conventional wisdom.[14]

However, there are problems in this way of thinking about
divisions within public opinion. One is that such analyses are
hostage to stereotypes whose plausibility is founded not so
much in evidence—for that would put the neatness of the
labels at risk—but in the repetition of the labels by others.
When poll evidence is used with care, the distribution of
respondent opinion is much more messy than the practice of
labelling types of Australians implies; sometimes the evidence
undermines the conventional wisdom on which the plausibility
of these labels rests. The currency of 'middle Australia' is an
example of such labels' persistent appeal—never mind that
those who use this phrase do not define their usage with any
clarity, much less cite one another's uses to make sure that
there is some consistency in the term's meaning.

Thinking about the typical 'old Labor' voter or the typical
'middle Australian' resides not so much in absence of evidence
but in the way the evidence is used; crucially, characteristics
believed to typify the *group* are used as if they must also be
characteristic of most *individuals* in the group.[15] In the case of
'old Labor', the characteristics of the group seem to include
voters who left school early but who then read widely; voters
committed to equality, dignity and solidarity; voters who
didn't just vote for the party but joined it; and so on. In
Ordinary People's Politics, Neil Falkland can be labelled 'old
Labor' precisely because he embodies each of these qualities.[16]
The logic is as seductive as it is unsound. Even if it were true
that most 'old Labor' voters left school early, that most 'old
Labor' voters believed in equality, and that most 'old Labor'

voters joined the Labor Party, it does not follow that most 'old Labor' voters, taken as individuals, left school early, believed in equality and joined the party. On the contrary, as the number of qualities characteristic of the group increases the number of individuals who embody them all necessarily falls away. The richer the portrait of Falkland, the less typical of 'old Labor' the portrait can claim to be.

While 'middle Australians' (unlike 'old Labor') are not *defined* by this logic, the same logic seems to have been deployed in an attempt to encapsulate how 'middle Australians' *think*. The 'predominant stereotype' held by 'middle Australia' of Australian Aborigines, we are told by ANOP, 'is of a primitive, nomadic people who are passive and lazy, and have become virtual alcoholics under the influence of white society'.[17] Even if the research had furnished evidence of 'middle Australians' thinking of Aborigines as 'primitive', 'nomadic', 'passive', 'lazy', and 'virtual alcoholics'—and, apart from a single quotation from one of the focus groups, we can find no evidence of this in the ANOP study—it would not follow that most 'middle Australians' subscribed to all or even most of the elements attributed to them. In short, this was ANOP stereotyping 'middle Australia'. It was not 'middle Australia' stereotyping Aborigines.

And if there were such an entity as a 'middle Australian', his or her thinking would not be unitary. It is much more plausible to assume that all humans have the capacity to articulate two (or more) apparently contradictory opinions at once. Certainly the evidence cited in this book (and in Brett and Moran's profiles) bears this out. For example, many surveys show respondents believing that all Australians are entitled to be treated the same way but that some (Indigenous) Australians have entitlements that no other Australians have. Do such people simply forget their answer to one question when another is posed? Not necessarily. Do such people care nothing for logical consistency? Not necessarily: the issues of

Indigenous affairs can be framed in more than one way. Attitudes to 'equality', in particular, are revealed by the public opinion studies to be complex. The answer to the question that our title poses—Divided Australia?—is not that Australia is an arena of competing and contesting political and cultural groups each with their own way of seeing the world, though in part this may be true. Rather, or at least in addition, Australians are divided in their own minds when they find that more than one framing of a complex matter makes sense to them. We should expect this to be so, and not only because polling (with its diverse framing of issues) is now so common. The coexistence in the one person of different ways of looking at a complex issue is not evidence of that person's forgetfulness or irrationality but of his or her openness and sophistication.

Political contests involve not only attempts by the various parties to get the public to focus on different issues—the issues that favour them rather than their opponents;[18] they are also contests over different ways of framing issues. Australia's political culture, saturated with ideas that derive from the Western liberal tradition, provides alternative frames. When pollsters write questions about Indigenous Australians' place in Australian society, they cannot help but use words such as 'equality' and 'responsibility'—words with contradictory possibilities in which liberal thought is deeply embedded.

Respondents have viewed Indigenous Australians as both equal and different. In the 1960s, high proportions of respondents attributed negative qualities to Aborigines, did not want to share certain public spaces with them and would not have been pleased had a relative chosen an Aboriginal spouse. At the same time, respondents conceded that, in a certain way, Aboriginal people were their equals. In short, at the time of the referendum and beyond there was a disjunction between what respondents thought Aborigines were like and what they thought Aborigines were entitled to. It may be that the disjunction persists to this day.

The significance of perceived differences—some negative, some not—can change according to context. In Chapter 2 we noted that the proportion of respondents prepared to concede 'land rights' to Indigenous Australians was greater when the issue was framed in such a way as to acknowledge certain differences between Indigenous and non-Indigenous Australians. From 1947 to the late 1990s we find examples of polls in which respondents were willing to honour 'Aboriginal culture' either as a good thing or, less respectfully perhaps, as a real thing governments would be foolish to ignore. In Chapter 3 we saw a surprisingly large proportion of respondents approve the High Court's *Mabo* judgment—surprising because polls on 'equal rights' and 'same rights' seemed to suggest that the notion of 'different' rights offended widely accepted understandings of 'fairness'. Equality is not a simple idea—it wears 'two faces', as Canadian public opinion on 'Aboriginal rights' shows[19]—and large proportions of Australian respondents have shown that they know this.

'Responsibility' is not a simple idea either. In liberal political thought, the word points to issues that have been discussed since late-Victorian political theorists, such as T. H. Green, reconsidered the legacy of mid-Victorian political theorists such as Herbert Spencer and John Stuart Mill: the duties of individuals towards the state and the duties of the state towards its citizens. How much should we expect individuals to take care of themselves? When is the state's help a condition of the individual's liberty? And when does the state stifle individual autonomy? In addition to these well-rehearsed questions there are the questions of 'responsibility' that arose in the twentieth century after nation-states became accountable to international law and morality and when states began to acknowledge their responsibility for nation-building processes—processes that have sometimes included such coercive and exclusionary practices as genocide and 'ethnic cleansing'. As a signatory to the Treaty of Versailles that concluded World War I, Australia entered this global conversation about the morality of nations nearly ninety years ago. Responding to the historical work produced since the 1960s, Australians have had to ask themselves about the nature of the responsibilities that their colonial past has conferred on them.

'Responsibility' is the most important word to have emerged from the Decade of Reconciliation. By the time the Council for Aboriginal Reconciliation began market researching 'reconciliation' in 1991, the word 'responsibility' had come to mark the intersection of several discourses about how Australians had lived in the past and should live in the future. Thus, while the idea that 'reconciliation' meant Aborigines becoming more 'responsible' was popular, it was also contested.

We quoted, in Chapter 2, Clyde Holding's remark that 'the history of white domination of Australian society … has scarred the Australian community. It leads to latent and overt forms of rac[ism] ….'[20] We agree that there is a heritage of racism in Australia and that negative racial stereotyping of certain minorities is a frequent recurrence. However, the evidence allows a more nuanced account of Australian public opinion about Indigenous affairs. When Australians think about Indigenous issues there is much more than 'racism' and 'enlightenment' in play, partly because the nature of the 'enlightenment' itself is debatable. In a political culture shaped by liberalism, discussions of rights and reconciliation are exchanges *within* a common intellectual heritage. They are exchanges about how to apply to our present circumstances the cherished values of 'equality', of respect for 'difference' and of a shared 'responsibility'.

Notes

Introduction

1 An inquiry into Indigenous Australian children 'forcibly removed from their families', from the very first days of European occupation to the present, was established by the Keating Government in August 1995. *Bringing Them Home*, the report prepared by the Human Rights and Equal Opportunity Commission (HREOC), was handed to the Howard Government early in April 1997 (*Sydney Morning Herald*, 5 April 1997). Its findings included that 'between one in three and one in ten Indigenous children were forcibly removed from their families between 1910 and 1970'. Following the United Nations Convention on Genocide, HREOC labelled these practices 'genocide'. State and federal governments must make reparation, HREOC urged, starting with 'acknowledgment and apology' (HREOC, 1997, pp. 4, 27, 34).

2 Gallup and Rae, *The Pulse of Democracy*, pp. 30–1; Gallup, *A Guide to Public Opinion Polls*, 1944, pp. 7–8, and *A Guide to Public Opinion Polls*, 1948, p. 8.

3 Bourdieu, 'Public Opinion Does Not Exist'; Osborne and Rose, 'Do the Social Sciences Create Phenomena?: The Example of Public Opinion Research'; Lewis, *Constructing Public Opinion*.

4 Fishkin, *Democracy and Deliberation*, p. 1. Farr, 'Framing Democratic Discussion', p. 388; Yankelovich, *Coming to Public Judgment*, chapter 2.

5 *Sydney Morning Herald*, 29 May 1997.

6 Tickner, *Taking a Stand*, p. 57. See also Manne, who found the 'Howard government resistant to the general mood' and suggests that 'the overwhelming reception' and 'culturally transforming impact' only changed later when 'critics of *Bringing Them Home* emerged'; 'The Howard Years', p. 19, and 'In Denial', pp. 5–6, reprinted in *Left, Right, Left*, p. 221.

7 Millett, et al., 'It Hurts Us', and Megalogenis, *Fault Lines*, p. 128, for the Prime Minister's views. For his explanation of his willingness to 'change public minds' on some issues but not on what Marr calls 'ordinary white resentment', see Marr, *The High Price of Heaven*, pp. 37–8.

8 Gunn, 'Public Spirit to Public Opinion', for an elaboration.

9 Elkin, *Citizenship for the Aborigines: A National Aboriginal Policy*, pp. 10–11, 17, 18–19.

10 Ibid., pp. 16–19.

11 Elkin, *Aborigines and Citizenship*, pp. 5, 9, 28–9.

12 Bennett, *Human Rights for Australian Aborigines*, p. 59.

13 Our contrast of public opinion, as expressed in Elkin, and public opinion represented by the polls is similar to but not the same as Ginsberg's well-known account of the transformation of public opinion wrought by the polls in 'Polling and the Transformation of Public Opinion'. Note, in particular, our emphasis on the way in which 'respondent opinion', as we call it, commodifies public opinion.

14 Gallup, 'The Quintamensional Plan of Question Design'; *A Guide to Public Opinion Polls*, pp. 40–9.

15 Jacobs and Shapiro, *Politicians Don't Pander*.

16 [Gallup], *The New Science of Public Opinion Measurement*, p. 3.

17 During the debate over *Mabo*, Gary Morgan agreed that the following words should accompany the Morgan poll published by *Time*: 'Statement of interest: The executive chairman of the Roy Morgan Research Centre, Gary Morgan, is also chairman of the WA mining company Haoma North West NL'; *Time*, 14 February 1994.

18 Bourdieu, 'Public Opinion Does Not Exist'.

19 Elkin himself was one of the pioneers and early promoters of survey research of various kinds though, so far as we know, not in relation to Aboriginal questions. See Elkin, *Our Opinions and the National Effort*, and his 'Study of Public Opinion'.

20 The term comes from Yankelovich, *Coming to Public Judgment*, p. 34.

21 Lippmann, *The Phantom Public*.

22 Andrew Markus is a notable exception; see *Race*. Nor are historians the only ones to have shown little interest. Writing about the state

of public opinion in the mid-1960s, Frank Jones noted that 'The Gallup polls around this time are mostly silent about race relations'; 'Changing Attitudes and Values in Post-War Australia', p. 104. More recently, John Western and his colleagues have argued that 'there is a parlous lack of survey research on political attitudes towards indigenous Australians'; Western, et al., 'The Importance of Visibility for Social Inequality Research', p. 130.

23 The graph does not include every poll discussed in this book; polls commissioned by governments, political parties and business lobbies are excluded. Sometimes, such polls become 'news' if they are leaked to journalists; the ANOP report commissioned by the Department of Aboriginal Affairs in 1984 (discussed in Chapter 3), the Saulwick focus group study of 1999 and the Newspoll survey of 1999 (both of which are noted in Chapter 4) were given wide publicity in this way.

24 Australian Gallup Polls, Survey 177, and Australian Gallup Polls (subscriber reports), nos 1872–1883.

25 Attwood and Markus, *The 1967 Referendum, or When Aborigines Didn't Get the Vote*, p. 35.

26 Hasluck, *Shades of Darkness*, p. 75.

1. The 1967 Referendum and the Politics of Inclusion

1 Established in 1941, Australian Public Opinion Polls (The Gallup Method) was owned by the Herald & Weekly Times but operated by Roy Morgan. Though Sylvia Ashby conducted polls in New South Wales for the *Daily Telegraph*, the Gallup Poll had the field to itself nationally until 1971, when it was joined by the Australian Sales Research Bureau (later, Irving Saulwick & Associates), for the Fairfax group, and Australian Nationwide Opinion Polls, for News Ltd; Beed, 'Opinion Polling and the Election', pp. 211–18, and Goot, 'Ashby, Sylvia Rose'.

2 Rowse, 'Introduction', pp. 2–3.

3 Native Welfare Conference, *The Policy of Assimilation*, p. 1. In 1965 this was amended to indicate that the 'policy of assimilation seeks that all persons of Aboriginal descent will *choose* to attain a similar manner and standard of living to that of other Australians …'; see Rowse, *Obliged to be Difficult*, p. 22 (emphasis added).

4 Haebich, *Broken Circles*, pp. 85–6. For a similar story in relation to the Aboriginal suffrage for Commonwealth elections, see Goot, 'The Aboriginal Suffrage and its Consequences', pp. 528–32.

5 Rowley, *Outcasts in White Australia*, p. 6.

6 Sawer, 'The Australian Constitution and the Australian Aborigine';
Smith, *The Aboriginal Population of Australia*, Table 3.1.1.

7 Bleakley, *The Aborigines of Australia*, p. 314.

8 Smith, *The Aboriginal Population of Australia*, p. 30; Parliament, 'Report
from the Select Committee on Voting Rights of Aborigines', p. 4.

9 Long, 'The Administration and the Part-Aboriginals of the Northern
Territory', pp. 194–5.

10 Rowse, *White Flour, White Power*, pp. 189–94.

11 Australian Gallup Polls (subscriber reports), nos. 1056–1069. In
Berinsky's terms we suspect the high level of refusals signifies a
question that was 'cognitively difficult' rather than one made 'socially
hard' by a climate of opinion that discouraged respondents from
affirming what they actually believed; 'The Dynamics of Racial
Policy Opinion, 1972–1994'.

12 Elkin, *Citizenship for the Aborigines*, pp. 45–7.

13 Ibid., p. 47.

14 Elkin, *The Australian Aborigines*, pp. 378–9.

15 Ibid., pp. 376, 378.

16 Writing in the early 1960s, Beckett said he would follow 'popular
usage in making no distinction between … full and part-aborigines';
'Aborigines, Alcohol, and Assimilation', p. 34.

17 Lippmann, *Words or Blows*, pp. 172–8.

18 On the difference between marriage and other situations in the
late 1960s and early 1970s, see also: 1968 data from Canberra and
New South Wales reported in Beswick and Hills, 'An Australian
Ethnocentrism Scale', p. 215; 1969 data from New South Wales and
Victoria reported in Beswick and Hills, 'A Survey of Ethnocentrism
in Australia', p. 157; 1971 data from married women, Australian-
born with Australian-born parents, reported in Buchanan, *Attitudes
towards Immigrants in Australia*, pp. 26–30; and Rump, 'Comparing
Australia and New Zealand on Colour Prejudice', based on a sample
of psychology students in Adelaide. Note, however, that in a study
of 'the junior grades of a boy's boarding school in northern New
South Wales', conducted in 1974, respondents were as reluctant
to share their 'lunch with an Aborigine' as they were to see their
'brother or sister' marry one; Smith, 'Racial Attitudes', p. 46. One way
of explaining this anomaly vis-à-vis other research is that a sharper
sense of the difference between the two situations only develops at
an older age. Another way of explaining the difference might be in
terms of class. For a sociologist's summary of 'racial consciousness'

in Australia at the time, based on a single anecdote that elides the difference between marriage and other situations, see Encel, *Equality and Authority*, p. 138. In a more recent study in Perth, conducted in 1990, respondents were less inclined to agree with the proposition 'I wouldn't like any member of my family to marry an Aborigine' (mean of 3.43 on a seven-point scale) than with the proposition 'I would not like an aborigine to be my boss' (4.23) or the proposition 'If an Aborigine sat next to me on a bus or train I would feel uncomfortable' (4.86); Walker, 'Attitudes to Minorities', p. 140. One way of interpreting these results is that sitting next to an Aborigine or even having an Aborigine as one's boss is seen as a more intimate relationship than having a relative marry one.

[19] Elkin, *The Australian Aborigines*, p. 378.

[20] Haebich, '"Between Knowing and Not Knowing"', pp. 85–6.

[21] Taft, 'Attitudes of Western Australians', Table 3.

[22] Ibid., p. 15.

[23] Western, 'What White Australians Think', Table 21.9, item 16. In Canberra ('Urbania'), 132 interviews were conducted; in Condobolin ('Bush Town'), 125; ibid., p. 246. The findings are also published in 'The Attitudes of White Australians to Australian Aborigines—Some Survey Results', Table 1, which reports the results of a similar survey conducted in 1967 in Melbourne (n = 204) and Brisbane (n = 257), and five rural towns (n = 471)—two (Murgon and Ayr) with Aboriginal inhabitants and three (Warragul, Laidley and Yass) with few if any; p. 63.

[24] Lippmann, *Words or Blows*, pp. 163–4.

[25] The contrast with attitudes to marrying Italians was striking; see Taft, 'Attitudes of Western Australians', p. 22, and Lippmann, *Words or Blows*, p. 177. For an attempt to argue that prejudice against 'part-aborigines' and Italians in Australia were similar because of 'the group life they lead', see Bell, 'Assimilation in New South Wales', p. 70. See also McGregor, for whom 'mass hostility' to 'racial minorities such as aborigines and Jews' largely reflected their failure to 'conform'; *Profile of Australia*, pp. 45–6. For an early, survey-based, attempt to demonstate that 'those who were prejudiced against dark people tended to be prejudiced against other ethinic groups', see Victorian Council of Social Service, *Dark People of Melbourne*, p. 12.

[26] Compare Colin Tatz's singular assessment: 'By 1965 it was clear that the aims of the 1951 policies had not in any way been realised'; 'The Aborigines', p. 32.

[27] Western, 'What White Australians Think', Table 21.7.

[28] Australian Gallup Polls (subscriber reports), nos. 1056–1069.

[29] Taft, 'Attitudes of Western Australians', pp. 17, 60. Even in a country town where 'the level of independent and successful functioning of the Aboriginal population' appeared 'to be considerably retarded', 57 per cent of the respondents interviewed in about 1974 agreed that 'aboriginal children' were 'equal to whites in ability'; Hill, *A Study of Aboriginal Poverty in Two Country Towns*, pp. v, 61. In 1968 and 1969, 85 to 89 per cent of respondents in Canberra, New South Wales and Victoria agreed that 'When he is given a fair chance, the Aborigine can live as decently as any white man'; Beswick and Hills, 'An Australian Ethnocentrism Scale', p. 215, and Beswick and Hills, 'A Survey of Ethnocentrism in Australia', p. 157.

[30] Parliament, 'Report from the Select Committee on Voting Rights of Aborigines', p. 4.

[31] Ibid., p. 1.

[32] Ibid., p. 8.

[33] Ibid., p. 4.

[34] Ibid., p. 9.

[35] Australian Gallup Polls (subscriber reports), nos. 1056–1069.

[36] Ibid. Survey 153. On the tendency of referenda to show diminished support for changes after debate, see Goot and Beed, 'The Referenda', p. 89.

[37] Taft, 'Attitudes of Western Australians', pp. 17, 59.

[38] Western, 'What White Australians Think', Table 21.9.

[39] Parliament, 'Report from the Select Committee on Voting Rights of Aborigines', p. 9.

[40] Australian Gallup Polls, Survey 134. For the Namatjira case, see Blackshield, 'Namatjira v. Raabe', and Strehlow, *Nomads in No-Man's Land*, pp. 20–1.

[41] Ibid., Survey 142. Support for the court's having discretion is also likely to have reflected support for discretion as a general principle of justice.

[42] Ibid., Survey 147. 'Had they been asked the same question about part-aborigines', Inglis suggests, 'it seems likely that the majority in favour of letting them drink would have been even greater'; '"The Dark People"', p. 63. However, the data on attitudes to 'full-blood' Aborigines and part-Aborigines, discussed above, suggests that any difference would have been modest.

[43] Flick and Goodall, *Isabel Flick*, pp. 17, 90, 92–3; Bell, 'The Aborigines of New South Wales: Racial Prejudice'; Calley, 'Race Relations on the North Coast of New South Wales'; Fink, 'The Caste Barrier'; Reay and Sitlington, 'Class and Status in a Mixed-Blood Community

(Moree, New South Wales)'; Rowley, *Outcasts in White Australia*, pp. 256, 262–4, 276–7; Curthoys, *Freedom Ride*. See also Kelly, 'The Reaction of White Groups in Country Towns of New South Wales to Aborigines'. For an overview, see Broome, 'Aborigines and the Caste Barrier'.

44 Taft, 'Attitudes of Western Australians', p. 14. See also: Bell, 'The Aborigines of New South Wales: Racial Prejudice'; Calley, 'Race Relations on the North Coast of New South Wales'; and Reay and Sitlington, 'Class and Status in a Mixed-Blood Community (Moree, New South Wales)'.

45 Compare the 1973 surveys in two country towns (reported in Hill, *A Study of Aboriginal Poverty in Two Country Towns*, p. 62), where the majority of respondents (70 per cent and 60 per cent) nominated 'alcohol' as a factor in creating negative attitudes to Aborigines; 'handouts and too much done for them' was nominated by 64 and 43 per cent respectively; 'lack of hygiene—dirty' was only mentioned by 30 per cent and 3 per cent. For a rare survey of Aborigines living in a town and on a station, taken in the mid-1950s and said to show 'that the natives' images of their group mirror many of the prevailing ideas which white people have about natives', see Fink, 'The Changing Status and Cultural Identity of Western Australian Aborigines', pp. 182, 187–90.

46 *Brown v. Board of Education*, 1954. 'I feel sure that there are many people like myself', a woman of 'liberal' opinion wrote to the *Sydney Morning Herald* in 1963, 'who simply feel that aborigines are a different race springing from a totally different civilization from our own, but the question of social inferiority never even enters our minds'; quoted in Hiatt, 'Aborigines in the Australian Community', p. 293. See also John Wilson's observation, based on a 1956 survey among 'white farmers in a prosperous mixed-farming area' in Western Australia; 'Assimilation to What?', pp. 158, 165 n17.

47 Contrast this with the concern expressed in the 1950s that 'no real attempt has been made to prepare the public' for assimilation's 'social implications', Taft and Walker, 'Australia', p. 138. Or contrast it with the claim in the mid-1960s that 'Assimilation finally means interbreeding', Horne, *The Lucky Country*, p. 117.

48 Taft, 'Attitudes of Western Australians', p. 24.

49 Compare Western, 'What White Australians Think', Table 21.9, with 'The Attitudes of White Australians to Australian Aborigines—Some Survey Results', Table 3.

50 Writing after Aborigines had been enfranchised by the Commonwealth, Les Hiatt noted that 'there is little doubt that within a short time

the political and legal status of aborigines will be the same as that of Europeans' but that 'How long aborigines will go on living together in separate groups ... is another matter'; 'Aborigines in the Australian Community', p. 293. Contrast this with Judy Inglis' view that 'To suggest that there might be parallel development of dark and white in separate communities brings to mind the "apartheid" policy of the South African government'; 'The Outback Aborigines', p. 48.

51 Stanner, *After the Dreaming*, p.38.

52 Attwood and Markus, *The 1967 Referendum*; Taffe, 'The Role of FCAATSI in the 1967 Referendum'.

53 Attwood and Markus, *The 1967 Referendum*, p. 44.

54 Taffe, 'The Role of FCAATSI in the 1967 Referendum', p. 286.

55 Ibid., p. 290.

56 Cited in Attwood and Markus, *The 1967 Referendum*, p. 93.

57 Taffe, 'The Role of FCAATSI in the 1967 Referendum', pp. 295–6.

58 Australian Gallup Polls, Survey 171. See also the poll taken in April 1965, which shows the same result and that a higher proportion of 'youth' than 'adult' respondents supported more money being spent on Aborigines; ibid. (subscriber reports), nos 1852–1871.

59 Ibid., Survey 177. Such a high level of support, two years ahead of the referendum, makes Marilyn Lake's claim that FCAATSI's Faith Bandler 'was vital for the successful outcome of the campaign' quite implausible; see *Faith*, p. 85.

60 Ibid. (subscriber reports), nos 1884–1899.

61 Ibid. (subscriber reports), nos 1961–1980.

62 Writing in 1968, Tatz claimed that the referendum had alerted the mass media to 'public interest in anything to do with Aborigines and scarcely a day passes without some sympathetic reference to them in the daily press, on television or on radio'; 'The Aborigines', p. 33.

63 This disjunction—more exactly, a failure to notice it—may explain why Prime Minister Harold Holt was 'astonished' that the referendum succeeded, let alone that it succeeded 'overwhelmingly'; Frame, *The Life and Death of Harold Holt*, p. 214 for Holt's private reaction.

2. Land Rights, the 'Backlash' and 'Middle Australia'

1 Australian Labor Party, *Platform, Constitution and Rules*, pp. 4–5. Woodward, *Aboriginal Land Rights Commission: First Report*; see also *Aboriginal Land Rights Commission: Second Report*.

[2] Hawke, *The Resolution of Conflict*, p. 15.

[3] Australian Labor Party, *Platform, Constitution and Rules*, p. 5. 'A Labor government', Hawke had declared in his 1983 policy speech, 'will not hesitate to use, where necessary, the constitutional powers of the Commonwealth to provide for Aboriginal people to own the land which has for years been set aside for them'; McAllister and Moore, *Party Strategy and Change*, p. 139, for the policy speech.

[4] 'I and PR, Brisbane', undated interview, Holding Press Cuttings, Vol. 1, AIATSIS Library.

[5] In telling the story we draw, in part, on Goot and Rowse, 1991, and Rowse, 1988.

[6] Mills, 'Holding Pledges Land Rights'.

[7] Published as a leaflet by the Department of Aboriginal Affairs; Holding Press Cuttings, Vol. 2, AIATSIS Library.

[8] Buckley, 'Holding Sees Land Rights as Reparation'.

[9] Terry, 'Govt to Introduce National Land Rights Within a Year'.

[10] *Sydney Morning Herald*, 12 November 1983.

[11] Ellis, 'Blitner: Dump Parts of Land Act'.

[12] Buckley, 'PM Asked to Block NSW Land Rights Bill'.

[13] Anon, 'NSW Land Bill: Qld Uneasy'; Anon, 'Minister Criticized on Rights'.

[14] In his Boyer Lectures, Hawke had made only fleeting reference to the need to make Aborigines 'equal'; *The Resolution of Conflict*, p. 40.

[15] Anon, 'Holding Takes Hard Line on Land Rights'.

[16] Holding Press Cuttings, Vol. 2, AIATSIS Library.

[17] Editorial, *Courier-Mail*, 22 November 1983. The phrase 'too far, too fast' constituted a warning of broader significance: it had been widely used to explain the defeat of the Whitlam Government.

[18] *Daily News*, 14 December 1983, for Holding. Anon, 'Land Policy "Will Split Nation"' [source indecipherable], 10 December 1983, for O'Connor, Holding Press Cuttings Vol. 2, AIATSIS Library; McCourt 'Holding Hits at "Racist" WA Libs', for Holding.

[19] Transcript of interview, 10 February 1984, Holding Press Cuttings, Vol. 3, AIATSIS Library.

[20] Fia Cumming reports the department's view in 'The Embattled Clyde Holding Continues to Fight'. Holding's comment on the polls is paraphrased in Libby, *Hawke's Law*, p. 27. In December 1983, the proportion of respondents in the Australian Gallup Poll saying that 'federal and state governments' were 'doing too much for Aborigines' (28 per cent) was almost the same as the proportion (32 per cent) saying that what governments were doing was 'not enough'. In

September 1981, the corresponding figures were 18 per cent and 50 per cent. See Australian Gallup Polls, September 1981, and Australian Gallup Polls, December 1983.

21 Campbell, 'Letter to the Federal Parliamentary Labor Party'; also cited in Libby, *Hawke's Law*, pp. 15–16.

22 Duncan, 'Rights Issue Seen as Land Mine in ALP'.

23 O'Neill, 'Holding to Blame for Attitude to Blacks: Lib'.

24 The report does not include the question and does not define 'potential swinging voter'; ANOP, 'Voter Attitude Study: Marginal Seat Research', Table 5.24. See also ANOP, 'Voter Attitude Study: Interim Summary Report', Table 36. None of the research undertaken by ANOP for the Labor Party attempted to model how positions on issues, the salience of issues, or perceived party differences on issues might change respondents' votes.

25 See Kelly, *The End of Certainty*, pp. 95–110, for the 'Liberal revolution'.

26 Quoted in O'Neill, 'Ad Campaign Will Fight Land Rights Backlash'.

27 O'Neill, 'Holding Hires an Expert to Fight League of Rights'. In his earlier pamphlet on the League, *Voices of Hate*, Gott notes its racism but makes no direct reference to its views on Aborigines. A later, more abstract, study also makes no reference to its position on Aborigines; see Campbell, *The Australian League of Rights*.

28 Margot O'Neill's words; 'Ad Campaign Will Fight Land Rights Backlash'.

29 Anon, 'Government Fearful of White Backlash'.

30 Cumming, 'The Embattled Clyde Holding Continues to Fight'.

31 Mayman, 'Prominent Aborigine Hits Rights "Fiasco"'.

32 Mayman, 'Land Rights Opponents in Racial Con: Holding'. The reference to the 'terror campaign' is from Libby, *Hawke's Law*, p. 41.

33 ANOP, 'Land Rights: Winning Middle Australia', pp. 1–5 and cover page.

34 Libby, *Hawke's Law*, p. 67.

35 Ibid., p. 105.

36 Ibid., pp. 109, 106. The five principles, articulated by Holding in the House of Representatives on 8 December 1983, are reprinted on p. 13. See also: Holding, 'Federal Government Policies and Initiatives', p. 5; Gruen and Grattan, *Managing Government*, p. 251; Dodson, Mowbray and Snowdon, 'Promise, Confrontation and Compromise in Indigenous Affairs', p. 299; or Ryan, 'Aboriginals and Islanders', p. 397.

37 ANOP, 'Voter Attitude Research: The Northern Suburbs of Perth', Tables 7, 9 and 10. The failure of the Federal Labor secretariat in

Canberra to include a marginal seat from Western Australia in its May and June poll (note 25 above) may well have reflected the fact that ANOP was polling in Western Australia for the State branch.

38 Ibid.; Libby, *Hawke's Law*, p. 95, for a paraphrase.

39 Ibid., p. 107. The reference to the 'eight seats' is in Altman and Dillon, 'Why Hawke's Model has no Backing'; whether the seats were seats in the national parliament (where Labor had only eight seats in the House of Representatives to lose) or in the State parliament is unclear.

40 Libby, *Hawke's Law*, pp. 109, 111.

41 Kelly, *The End of Certainty*, p. 148; McAllister and Moore, *Party Strategy and Change*, pp. 139 and 145 for the speeches; Gruen and Grattan, *Managing Government*, p. 252, for Burke.

42 Libby, *Hawke's Law*, p. 95.

43 Anon, 'Majority Must Accept Land Rights: Holding'. He repeated this insistence on majority support in the *Bulletin*, 'Land Rights Policy Merely a Model', and on the ABC's 'PM' program, 13 May 1985.

44 *Sydney Morning Herald*, 15 February 1985.

45 MacCallum, 'Aborigines Caught in a Holding Pattern'.

46 Buckley, 'Clyde Holding's Fight Against Time and Tide'.

47 O'Neill, 'Holding Goes on a Talkabout'.

48 Nihill, 'Holding Plans WA Land-Rights Talks'.

49 Fewster and Terry, 'Canberra to Override States on Land Rights'.

50 Transcript of 'National Today Show', 16 October 1985; Holding Press Cuttings, Vol. 4, AIATSIS Library.

51 Legge, 'Coombs Stamp on Land for Aborigines'.

52 'AM' (ABC Radio) transcript, 13 February 1985; Holding Press Cuttings, Vol. 4, AIATSIS Library.

53 Legge, 'Coombs Stamp on Land for Aborigines'.

54 MacCallum, 'Clyde Holding Penthouse Interview', *Penthouse*, September 1985.

55 Buckley, 'Clyde Holding's Fight Against Time and Tide'.

56 Nonetheless, critics such as Eve Fesl and Andrew Markus held Holding responsible for allowing 'a wholly negative interpretation' of ANOP's research 'to go unchallenged' and held the government responsible for not heeding ANOP's plea for 'a campaign to inform and lead public opinion'; 'Land Rights: The Wrong Numbers'.

57 O'Callaghan, 'Land Rights Gone Wrong'.

58 The Hawke speech and Holding interview were reported widely; see *Canberra Times*, Launceston *Examiner*, Melbourne *Sun*, and *West Australian*, 10 March 1986.

[59] Transcript of ABC TV 'Four Corners', 17 March 1986; Holding Press Cuttings, Vol. 5, AIATSIS Library.

[60] *Commonwealth Parliamentary Debates*, House of Representatives, Vol. 60, p. 15, 13 August 1968.

[61] Tiffen, *Communications and Politics*, p. 44, for the survey results, and 'Symbolic Processes of Out-Group Politics', p. 166, for the sampling. For McMahon, see Rowse, *Obliged to be Difficult*, p. 67.

[62] Saulwick, *Age* Poll, November 1978.

[63] *News* (Adelaide), 29 May 1980. The exact question was not published.

[64] Saulwick, *Age* Poll, October 1980.

[65] Morgan Gallup Poll, Finding No. 1096; Committee, AVSS, et al., 'Australian Values Study Survey'

[66] Australian Gallup Polls, September 1981.

[67] The ads are reproduced in Libby, *Hawke's Law*, pp. 78–9.

[68] ANOP, 'Land Rights: Winning Middle Australia', p. 60.

[69] Australian Gallup Polls (subscriber reports) nos 406–415, for February 1947, and survey 123, for February 1957. See also the discussion in Murphy, *Imagining the Fifties*, p. 172.

[70] Australian Gallup Polls, October 1984.

[71] Up to and including the 1966 Census, Australia's statisticians sorted people of Aboriginal descent into 'caste' categories. The almost universal belief that the 1967 referendum mandated the counting of Aborigines for the first time is mistaken.

[72] Although 'descendants of full blood' does not really specify a sub-group of Aborigines (as all Aborigines claim that descent, to some degree), it may have seemed to do so, in a State in which the authenticity of the resident Aborigines was much in dispute.

[73] ANOP, 'Land Rights: Winning Middle Australia', pp. 58, 61, 63.

[74] Ibid., p. 22.

[75] Libby, *Hawke's Law*, p. 83; Terry, 'Trouble for Govt. on Land Rights Law'.

[76] ANOP, 'Land Rights: Winning Middle Australia', p. 1.

[77] See Cornwall, *Just for the Record*, pp. 85–9.

[78] ANOP, 'Land Rights: Winning Middle Australia', p. 13; p. 36 also reports 'attitude change'.

[79] In *The Hawke-Keating Hijack*, p. 116, Jaensch argues from the premise that 'Burke faced an electorate in which a clear majority was opposed to Land Rights' to the conclusion that in heeding this majority he 'placed his electoral future above the policy of his party'. But an unpopular land rights policy would not in itself have damaged Labor's electoral prospects: a party's prospects are a function of how

opinions are mobilised not a function of how opinion is distributed; compare Libby, *Hawke's Law*, p. 84.

80 ANOP, 'Land Rights: Winning Middle Australia', pp. 2, 5, 36. For alternative conceptions of 'middle Australia', compare: Mackay, *The MacKay Report*, p. 3; Greig, Lewins and White, *Inequality in Australia*, pp. 95ff; Pusey, *The Experience of Middle Australia*, pp. 14–16; and Brett and Moran, *Ordinary People's Politics*, pp. 312–13.

81 ANOP, 'Land Rights: Winning Middle Australia', p. 58.

82 Ibid., pp. 2, 5, 35.

83 Ibid., pp. 5, 6, 35.

84 Ibid., p. 5.

85 In finding the *Australian*'s headline—'Few Support Aboriginal Land Rights' (28 August 1985)—of the ANOP report 'misleading' and designed to reflect 'the least favourable interpretation' of the findings, the Australian Press Council suggested that the 'striking result of the poll was that the majority of Australians did not have strong views one way or another'; *Annual Report*, pp. 60–1. While ANOP's report insists that those with 'reservations' had 'a greater propensity to harden than to turn to sympathy', it also suggested that 'community attitudes will harden and divide further' only if the '[c]ontinued silence of government' allows 'those with vested interests in opposing land rights' to 'retain the initiative'; ibid., pp. 5, 60. One would have thought a greater division of opinion, provided it boosted the pro-land rights side, was something ANOP would have welcomed.

86 Ibid., pp. 2–3.

87 Ibid., p. 58. In July 1985, ANOP research in Western Australian marginal seats reported almost the same proportion (42 per cent) 'strongly opposed' to land rights; 'Voter Research in Marginal Seats in Western Australia', Table 15.

88 Ibid., pp. 62–4.

89 Brett, 'Australia', p. 192.

90 See, Brett and Moran, *Ordinary People's Politics*, p. 324, where respondents grapple with the choice between 'equality' and 'special rights'.

91 It also occasioned other research. One of the responses to the ANOP findings was the development of a research project by the Australian Institute of Aboriginal Studies (AIAS) to investigate and analyse 'the social, economic and political forces which shape public opinion about Aborigines today'; Edmunds, *They Get Heaps,* was one of the fruits (p. xiv for the quote).

92 Letter to agencies from K.C. Martin on behalf of the Secretary of the Department of Aboriginal Affairs, 22 April 1985; authors' collection.

93 Department of Aboriginal Affairs, 'Brief for Advertising/Public Relations Firms for a National Communications Campaign on Aboriginal Affairs', pp. 1–2.

94 Ibid., p. 2.

95 Stokes, 'Special Interests or Equality?', pp. 73–4.

96 Miller, *Report of the Committee of Review of Aboriginal Employment and Training Programs*, p. 7.

97 Jennett, 'Politics, the Law and Aborigines: Modern Politics', p. 232. See also Parkin and Summers, 'Ethnic Groups and Aborigines', pp. 283 and 286 n29, who cite an April 1986 AGB-McNair Gallup poll reporting majority opposition to 'the granting of uniform land rights' to argue that 'in the mid-1980s' there was 'a shift in public opinion against the granting of land rights'.

98 Perkins, 'The Administration of Aboriginal Development'.

99 Riley, 'Reconciliation?'.

100 Australian Institute of Aboriginal Studies, 'Circular Outlining Proposed Study of Formation of Opinion on Aborigines' (undated); Rowse's files.

101 Chaney, 'Advancement Through Self-help'.

102 Kelly, *100 Years*, p. 181. See also Rickard, *Australia: A Cultural History*, p. 241, and Summers, 'Federalism and Commonwealth-State Relations', p. 108.

103 Australian Labor Party, 'Conference Resolution Pertaining to the Platform', in *Platform, Constitution and Rules*; Mills, *The Hawke Years*, p. 73.

104 In this sense, Maddox's accusation of bad faith on Hawke's part—that his Government was responding 'not to popular opinion' but to the 'mining industry'—is misleading. It also sits ill with Maddox's view that Hawke's main concern as Prime Minister was that his Government should take decisions that will 'not be unpopular'. Maddox appears to have been unaware of ANOP's research; see, *The Hawke Government and the Labor Tradition*, pp. 15–16, 94–5. In his memoirs, Hawke fails to mention his decision not to legislate national land rights. But he does recall the contempt with which he treated the mining industry's attempt to mobilise public support for mining in Coronation Hill in the Northern Territory (where only one seat was at risk); Hawke, *The Hawke Memoirs*, pp. 507–10. There is an account of the relevant Cabinet meeting, with Hawke 'doing a job for his mate Brian Burke', in Uren, *Straight Left*,

pp. 366–7. Tickner, *Taking a Stand*, p. 29, stresses the lack of a
'political movement'. Dodson, Mowbray and Snowdon, 'Promise,
Confrontation and Compromise in Indigenous Affairs', pp. 299–300,
highlight ANOP's research and claims about the issue not being
'electorally popular'.

3. Native Title and Reconciliation

[1] Pratt, *Practising Reconciliation?*, p. 3.
[2] Donovan Research, 'Research Report: Aboriginal Reconciliation
     Research: Vol. I', pp. 17, 23; emphasis in the original.
[3] Ibid., pp. 21, 31, 32.
[4] Blainey, *A Shorter History of Australia*, p. 236. See also the discussion in
     Povinelli, *The Cunning of Recognition*, p. 174.
[5] For narratives of the debate, see Gardiner-Garden, 'The Mabo Debate—
     A Chronology', and Rowse, 'How We Got a Native Title Act'.
[6] The discussion of the polls in relation to *Mabo* draws on Goot, 'Polls
     as Science, Polls as Spin: Mabo and the Miners'.
[7] 'Attorney-General's Commentary on the Native Title Act 1993',
     p. 270.
[8] AMR:Quantum, 'National Opinion Survey on Aboriginal Issues'.
[9] Ibid; see also 'National Opinion Survey on Aboriginal Issues: Wave III
     [sic]'
[10] AMR:Quantum, 'National Opinion Survey on Aboriginal Issues',
     p. 8. In the subsequent survey, conducted in November, the
     corresponding figures were virtually the same: 30 per cent and 20 per
     cent; 'National Opinion Survey on Aboriginal Issues: Wave III [sic]',
     p. 14.
[11] AMR:Quantum, 'National Opinion Survey on Aboriginal Issues',
     p. 31, and 'National Opinion Survey on Aboriginal Issues: Wave III
     [sic]', p. 38.
[12] AMR:Quantum, 'National Opinion Survey on Aboriginal Issues',
     pp. 48, 50, and 'National Opinion Survey on Aboriginal Issues: Wave
     III [sic]', pp. 53, 55; emphasis in the original.
[13] Morgan Poll Finding No. 2405 and No. 2543.
[14] Morgan Poll Finding No. 2370.
[15] Ibid.
[16] *Time*, 25 January 1993, 5 April 1993, 7 June 1993, 6 September 1993
     and 14 February 1994.

[17] See Beed et al., *Australian Opinion Polls 1941–1977*, pp. 135ff; Goot et al., *Australian Opinion Polls 1977–1990*, pp. 134ff. See also the graph in our Introduction, with its 1993 spike. It was the debate around *Mabo* that prompted Newspoll, in November 1993, to add 'Aboriginal and native title issues' to the list of issues on which respondents are asked to judge the government and opposition from time to time and to say whether the issue was 'very important, fairly important or not very important' to how they 'would vote in a federal election'.

[18] Morgan Poll Finding No. 2405; *Time*, 25 January 1993; AMR: Quantum, 'National Opinion Survey on Aboriginal Issues', p. 22.

[19] Morgan Poll Finding No. 2543; *Time*, 14 February 1994.

[20] McQueen's view, that Mabo 'stiffened white resentments', might be correct but it begs the question about the impact of the decision on those who were not resentful; *Social Sketches of Australia*, p. 353.

[21] AMIC & WACME, 'Mabo Doubts Remain High'; AMR:Quantum, 'National Opinion Survey on Aboriginal Issues: Wave III [sic]', p. 60.

[22] Saulwick *Age* Poll, 27 July 1993.

[23] The only exception, and we will come to this later, were certain grants of Crown land that had been made after 31 October 1975, the day that the *Racial Discrimination Act* came into force. Native titleholders, if they could be found, would have to be compensated for these losses.

[24] AGB McNair, 'Project Land'.

[25] Saulwick *Age* Poll, 27 July 1993.

[26] AGB McNair, 'Aust Backs Black Title', and John Mitchell for the wording; pers. comm. 19 October 1993.

[27] Morgan Poll Finding No. 2405.

[28] Taylor, 'Newspoll: People Turn Against Mabo Plan'.

[29] AGB McNair, 'Aust Backs Black Title', and John Mitchell for the wording; pers. comm. 19 October 1993; Taylor, 'Newspoll: People Turn Against Mabo Plan'.

[30] Goot and Rowse, 'The "Backlash" Hypothesis and the Land Rights Option', pp. 7–8.

[31] Morgan Poll Finding No. 2405 and No. 2543.

[32] AMR:Quantum, 'National Opinion Survey on Aboriginal Issues June 1993', p. 39.

[33] Gill and Wilson, 'Native Title Tribunal Will Give Rulings "Within Weeks"'.

[34] AMIC & WACME, 'Mabo: Concern and Equal Rights'.

35 See, for example: *Sydney Morning Herald* and *Weekend Australian*, 14 August 1993; *Age* and *Australian*, 17 August 1993.

36 Morgan Poll Finding No. 2370.

37 Can we estimate what proportion of people thought in this way? If we assume that, in Morgan's national poll, in January, all those who favoured 'more' rights for Aborigines and none of those who favoured 'less' rights (or were 'undecided') supported the High Court's decision, then 19 per cent (38 per cent who backed the High Court less the 19 per cent who favoured 'more' rights) of the 70 per cent—that is, 27 per cent of those in favour of 'same rights'—must have supported *Mabo*. If we assume that all those in favour of 'less' rights and none of those in favour of 'more' (or 'undecided') opposed the judgment, then 27 per cent (the 32 per cent who opposed the High Court less the 5 per cent who wanted 'less' rights) of the 70 per cent—that is, no more than 39 per cent of those in favour of 'same rights'—would have opposed *Mabo*. And if we assume that all of the 'undecided' on the 'rights' question but none of those in favour of 'greater' or 'lesser' rights were 'undecided' on the Court's finding, then 23 per cent (the 30 per cent 'undecided' on *Mabo* less the 7 per cent 'undecided' on 'equal rights') of the 70 per cent—that is, 33 per cent of those in favour of 'same rights'—must have been 'undecided' on *Mabo*. In short, it is likely that those in favour of 'equal rights' divided roughly 27 (in favour):39 (against):33 (don't know) over the issue. On this evidence attitudes to 'equal rights' correlate with reactions to *Mabo*, but not very strongly. In Morgan's only other attempt to report on national attitudes to both equality and *Mabo*, a year later, the correlation (calculated in this way) disappears altogether. Thus, 35 per cent (45 per cent less 10 per cent) of the 80 per cent in favour of 'same rights'—that is, 44 per cent—would have supported the Court; 32 per cent (38 per cent minus 6 per cent) of the 80 per cent—that is, 40 per cent of those in favour of 'same rights'—would have opposed it. See Morgan Poll Finding No. 2370 and No. 2543.

38 Saulwick *Age* Poll, 27 July 1993.

39 AMR:Quantum, 'National Opinion Survey on Aboriginal Issues: Wave III [sic]', pp. 39, 46.

40 Cited in the *Bulletin*, 9 November 1993. Asked by Newspoll whether they agreed or disagreed that 'a referendum should be held to decide the outcome of the native title issue', two-thirds (67 per cent) of those interviewed in November agreed; Taylor, 'Majority Back Referendum on Native Title Issue'.

[41] Morgan Poll Finding No. 2425.

[42] *Age*, 21 August 1993; *Weekend Australian*, 21–22 August 1993.

[43] Morgan Poll Finding No. 2425.

[44] Even AMR:Quantum—though it sought respondents' estimates of the Aboriginal population, of how much land Aborigines controlled and of how much they 'might try to claim'—drew a line at asking what proportion of the land Aborigines should have; 'National Opinion Survey on Aboriginal Issues: Wave III [sic]', pp. 31, 57, for the results from both surveys.

[45] For a more elaborate critique of the idea that one might assess the entitlement of Aborigines on the basis of their numbers, see Maddock, *Your Land Is Our Land*, pp. 187–9. Morgan's conclusion— that the current level of ownership was widely accepted—was based on a series of assumptions, none of them persuasive. Firstly, it assumed that the appropriate measure for comparing responses to the two questions was the mean. But, as any student of statistics knows, the mean gives disproportionate weight to the extreme scores or outliers. Asked 'what percentage of the Australian population are Aborigines?', 55 per cent nominated a figure of 10 per cent or less while 28 per cent nominated a figure in excess of this—17 per cent imagining that at least a quarter of the population was Aboriginal; the rest, 17 per cent, didn't venture a figure. Morgan's mean, a figure well in excess of the majority's understanding, was clearly affected by this. Similarly, though less acutely, with the question of 'what percentage of Australia's land should Aborigines be granted or given title to?': there were more respondents who said 9 per cent or less than said 10 per cent or more, but among the latter the largest proportion gave a number in the range 20 to 49 per cent; Morgan Poll Finding No. 2425. This, too, pushed out the mean. While substituting a more appropriate measure (say, the median) would help, it would hardly go to the heart of the matter. For there is surely something odd in elevating a figure of 12 per cent (or 9 per cent) to represent a verdict about the 'appropriate' level of Aboriginal land ownership, when much larger proportions of those interviewed appeared to have wanted considerably more Aboriginal ownership or considerably less. The most one could say is that the figure represented a compromise. A less tendentious answer would describe public opinion as divided.

[46] Bartlett, *The Mabo Decision*, p. 7.

[47] Morgan Poll Finding No. 2370 and No. 2543.

[48] Morgan Poll Finding No. 2434.

[49] Morgan Poll Finding No. 2467.

50 Tickner, 'Mabo a Mystery to Most of WA', 'WA Learns What Mabo is All About', and Patterson Market Research.

51 AMR:Quantum, 'National Opinion Survey on Aboriginal Issues June 1993', p. 60, and 'National Opinion Survey on Aboriginal Issues: Wave III [sic]', p. 67.

52 Milne, 'Community Divided on Native Title but Most Oppose Compensation'.

53 Morgan Poll Finding No. 2467.

54 Milne, 'Community Divided on Native Title but Most Oppose Compensation'.

55 Tickner, 'WA Learns What Mabo is All About'.

56 Morgan Poll Finding No. 2467.

57 Tickner, 'Mabo a Mystery to Most of WA'.

58 Tickner, 'Mabo a Mystery to Most of WA' and 'WA Learns What Mabo is All About'.

59 AMIC & WACME, 'Mabo: Concern and Equal Rights' and 'Mabo Doubts Remain High'.

60 Ibid.

61 AMR:Quantum, 'National Opinion Survey on Aboriginal Issues June 1993', p. 54, and 'National Opinion Survey on Aboriginal Issues: Wave III [sic]', p. 60.

62 AMR:Quantum, 'National Opinion Survey on Aboriginal Issues June 1993', p. 58, and 'National Opinion Survey on Aboriginal Issues: Wave III [sic]', p. 65.

63 Saulwick *Age* Poll, 27 July 1993; see also AGB McNair, 'Project Land'.

64 AGB McNair, 'Aust Backs Black Title'.

65 Tickner, 'Mabo a Mystery to Most of WA' and 'WA Learns What Mabo is All About'.

66 AGB McNair, 'Aust Backs Black Title'.

67 See Taylor, 'Majority Back Referendum on Native Title Issue', for Newspoll, and Morgan Poll Finding No. 2543.

68 Morgan Poll Finding No. 2370.

69 Roy Morgan Research Centre, 'Defer Mabo to Full Senate Hearing'.

70 Morgan Poll Finding No. 2467 and No. 2370.

71 AMR:Quantum, 'National Opinion Survey on Aboriginal Issues: Wave III [sic]', p. 62.

72 Morgan Poll Finding No. 2434 and No. 2467; Roy Morgan Research Centre, 'Defer Mabo to Full Senate Hearing'.

73 Tickner, 'Mabo a Mystery to Most of WA' and 'WA Learns What Mabo is All About'.

[74] Roy Morgan Research Centre, 'Defer Mabo to Full Senate Hearing'.

[75] Ibid.

[76] Morgan Poll Finding No. 2543.

[77] For an extended discussion of the items on which opinion in Western Australia (and Queensland) differed from opinion in the other states, see Goot, 'The Wild West? Yes, No and Maybe', pp. 194–202.

[78] Roy Morgan Research Centre, 'Defer Mabo to Full Senate Hearing'; Morgan Poll Finding No. 2543.

[79] Donovan Research, 'Research Report: Aboriginal Reconciliation Tracking Research', p. 6; emphasis in the original.

[80] Council for Aboriginal Reconciliation, *Walking Together*, p. 51. Reproduced as Appendix 1 of Council for Aboriginal Reconciliation, 'Reconciliation: Australia's Challenge', pp. 109–114.

[81] Donovan Research, 'Research Report: Aboriginal Reconciliation Tracking Research', p.14; emphasis in original.

[82] Council for Aboriginal Reconciliation, *Walking Together*, pp. 53, 59.

4. Reconciliation and Responsibility

[1] Reproduced as Appendix 1 of Council for Aboriginal Reconciliation, *Reconciliation: Australia's Challenge*, pp. 109–14.

[2] Ibid., p. vii.

[3] Donovan Research, 'Aboriginal Reconciliation Study November/ December 1991'; 'Aboriginal Reconciliation Study February 1993'; 'Aboriginal Reconciliation Study September 1993'; 'Aboriginal Reconciliation Study March 1994'; Aboriginal Reconciliation Tracking Study August 1994'; and 'Aboriginal Reconciliation Tracking Research May 1995'.

[4] Donovan Research, 'Aboriginal Reconciliation: Qualitative Research Update'.

[5] Sweeney, 'A New Beginning', based on 31 focus groups; 'Report on Supplementary Qualitative Research Study', based on 12 focus groups conducted in Sydney and Dubbo, Melbourne and Ballarat, Brisbane and Alice Springs; and 'A Report on a National Quantitative Survey'. For a highly selective summary, see Johnson, *Unfinished Business*, and for a critique of Johnson's handling of Sweeney's question on support for the process of Aboriginal Reconciliation, see Donovan, 'Increased Support for Aboriginal Reconciliation: Fact or Artefact?'

6 Ponting, 'Processing Public Opinion on Reconciliation in Australia', p. 111. For the view of the Council's deputy chairman on what the 'community consultation' produced, see Nossal, 'The Next Steps in the Long March to Reconciliation'.

7 Brennan, *Sharing the Country*, p. 7.

8 Ponting, 'Processing Public Opinion on Reconciliation in Australia', pp. 111–12.

9 Saulwick, 'Research into Issues Related to a Document of Reconciliation'; Newspoll, 'Quantitative Research into Issues Relating to a Document of Aboriginal Reconciliation'; Newspoll, 'Quantitative Research into Issues Relating to a Document of Aboriginal Reconciliation: Summary of Findings'; Newspoll, 'Quantitative Research into Issues Relating to a Document of Aboriginal Reconciliation: Stage I—Tables'; Newspoll, 'Quantitative Research into Issues Relating to a Document of Aboriginal Reconciliation: Stage II—Tables'; and Saulwick, 'Report No. 2 Indigenous Qualitative Research'. The most readily accessible accounts are in Newspoll, Saulwick & Muller and Mackay, 'Public Opinion on Reconciliation', pp. 33–45. For an account of the workings of the Council and the Department of Prime Minister and Cabinet in relation to the Newspoll and Saulwick surveys, see Ponting, 'Processing Public Opinion on Reconciliation in Australia'.

10 Wright and Overington , 'PM Backs Survey on Aborigines'; Peake, 'Howard Denies Being Poll-Driven on Reconciliation'.

11 Elsewhere, there was a piece in the *Australian Financial Review*, one in Sydney's *Sunday Telegraph*, and one in the pages of its rival, the *Sun-Herald*.

12 The *Australian* published fourteen pieces—news items, editorials or other articles—over a period two weeks commencing 28 February; it published seven letters as well. The *Sydney Morning Herald*, which picked up the story a day later, also published fourteen pieces and no fewer than eighteen letters. The *Canberra Times* generated nine pieces. The Melbourne *Age*, whose coverage petered out after a week, had eight stories or commentaries.

13 Scalmer and Goot, 'Elites Constructing Elites', p. 143, for a comparison between the *Australian*, *Courier-Mail* and *Daily Telegraph*.

14 In Newspoll surveys about election-relevant issues, better educated respondents are not as likely as poorly educated respondents to think of 'Aboriginal issues' as 'extremely important'; Sol Lebovic, pers comm. Newspoll data for Donovan Research show 'white-collar' respondents slightly more likely than 'blue-collar' respondents to regard 'Aboriginal reconciliation' as 'important'; there are no data

for professional–managerial middle-class respondents. The same surveys show a much bigger gap between those who left school at seventeen plus compared to those who left at sixteen years or less; again, however, there are no data for those who went on to tertiary education. Bulbeck claims that, among the young people in South Australia who filled out questionnaires for her in 2002–03, those from professional and managerial households evinced 'a more liberal attitude' than did those from other households on 'land rights/Aboriginal people'. However, the relationships with mothers' and fathers' occupations are mixed; the analysis treats responses to Aboriginal 'land rights' and the idea that Aborigines should be 'treated fairly' as the same; and the difference does not surface in relation to whether the Prime Minister should apologise; Bulbeck, 'The "White Worrier" in South Australia', pp. 346–9.

15 Saulwick, 'Research into Issues Related to a Document of Reconciliation', pp. 5, 7.

16 Ibid., p. 35.

17 Ibid., p. 68.

18 Grattan, *Reconciliation*; 'We Are a Nation of John Howards'.

19 Gordon, 'An Issue He Didn't Believe In'.

20 Kelly, 'Howard's Views on Aborigines Shared by Majority of Public'.

21 Peake, 'Howard Denies Being Poll-Driven on Reconciliation'; *Canberra Times,* 5 March 2000.

22 'New Light on Reconciliation', *Sydney Morning Herald*, 6 March 2000.

23 Contractor, 'PM's Tax Break for New Black Body'.

24 Jopson, 'Howard's Far Horizon'.

25 Grattan and Kingston, 'The Past is the Past: Most Reject Apology to Aborigines'.

26 Ibid.

27 Kelly, 'Howard's Views on Aborigines Shared by Majority of Public'.

28 Grattan and Kingston, 'The Past is the Past: Most Reject Apology to Aborigines'.

29 Contractor, 'PM's Tax Break for New Black Body'.

30 Grattan, 'We Are a Nation of John Howards'.

31 'New Light on Reconciliation', *Sydney Morning Herald,* 6 March 2000.

32 Kingston and Vaughan, '"Failure" on Blacks Puts PM on Notice'. It is not clear where their figures come from. In the quantitative survey, 57 per cent agreed that 'the process of reconciliation could be helped through some form of document of reconciliation'; Newspoll, 'Quantitative Research into Issues Relating to a Document of Aboriginal Reconciliation: Stage I—Tables', Table 73.

33 Kelly, 'Howard's Views on Aborigines Shared by Majority of Public';
   McGuiness, 'Slow, Gradual Path to Reconciliation'; Grattan and
   Kingston, 'The Past is the Past: Most Reject Apology to Aborigines'.
34 Saulwick, 'Research into Issues Related to a Document of
   Reconciliation', pp. 164–6.
35 A group of sociologists, led by the President of The Australian
   Sociological Association, tried to counter the misleading reporting
   of Saulwick's work. Headlines referring to 'majority' opinion were
   misleading, they argued, as focus groups were 'not designed to
   produce reliable indicators of the distribution of views and attitudes
   across the community'; they called upon Saulwick 'to correct the
   widespread misinterpretations' of its research; Crook et al., 'Media
   Distorted the Reconciliation Poll'. And see Cox, 'Why We are Far
   From Reconciled'; her complaint about 'press distortion' was directed
   specifically at the sub-editor's headline in Kelly, 'Howard's Views on
   Aborigines Shared by Majority of Public'.
36 Kelly, 'Howard's Views on Aborigines Shared by Majority of Public'.
37 Ponting, 'Processing Public Opinion on Reconciliation in Australia',
   pp. 109–10, 115.
38 Taylor, 'Show Courage, Howard Told'; Scott, 'The People Will Have
   the Final Say'.
39 Ponting, 'Processing Public Opinion on Reconciliation in Australia',
   p. 110.
40 Newspoll, 'Quantitative Research into Issues Relating to a Document
   of Aboriginal Reconciliation: Summary of Findings', 2. Methodology.
41 Kelly, 'We Want to Get it Right on Race'; see also the editorial,
   'Society Needs Leadership on Aborigines', *Australian*, 8 March 2000.
42 Contractor, 'Majority Support Aborigines in Survey'.
43 Kelly, 'We Want to Get it Right on Race'.
44 Gordon, 'Nation Divides Over Reconciliation Issue'.
45 Grattan, 'Senate Dumps on PM over Reconciliation'.
46 Shanahan, 'Howard Abandons Deadline—No Reconciliation by
   Centenary'. Earlier, at a meeting of Coalition MPs, the Prime
   Minister had 'reaffirmed his opposition to a formal apology'. In doing
   so he was said to have cited 'an elder' who 'told him he was right not
   to say sorry'; Gordon, 'PM Says No to Apology, Again'.
47 Ibid.
48 'Howard Goes Back on Reconciliation', *Australian*, 28 February 2000.
49 Taylor, 'Show Courage, Howard Told'; see also Gordon, 'The Tax
   Reformer Finds Reconciliation too Taxing'.
50 'The Prime Minister and Reconciliation', *Age*, 29 February 2000.

51 Seccombe, 'Kookaburra'; Kingston and Vaughan, '"Failure" on Blacks Puts PM on Notice'.

52 Contractor, 'PM's Tax Break for New Black Body'; 'Deeds as Empty as Promises', *Canberra Times*, 4 March 2000.

53 Gordon, 'PM says No to Apology, Again'; 'An Issue He Didn't Believe In'. See also Wright, 'Howard Is Single-minded About Changing His Views'; 'New Light on Reconciliation', *Sydney Morning Herald*, 6 March 2000.

54 Seccombe, 'The PM's Man Who is Master at Massaging Words'.

55 Grattan, 'Blotting Out Past a Blot on Howard'; 'We are a Nation of John Howards'.

56 Devine, 'Equivocal Support for Redress'.

57 Quoted in Wright and Overington, 'PM Backs Survey on Aborigines'.

58 Megalogenis, 'Reality Check'.

59 And not just then. See, for example, Carney's conclusion that Howard's 'outright rejection of an apology … meant that the process [of reconciliation] had nowhere meaningful to go', and Hage's insistence that Howard 'destroyed the process of reconciliation'; Carney, *Peter Costello*, p. 275, and Hage, *Against Paranoid Nationalism*, p. xii.

60 According to Megalogenis, 'Opinion polls confirm majority support for Howard's brand of no-fault reconciliation that says no formal apology is necessary'; *Faultlines*, p. 126. But this is misleading: since 1997 there have been at least nine polls on an apology for things that happened in the past, but none explicitly about an apology for the 'Stolen Generations'. As John Hirst observes, asking respondents whether 'governments should apologise to Aboriginal people for what's happened in the past'—as the Council did—is a more unreasonable proposition than asking whether they should apologise for '"injustices"'; 'How Sorry Can We Be?', p. 96. This point also goes some way to resolving the 'paradox' Rosemary Neill observes in the Council's research, which showed 'overwhelming' acknowledgment of Aboriginal people being 'treated harshly and unfairly in the past' but only half that level of support for the idea that 'today's governments should apologise'; *White Out*, p. 8.

61 Donovan, 'Aboriginal Reconciliation Research: Vol. I Main Report', p. 23.

62 Muller, 'Most Say Blacks Lack Equality'.

63 Muller, 'Two out of Three Support a Treaty'.

64 McAllister et al., 'Australian Election Study, 1990'; Galligan et al., 'Rights in Australia 1991–1992'.

[65] Muller, 'Treatment of Aborigines Leads to Conflict: Survey'.

[66] Kelley et al., 'National Social Science Survey 1988–89'; 'National Social Science Survey 1993'; and 'International Social Science Surveys: Australia 1994'.

[67] McAllister et al., 'Australian Election Study, 1990'; Galligan et al., 'Rights in Australia 1991–1992: Jones et al., 'Australian Election Study, 1993'. For a brief report on the Rights in Australia survey, including data from a survey of politicians, see Galligan, 'Public Attitudes to Aboriginal Issues'.

[68] Donovan, 'Aboriginal Reconciliation Study November/December 1991', Table 17. The fieldwork for this and subsequent surveys was conducted by Newspoll.

[69] Donovan, 'Research Report: Aboriginal Reconciliation Tracking Research', 93058, p. 22; emphasis in the original.

[70] Donovan, 'Research Report: Aboriginal Reconciliation Research: Vol. I Main Report', pp. 25, 28; emphasis in the original.

[71] McAllister et al., 'Australian Election Study, 1990'; Galligan et al., 'Rights in Australia 1991–1992'.

[72] Donovan, 'Aboriginal Reconciliation Study November/December 1991', Table 58; 'Aboriginal Reconciliation Study February 1993', Table 45; 'Aboriginal Reconciliation Study September 1993', Table 45; 'Aboriginal Reconciliation Study March 1994', Table 45; and 'Aboriginal Reconciliation Tracking Study August 1994', Table 44.

[73] Donovan, 'Aboriginal Reconciliation Study November/December 1991', Table 60; 'Aboriginal Reconciliation Study February 1993', Table 47; 'Aboriginal Reconciliation Study September 1993', Table 47; 'Aboriginal Reconciliation Study March 1994', Table 47; and 'Aboriginal Reconciliation Tracking Study August 1994', Table 46.

[74] Pratt, *Practising Reconciliation?* Figure 3.1, p. 61. Lest this be seen as a sign of ignorance, indifference or thoughtlessness, note that Henry Reynolds' appeal to 'true reconciliation' also leaves the term undefined; *This Whispering in Our Hearts*, p. 251. See also the declaration by Bob Hodge and John O'Carroll that: 'Without a reconciliation between Aboriginal Australians and all later comers, Australia and its multiculture would be forever flawed, incomplete, lacking legitimacy'; *Borderwork in Multicultural Australia*, p. 18.

[75] Donovan, 'Aboriginal Reconciliation Study November/December 1991', Table 14; 'Aboriginal Reconciliation Study February 1993', Table 14; 'Aboriginal Reconciliation Study September 1993', Table 14; 'Aboriginal Reconciliation Study March 1994', Table 14; and 'Aboriginal Reconciliation Tracking Study August 1994', Table 14.

76 Donovan, 'Research Report: Aboriginal Reconciliation Tracking Research', 93169, p. 20.

77 Donovan, 'Aboriginal Reconciliation Study November/December 1991', Table 17; 'Aboriginal Reconciliation Study February 1993', Table 17; 'Aboriginal Reconciliation Study September 1993', Table 17; 'Aboriginal Reconciliation Study March 1994', Table 17; and 'Aboriginal Reconciliation Tracking Study August 1994', Table 17.

78 This is broadly consistent with a recent (undated) study in Western Australia where, asked to 'describe how you feel about Australian Aborigines', only 12 per cent of the respondents (n = 650) mentioned that 'being Indigenous entitled a person to more privileges' than if they 'were not Indigenous', responses assumed to represent negative feelings; Pedersen et al., 'Attitudes Toward Indigenous Australians', p. 87.

79 Donovan, 'Research Report: Aboriginal Reconciliation Tracking Research', Job No. 94079, p. 7.

80 Ibid., p. 14; emphasis in the original. For the data, see Donovan, 'Aboriginal Reconciliation Study November/December 1991', Table 17; 'Aboriginal Reconciliation Study February 1993', Table 17; 'Aboriginal Reconciliation Study September 1993', Table 17; 'Aboriginal Reconciliation Study March 1994', Table 17; and 'Aboriginal Reconciliation Tracking Study August 1994', Table 17.

81 Council for Aboriginal Reconciliation, *Going Forward*; Dodson quoted in Pratt, *Practising Reconciliation?* p. 95.

82 Pratt, *Practising Reconciliation?* Figure 4.1, p. 87. Contrast Pratt's research with Megalogenis' impression that getting 'closer to knowing one another' was 'what all sides agree should be the ultimate goal of reconciliation'; *Faultlines*, p. 133.

83 Donovan, 'Aboriginal Reconciliation Study November/December 1991', Table 50. According to Ponting, some council members thought the question on disadvantage 'phrased in a manner biased against Indigenous people', but he doesn't elaborate; 'Processing Public Opinion on Reconciliation in Australia', p. 115.

84 Donovan, 'Aboriginal Reconciliation Study, November/December 1991', Table 52.

85 Newspoll, 'Quantitative Research into Issues Relating to a Document of Aboriginal Reconciliation: Stage I—Tables', Tables 4 and 7.

86 In the 1990 Australian Candidates Study, 42 per cent of Coalition candidates said that on 'help for Aborigines' the Government had gone 'too far' or 'much too far'; Megalogenis, *Faultlines*, pp. 131–2. In the 1996 Candidates Study, Coalition candidates were

overwhelmingly 'racially conservative', inclined to think 'land rights' and government help for Aborigines had 'gone too far'; Jackman, 'Pauline Hanson, the Mainstream, and Political Elites', p. 181.

87 See, for example, Hancock, *Australia*, pp. 33, 80; Shaw, *The Story of Australia*, pp. 246–7; Bleakley, *The Aborigines of Australia*, ch. 5; Strehlow, *Assimilation Problems*, pp. 6, 8ff; Berndt, *Looking Ahead Through the Past*, pp. 13–14.

88 For an analysis of the talk of eight first-year psychology students, in which Aboriginal 'failure to adapt' is a central organising framework in understanding Aboriginal 'problems', see Augoustinos, Tuffin and Sale, 'Race Talk', p. 96.

89 Donovan, 'Aboriginal Reconciliation Study November/December 1991', Table 20.

90 Donovan, 'Aboriginal Reconciliation Tracking Study August 1994', Table 42.

91 Council for Aboriginal Reconciliation, *Going Forward*, p. 2.

92 Sweeney, 'A Report on a National Quantitative Survey of Community Attitudes Towards Aboriginal Reconciliation', Table 13.

93 Newspoll, 'Quantitative Research into Issues Relating to a Document of Aboriginal Reconciliation: Stage I—Tables', Tables 11 and 14. Long before the emergence of a revisionist history, Hancock called the opening chapter of *Australia*, 'The Invasion of Australia'.

94 *Commonwealth Parliamentary Debates*, House of Representatives, Vol. 29 October 1996, p. 5976 and 30 October 1996, p. 6155ff. For the phrase 'the Black Armband view of history', Howard was indebted to Blainey; 'Drawing up a Balance Sheet of Our History', p. 11.

95 Goot and Watson, 'Immigration, Multiculturalism and National Identity', p. 190 for survey data.

96 'The Fight for Aboriginal Rights', pp. 264–5. See also: Horne, *Looking for Leadership*, p. 211, with his Gradgrind-like insistence that reconciliation is about '*recognising the facts*' (emphasis in the original); McGregor, et al., *Imagining Australia*, p. 33, who argue that 'The key to reconciliation is understanding … Indigenous cultures, understanding Indigenous links with the land and understanding Indigenous history'; and Tickner, *Taking a Stand*, p. 29. In parliamentary debates on 'practical reconciliation', links to 'Indigenous history, culture, heritage' were more commonly made not by Labor speakers but by Coalition MPs; Pratt, *Practising Reconciliation?* p. 137.

97 Gaita, 'Guilt, Shame & Community'; Manne, *Left, Right, Left*, pp. 202–04. Arguments for the importance of 'guilt' are advanced in: Mulgan, 'Citizenship and Legitimacy in Post-colonial Australia';

Little, *The Public Emotions*, pp. 210–12; and Williams, '"Why Should I Feel Guilty?"'. For evidence connecting a sense of guilt with more 'positive' attitudes to Aborigines, including support for the Government's saying 'sorry', see: McGarty et al., 'Group-based Guilt'; and Pedersen et al., 'Attitudes Toward Indigenous Australians: The Role of Empathy and Guilt'. However, the same or other research suggests that a sense of 'collective guilt' is not widely shared, is 'counterproductive' to 'reconciliation', or is not as useful as a sense of 'shame' or 'regret'. See: Williams, '"Why Should I feel Guilty?"'; McGarty et al., 'Group-based Guilt'; Augoustinos and LeCouteur, 'On Whether to Apologise to Indigenous Australians'; and Halloran, 'Indigenous Reconciliation in Australia'.

98 Donovan, 'Research Report: Aboriginal Reconciliation Research: Vol. I Main Report', p. 22.

99 'I do not believe, and I have always strongly rejected, notions of intergenerational guilt'; *Commonwealth Parliamentary Debates*, House of Representatives, 30 October 1996, p. 6158.

100 Donovan, 'Aboriginal Reconciliation Study November/December 1991', Table 20; Newspoll, 'Quantitative Research into Issues Relating to a Document of Aboriginal Reconciliation: Stage I—Tables', Table 39.

101 Donovan, 'Research Report: Aboriginal Reconciliation Research: Vol I Main Report', p. 25.

102 Newspoll, 'Quantitative Research into Issues Relating to a Document of Aboriginal Reconciliation: Stage I—Tables', Tables 64 and 23.

103 Ibid., Table 23.

104 Ibid.

105 Ponting, 'Processing Public Opinion on Reconciliation in Australia', pp. 101, 118; emphasis added.

106 Brett and Moran, *Ordinary People's Politics*, p. 326.

107 The idea that Aborigines would secure their future by all of these means was foreseen, a year after the 1967 referendum, by the Chairman of the Council of Aboriginal Affairs, H.C. Coombs; see Tatz, 'The Aborigines', p. 38.

108 Galligan, 'Rights in Australia'.

109 Donovan, 'Aboriginal Reconciliation Tracking Study August 1994', Table 30.

110 Sweeney, 'A Report on a National Quantitative Survey of Community Attitudes Towards Aboriginal Reconciliation', Table 19 and Appendix Two, p. 6.

111 Newspoll, 'Quantitative Research into Issues Relating to a Document of Aboriginal Reconciliation: Stage II—Tables', Tables 55–7, and

60–1. For the draft Declaration for Reconciliation, see Newspoll, 'Quantitative Research into Issues Relating to a Document of Aboriginal Reconciliation: Summary of Findings', Executive Summary.

Conclusion

1. Goot, 'Politicians, Public Policy and Poll Following: Conceptual Difficulties and Empirical Realities'.
2. Schultz, *Reviving the Fourth Estate*, pp. 250–1.
3. Cited in Pratt, *Practising Reconciliation?*, p. 37.
4. Rowse, 'The Modesty of the State: Hasluck and the Anthropological Critics of Assimilation'.
5. Rowley, 'Aboriginals in Australian Society', p. 113.
6. Mackay, 'Vox Populi', p. 45.
7. Mackay, *Turning Point*, pp. 134–5.
8. Goot, 'Politicians, Public Policy and Poll Following: Conceptual Difficulties and Empirical Realities', p. 200.
9. Donovan Research, 'Research Report: Aboriginal Reconciliation Tracking Research' 95052, Table 17.
10. See, for example, Lawrence, *Fear and Politics*, p. 106, who refers to 'so-called "practical reconciliation"'; Duncan, et al., *Imagining Australia*, p. 32, who insist that 'The parlous living conditions of Indigenous Australians is a problem that requires different solutions and different thinking'; and Lucy and Mickler, *The War on Democracy*, p. 9, who refer to Howard's 'deceitfully illiberal "practical reconciliation"'. Contrast these positions with Grattan, 'Introduction', p. 5, who argues that reconciliation 'vitally involves material progress'; Dodson, 'Indigenous Australians', p. 135; and Brennan et al., *Treaty*, pp. 42–3, for whom 'practical reconciliation' is necessary but not sufficient.
11. For one remarkable occasion—importantly, on the Labor side—see *The Latham Diaries*, p. 369, where Mark Latham says he was advised by Labor's New South Wales State Secretary, Mark Arbib, to 'find new issues, like attacking land rights, get stuck into all the politically correct Aboriginal stuff—the punters love it'.
12. As did Michael Duffy, *Latham and Abbott*, p. 104. Latham's unhesitating support for 'Aboriginal reconciliation', his hostility to Keating's agenda notwithstanding, is noted in McGregor, *Australian Son*, p. 192.
13. Donovan Research, 'Aboriginal Reconciliation: Qualitative Research Update on Attitudes Toward Reconciliation Related Issues', p. 11.

[14] Brett and Moran, *Ordinary People's Politics*, pp. 9–10. Brett and Moran's other typifications of their interviewees include 'the country doctor', 'the Italian migrant', 'the Vietnam veteran' and 'number one son'.

[15] Goot, 'The Identikit Fallacy'.

[16] Brett and Moran, *Ordinary People's Politics*, Chapter 3.

[17] ANOP, 'Land Rights: Winning Middle Australia', p. 13.

[18] See Budge et al., *Mapping Policy Preferences*.

[19] Sniderman et al., *The Clash of Rights*, p. 121.

[20] 'I and PR, Brisbane', undated interview, Holding Press Cuttings, Vol. 1, AIATSIS Library.

Bibliography

AGB McNair, 'Project Land', 12–13 June 1993.

——, 'Aust Backs Black Title', *Bulletin*, 26 October 1993, p. 15.

——, *Sydney Morning Herald*, 27 May 1997.

Altman, John and Michael Dillon, 'Why Hawke's Model Has No Backing', *Australian Society*, vol. 4 no. 6, June 1985, pp. 26–8.

AMIC & WACME, 'Mabo: Concern and Equal Rights', Joint Media Statement, Australian Mining Industry Council and the Chamber of Mines and Energy of Western Australia, 11 July 1993.

——, 'Mabo Doubts Remain High', Joint Media Statement, Australian Mining Industry Council and the Chamber of Mines and Energy of Western Australia, 21 November 1993.

AMR:Quantum, 'National Opinion Survey on Aboriginal Issues June 1993', Prepared for the Australian Mining Industry Council and the Chamber of Mines and Energy of Western Australia.

——, 'National Opinion Survey on Aboriginal Issues: Wave III [sic]', Prepared for the Australian Mining Industry Council and the Chamber of Mines and Energy of Western Australia.

Anon, 'NSW Land Bill: Qld Uneasy', *Northern Territory News*, 29 March 1983.

——, 'Minister Criticized on Rights', *Canberra Times*, 29 March 1983.

——, 'Holding Takes Hard Line on Land Rights', *Sydney Morning Herald*, 19 April 1983.

——, 'Land Policy "Will Split Nation"' [source indecipherable], 10 December 1983.

——, 'Government Fearful of White Backlash', *Canberra Times*, 17 August 1984.

——, 'Majority Must Accept Land Rights: Holding', *Mercury*, 10 March 1985.

ANOP, 'Voter Attitude Research: The Northern Suburbs of Perth', mid-1984. [Goot collection]

——, 'Voter Attitude Study: Interim Summary Report of Marginal Seat Research Wave One: Deakin, Kingston, Leichhardt', June 1994. [Goot collection]

——, 'Voter Attitude Study: Marginal Seat Research Waves One and Two: Tabular Results', July 1984. [Goot collection]

——, 'Land Rights: Winning Middle Australia. An Attitudes and Communications Research Study', Australian Nationwide Opinion Polls, Crows Nest, NSW, 1985.

——, 'Voter Research in Marginal Seats in Western Australia', July 1985. [Goot collection]

[Attorney-General], 'Attorney-General's Commentary on the Native Title Act 1993', reprinted in M. Goot and T. Rowse (eds), *Make a Better Offer: The Politics of Mabo*, Pluto, Leichhardt, NSW, 1994, pp. 244–82.

Attwood, Bain and Andrew Markus, *The 1967 Referendum, or When Aborigines Didn't Get the Vote*, Australian Institute of Aboriginal and Torres Strait Islander Studies, Canberra, 1997.

——, 'The Fight for Aboriginal Rights', in R. Manne (ed.), *The Australian Century: Political Struggle in the Building of a Nation*, Text Publishing, Melbourne, 1999, pp. 265–92.

Augoustinos, Martha, Keith Tuffin and Lucida Sale, 'Race Talk', *Australian Journal of Psychology*, vol. 51 no. 2, 1999, pp. 90–7.

Augoustinos, Martha and Amanda LeCouteur, 'On Whether to Apologise to Indigenous Australians: The Denial of White Guilt', in N. R. Branscombe and B. Doosje (eds), *Collective Guilt: International Perspectives*, Cambridge University Press, Cambridge, 2004, pp. 236–61. Exeter 301.11 BRA.

Australian Gallup Polls, Survey 123, 9 February 1957 [computer file]. Canberra: Australian Social Science Data Archive, Australian National University, 1989.

——, Survey 134, 28 October 1958 [computer file]. Canberra: Australian Social Science Data Archive, Australian National University, 1989.

——, Survey 142, 5 February 1960 [computer file]. Canberra: Australian Social Science Data Archive, Australian National University, 1986.

——, Survey 147, 9 December 1960 [computer file]. Canberra: Australian Social Science Data Archive, Australian National University, 1989.

——, Survey 153, 10 November 1961 [computer file]. Canberra:

Australian Social Science Data Archive, Australian National University, 1989.

——, Survey 171, 21 August 1964 [computer file]. Canberra: Australian Social Science Data Archive, Australian National University, 2004.

——, Survey 177, 7 May 1965 [computer file]. Canberra: Australian Social Science Data Archive, Australian National University, 2004.

——, September 1981 [computer file]. Canberra: Australian Social Science Data Archive, Australian National University, 1984.

——, December 1983 [computer file]. Canberra: Australian Social Science Data Archive, Australian National University, 1986.

——, October 1984 [computer file]. Canberra: Australian Social Science Data Archive, Australian National University, 1987.

Australian Gallup Polls (subscriber reports), nos 406–415, Feb.–March 1947. Australian Public Opinion Polls, Melbourne.

——, nos 1056–1069, Dec. 1954–Jan. 1955. Australian Public Opinion Polls, Melbourne.

——, nos 1852–1871, Sept.–Dec. 1965. Australian Public Opinion Polls, Melbourne.

——, nos 1872–1883, Dec. 1965–Jan. 1966. Australian Public Opinion Polls, Melbourne.

——, nos 1884–1899, Feb.–April 1966. Australian Public Opinion Polls, Melbourne.

——, nos 1961–1980, Feb.–June 1967. Australian Public Opinion Polls, Melbourne.

Australian Labor Party, *Platform, Constitution and Rules as Approved by the 35th National Conference*, Australian Labor Party National Secretariat, Canberra, 1982.

Australian Press Council, *Annual Report*, No. 10, 30 June 1986.

Bartlett, R. H., *The Mabo Decision*, Butterworths, Sydney, 1993.

Beckett, Jeremy, 'Aborigines, Alcohol, and Assimilation', in M. Reay (ed.), *Aborigines Now: New Perspective in the Study of Aboriginal Communities*, Angus & Robertson, Sydney, 1964, pp. 32–47.

Beed, T. W., 'Opinion Polling and the Elections', in H. R. Penniman (ed.), *Australia at the Polls: The National Elections of 1975*, American Enterprise Institute for Public Policy Research and Australian National University Press, Washington, DC and Canberra, 1977, pp. 211 56.

Beed, T. W., Murray Goot, Stephen Hodgson and Peggy Ridley (eds), *Australian Opinion Polls 1941–1977*, Hale & Iremonger, Sydney, 1978.

Bell, J. H., 'The Aborigines of New South Wales: Introduction', Discussion Course D.265, mimeo, c. 1958 [Goot collection]

——, 'The Aborigines of New South Wales: Racial Prejudice towards the Mixed-Blood Aborigines', Lecture 4, Discussion Course D.265, mimeo, c. 1958 [Goot collection]

Bell, James H., 'Assimilation in New South Wales', in M. Reay (ed.), *Aborigines Now: New Perspective in the Study of Aboriginal Communities*, Angus & Robertson, Sydney, 1964, pp. 59–71.

Bennett, Mary M., *Human Rights for Australian Aborigines: How Can They Learn Without a Teacher?* [Author, Brisbane, 1957]

Berensky, Adam J., 'The Dynamics of Racial Policy Opinion, 1972–1994', in *Silent Voices. Public Opinion and Political Participation in America,* Princeton University Press, 2004, pp. 51–83.

Berndt, Ronald M., 'Native Welfare in Western Australia since the "Warburton Controversy" of 1957', *Australian Quarterly*, vol. XXXI no. 3, 1959, pp. 57–72.

——, 'The Concept of Protest within an Australian Aboriginal Context', in R. M. Berndt (ed.), *A Question of Choice: An Australian Aboriginal Dilemma*, University of Western Australia Press, Nedlands, WA, 1971, pp. 25–43.

——, *Looking Ahead Through the Past*, The Wentworth Lecture 1982, Australian Institute of Aboriginal Studies, Canberra, 1984.

Beswick, D. G. and M. D. Hills, 'An Australian Ethnocentrism Scale', *Australian Journal of Psychology*, vol. 21 no. 3, 1969, pp. 211–25.

——, 'A Survey of Ethnocentrism in Australia', *Australian Journal of Psychology*, vol. 24 no. 2, 1972, pp. 153–63.

Blackshield, Tony, 'Namatjira v Raabe', in T. Blackshield, M. Coper and G. Williams (eds), *The Oxford Companion to the High Court of Australia*, Oxford University Press, South Melbourne, 2001, pp. 491–2.

Blainey, Geoffrey, 'Drawing up a Balance Sheet of Our History', *Quadrant*, vol. 37 nos 7–8, July–August 1993, pp. 10–15.

——, *A Shorter History of Australia*, William Heinemann Australia, Port Melbourne, 1994.

Bleakley, J. W., *The Aborigines of Australia*, Jacaranda Press, Brisbane, 1961.

Bourdieu, Pierre, 'Public Opinion Does Not Exist', in A. Mattelart and S. Siegelaub (eds), *Communication and Class Struggle*, Vol. 1, International General, New York, 1979, pp. 124–30; also in *Sociology in Question*, Sage, 1993, pp. 149–57.

Brennan, Frank, *Sharing the Country*, Penguin, Ringwood, Vic., 1991.

Brennan, Sean, Larissa Behrendt, Lisa Strelein and George Williams, *Treaty*, Federation Press, Annandale, NSW, 2005.

Brett, Judith, 'Australia', in A. Milner and M. Quilty (eds), *Communities of Thought*, Oxford University Press, Melbourne, 1996, pp. 184–202.

Brett, Judith and Anthony Moran, *Ordinary People's Politics: Australians Talk about Life, Politics, and the Future of Their Country*, Pluto Press, North Melbourne, 2006.

Broome, Richard, 'Aborigines and the Caste Barrier', in *Aboriginal Australians*, Allen & Unwin, St Leonards, NSW, 1982/1994, ch. 9.

Buchanan, M. E., *Attitudes Towards Immigrants in Australia*, Australian Government Publishing Service, Canberra, 1976.

Buckley, Amanda, 'PM Asked to Block NSW Land Rights Bill', *Sydney Morning Herald*, 21 March 1983.

——, 'Holding Sees Land Rights as Reparation', *Sydney Morning Herald*, 25 July 1983.

——, 'Clyde Holding's Fight Against Time and Tide', *Sydney Morning Herald*, 30 March 1985.

Budge, Ian, Hans-Dieter Klingemann, Andrea Volkens, Judith Bara and Eric Tanenbaum, *Mapping Policy Preferences: Estimates for Parties, Electors, and Governments, 1945–1998*, Oxford University Press, Oxford, 2001.

Bulbeck, Chilla, 'The "White Worrier" in South Australia: Attitudes to Multiculturalism, Immigration and Reconciliation', *Journal of Sociology*, vol. 40 no. 1, 2004, pp. 341–61.

Calley, Malcolm J. C., 'Race Relations on the North Coast of New South Wales', *Oceania*, vol. 27, 1956/1957, pp. 190–209.

Campbell, Andrew A., *The Australian League of Rights: A Study of Political Extremism and Subversion*, Outback Press, Collingwood, Vic., 1978.

Campbell, Graeme, 'Letter to the Federal Parliamentary Labor Party', in K. Baker (ed.), *The Land Rights Debate: Selected Documents*, Institute of Public Affairs, Melbourne, 1985. [Originally circulated 28 March 1984]

Carney, Shaun, *Peter Costello: The New Liberal,* Allen & Unwin, Crows Nest, NSW, 2001.

Catholic Commission for Justice and Peace, *Aborigines: A Statement of Concern*, 1978.

Chaney, Fred, 'Advancement Through Self-help', *Wikaru,* no. 15, July 1987, p. 47.

Committee, AVSS, et al., 'Australian Values Study Survey, 1983' [computer file], Canberra: Australian Social Science Data Archive, Australian National University.

Contractor, Aban, 'PM's Tax Break for New Black Body', *Canberra Times*, 2 March 2000.

——, 'Majority Support Aborigines in Survey', *Canberra Times*, 8 March 2000.

Cornwall, John, *Just for the Record: The Political Recollections of John Cornwall*, Wakefield Press, Kent Town, SA, 1989.

Council for Aboriginal Reconciliation, *Walking Together: The First Steps,* Australian Government Publishing Service, Canberra, 1994.

——, *Going Forward: Social Justice for the First Australians,* Australian Government Publishing Service, Canberra, 1996.

——, *Reconciliation: Australia's Challenge,* [Canberra], 2000.

Cox, Eva, 'Why We are Far From Reconciled', *Australian,* 6 March 2000.

Crook, Stephen, Jan Pakulski, Malcolm Waters and John Western, 'Media Distorted the Reconciliation Poll', *Age,* 7 March 2000.

Cumming, Fia, 'The Embattled Clyde Holding Continues to Fight', *Bulletin,* 11 September 1984.

Curthoys, Ann, *Freedom Ride: A Freedom Rider Remembers,* Allen & Unwin, Crows Nest, NSW, 2002.

Department of Aboriginal Affairs, 'Brief for Advertising/Public Relations Firms for a National Communications Campaign on Aboriginal Affairs', Information Branch [April 1985]. [Goot collection]

Devine, Frank, 'Equivocal Support for Redress', *Australian,* 9 March 2000.

ɯ Dodson, Mick, 'Indigenous Australians', in R. Manne (ed.), *The Howard Years,* Black Inc., Melbourne, 2004, pp. 119–43.

Dodson, P., M. Mowbray and W. Snowdon, 'Promise, Confrontation and Compromise in Indigenous Affairs', in S. Ryan and T. Bramston (eds), *The Hawke Government: A Critical Perspective,* Pluto Press, North Melbourne, 2003, pp. 296–310.

Donovan, Robert J., 'Increased Support for Aboriginal Reconciliation: Fact or Artefact? The Validity of Comparisons Between Questions with Different Wording', *Australasian Journal of Market Research,* vol. 6 no. 1, 1998, pp. 13–25.

Donovan Research, 'Aboriginal Reconciliation Study November/ December 1991', Job No. 1121, West Perth.

——, 'Research Report: Aboriginal Reconciliation Research: Vol. I Main Report', Job No. 91134, West Perth, January 1992.

——, 'Aboriginal Reconciliation Research: Vol. II Appendices', Job No. 91134, West Perth, January 1992.

——, 'Aboriginal Reconciliation Study February 1993', Job No. 3021, West Perth.

——, 'Research Report: Aboriginal Reconciliation Tracking Research', Job No. 93058, West Perth, March 1993.

——, 'Aboriginal Reconciliation Study September 1993', Job No. 3092, West Perth.

——, 'Research Report: Aboriginal Reconciliation Tracking Research', Job No. 93169, West Perth, October 1993.

——, 'Aboriginal Reconciliation Study March 1994', Job No. 4031, West Perth.

——, 'Research Report: Aboriginal Reconciliation Tracking Research', Job No. 94079, West Perth, April 1994.

——, 'Aboriginal Reconciliation Tracking Study August 1994', Job No. 4082, West Perth.

——, 'Research Report: Aboriginal Reconciliation Tracking Research' Job No. 95052, May 1995, West Perth.

——, 'Aboriginal Reconciliation: Qualitative Research Update on Attitudes Toward Reconciliation Related Issues', West Perth, July 1995.

Duffy, Michael, *Latham and Abbott: The Lives and Rivalries of the Two Finest Politicians of their Generation*, Random House, Milsons Point, NSW, 2004.

Duncan, MacGregor, Andrew Leigh, David Madden and Peter Tynan, *Imagining Australia: Ideas For Our Future*, Allen & Unwin, Crows Nest, NSW, 2004.

Duncan, T., 'Rights Issue Seen as Land Mine in ALP', *Bulletin*, 4 May 1984.

Edmunds, Mary, *They Get Heaps: A Study of Attitudes in Roebourne, Western Australia*, Aboriginal Studies Press, Canberra, 1989.

Elkin, A. P., *Our Opinions and the National Effort*, Australasian Publishing, Sydney, 1941.

——, 'Study of Public Opinion', *Australian Journal of Science*, vol. V, no. 1, 1942, pp. 16–18.

——, *Citizenship for the Aborigines: A National Aboriginal Policy*, Australasian Publishing, Sydney, 1944.

——, *Aborigines and Citizenship*, Association for the Protection of Native Races, [Sydney], [1958].

——, *The Australian Aborigines*, Fourth ed., Angus & Robertson, Sydney, 1964.

Ellis, Jack, 'Blitner: Dump Parts of Land Act', *Northern Territory News*, 21 April 1983.

Encel, S., *Equality and Authority: A Study of Class, Status and Power in Australia*, F. W. Cheshire, Melbourne, 1970.

Farr, James, 'Framing Democratic Discussion', in G. E. Marcus and R. L. Hanson (eds), *Reconsidering the Democratic Public*, Pennsylvania University State Press, University Park, Pennsylvania, 1993, pp. 379–91.

Fesl, Eve and Andrew Markus, 'Land Rights: The Wrong Numbers', *Australian Society*, vol. 5 no. 5, May 1986, pp. 3–5.

Fewster, Alan and Peter Terry, 'Canberra to Override States on Land Rights', *Australian*, 14 August 1985.

Fink, Ruth A., 'The Caste Barrier—An Obstacle to the Assimilation of Part-Aborigines in North-West New South Wales', *Oceania*, vol. 28, 1957/1958, pp. 100–10.

——, 'The Changing Status and Cultural Identity of Western Australian Aborigines: A Field Study of Aborigines in the Murchison District, Western Australia 1955–1957', unpublished PhD thesis, Columbia University, 1960.

Fishkin, James, *Democracy and Deliberation: New Directions for Democratic Reform*, Yale University Press, New Haven, Connecticut, 1991.

Flick, Isabel, and Heather Goodall, *Isabel Flick: The Many Lives of an Extraordinary Aboriginal Woman,* Allen & Unwin, St Leonards, NSW, 2004.

Frame, Tom, *The Life and Death of Harold Holt*, Allen & Unwin, Crows Nest, NSW, 2005.

Gaita, Raimond, 'Guilt, Shame & Community', in *A Common Humanity*, Text Publishing, Melbourne, 1999/2000, pp. 87–106.

Galligan, Brian, 'Public Attitudes to Aboriginal Issues', in C. Fletcher (ed.), *Aboriginal Self-Determination in Australia*, Aboriginal Studies Press, Canberra, 1994, pp. 99–105.

Galligan, Brian, Roger Jones, Joseph Fletcher and Ian McAllister, 'Rights in Australia 1991–1992: National Household Sample', User's Guide for the Machine-Readable Data File, Australian Social Science Data Archives, Australian National University, Canberra, 1993.

[Gallup, George], *The New Science of Public Opinion Measurement*, American Institute of Public Opinion, Princeton, New Jersey, [1938].

Gallup, George, *A Guide to Public Opinion Polls*, Princeton University Press, Princeton, New Jersey, 1944.

——, *A Guide to Public Opinion Polls*, Second edition, Princeton University Press, Princeton, New Jersey, 1948.

——, 'The Quintamensional Plan of Question Design', *Public Opinion Quarterly*, vol. 11, 1947, pp. 385–93.

Gallup, George and Saul Forbes Rae, *The Pulse of Democracy: The Public Opinion Poll and How It Works*, Simon and Schuster, New York, 1940.

Gardiner-Garden, John, 'The Mabo Debate—A Chronology', in *Mabo Papers*, Parliamentary Research Service, Subject Collection No. 1, Australian Government Publishing Services, Canberra, 1994, pp. 141–93.

Gill, Peter and Nigel Wilson, 'Native Title Tribunal Will Give Rulings "Within Weeks"', *Australian Financial Review*, 2 August 1993.

Ginsberg, Benjamin, 'Polling and the Transformation of Public Opinion', in *The Captive Public: How Mass Opinion Promotes State Power*, Basic Books, New York, 1986, pp. 59–85; also reprinted in M. Margolis and G. A. Mauser (eds), *Manipulating Public Opinion: Essays on Public Opinion as a Dependent Variable*, Brooks/Cole, Pacific Grove, California, 1989, pp. 271–93.

Goot, Murray, 'Ashby, Sylvia Rose', in J. Ritchie (ed.), *Australian Dictionary of Biography*, vol. 13, Melbourne University Press, Carlton, Vic., 1993, pp. 77–8.

——, 'Polls as Science, Polls as Spin: Mabo and the Miners', in M. Goot and T. Rowse (eds), *Make a Better Offer: The Politics of Mabo,* Pluto, Leichhardt, NSW, 1994, pp. 133–56.

——, 'The Wild West? Yes, No and Maybe', in M. Goot and T. Rowse (eds), *Make a Better Offer: The Politics of Mabo,* Pluto, Leichhardt, NSW, 1994, pp. 194–202.

——, 'Australia's "Stolen Children": Which Poll Would a Poll-Following Prime Minister Have Followed?' *International Journal of Public Opinion Research,* vol. 10 no. 4, 1998, pp. 349–64.

——, 'The Identikit Fallacy … or the Problem with "Phil and Jenny"', *Australian Journalism Review*, vol. 23 no. 2, 2001, pp. 119–27.

——, 'Politicians, Public Policy and Poll Following: Conceptual Difficulties and Empirical Realities', *Australian Journal of Political Science*, vol. 40 no. 2, 2005, pp. 189–205.

——, 'The Aboriginal Franchise and its Consequences', *Australian Journal of Politics and History*, vol. 52 no. 4, 2006, pp. 517–61.

——, 'Public Opinion', in B. Galligan and W. Roberts (eds), *The Oxford Companion to Australian Politics*, Oxford University Press, Melbourne (in press).

Goot, Murray, Peggy Ridley, Peter Day, Leonie Gibbins, Ian McNair and Terence W. Beed (eds), *Australian Opinion Polls 1977–1990,* D. W. Thorpe, Port Melbourne, 1993.

Goot, Murray and Terence W. Beed, 'The Referenda: Pollsters and Predictions', *Politics,* vol. XII no. 2, 1977, pp. 86–95.

Goot, Murray and Tim Rowse, 'The "Backlash" Hypothesis and the Land Rights Option', *Australian Aboriginal Studies*, no. 1, 1991, pp. 3–12.

Goot, Murray and Ian Watson, 'Immigration, Multiculturalism and National Identity', in S. Wilson et al. (eds), *Australian Social Attitudes: The First Report*, University of New South Wales Press, Sydney, 2005, pp. 182–203.

Gordon, Michael, 'Black Apology Splits Voters', *Australian*, 3 June 1997.

——, 'PM says No to Apology, Again', *Age*, 17 February 2000.

——, 'The Tax Reformer Finds Reconciliation Too Taxing', *Age*, 29 February 2000.

——, 'An Issue He Didn't Believe In', *Age*, 4 March 2000.

——, 'Nation Divides Over Reconciliation Issue', *Age*, 8 March 2000.

Gott, K. D., *Voices of Hate: A Study of the Australian League of Rights and its Director Eric D. Butler*, Dissent, Melbourne, 1965.

Grattan, Michelle, 'Blotting Out Past a Blot on Howard', *Sydney Morning Herald*, 29 February 2000.

——, 'We are a Nation of John Howards', *Sydney Morning Herald*, 3 March 2000.

——, 'Senate Dumps on PM over Reconciliation', *Sydney Morning Herald*, 8 March 2000.

——, 'Introduction', in M. Grattan (ed.), *Reconciliation: Essays on Reconciliation in Australia*, Black Inc., Melbourne, 2000, pp. 3–8.

Grattan, Michelle (ed), *Reconciliation: Essays on Reconciliation in Australia*, Black Inc., Melbourne, 2000.

Grattan, Michelle, and Margot Kingston, 'The Past is the Past: Most Reject Apology to Aborigines', *Sydney Morning Herald*, 3 March 2000.

Greig, A., F. Lewins, and K. White, *Inequality in Australia*, Cambridge University Press, Cambridge, 2003.

Gruen, F., and M. Grattan, *Managing Government: Labor's Achievements and Failures*, Longman Cheshire, Melbourne, 1993.

Gunn, J. A. W., 'Public Spirit to Public Opinion', in *Beyond Liberty and Property*, McGill-Queens University Press, Kingston, Ontario, and Montreal, Quebec, 1983, pp. 260–315.

——, 'Public Opinion', in T. Ball, J. Farr and R. L. Hanson (eds), *Political Innovation and Conceptual Change*, Cambridge University Press, Cambridge, 1989, pp. 247–65.

Haebich, Anna, *Broken Circles: Fragmenting Indigenous Lives 1800–2000*, Fremantle Arts Centre Press, South Fremantle, WA, 2000.

——, '"Between Knowing and Not Knowing": Public Knowledge of the Stolen Generations', *Aboriginal History*, vol. 25, 2001, pp. 70–90.

Hage, Ghassan, *Against Paranoid Nationalism: Searching for Hope in a Shrinking Society*, Pluto Press, Annandale, NSW, 2003.

Halloran, Michael J., 'Indigenous Reconciliation in Australia: Do Values, Identity and Collective Guilt Matter?' *Journal of Community & Applied Social Psychology*, vol. 17, 2007, pp. 1–18.

Hancock, W. K., *Australia*, Ernest Benn, London, 1930.

Hasluck, Paul, *Shades of Darkness: Aboriginal Affairs 1925–1965*, Melbourne University Press, Melbourne, 1988.

Hawke, R. J. L., *The Resolution of Conflict*, Australian Broadcasting Commission, Sydney, 1979.

——, *The Hawke Memoirs*, William Heinemann, Port Melbourne, 1994.

Hiatt, L. R., 'Aborigines in the Australian Community', in A. F. Davies and S. Encel (eds), *Australian Society: A Sociological Introduction*, F. W. Cheshire, Melbourne, 1965, pp. 274–95.

Hill, Kathleen F., *A Study of Aboriginal Poverty in Two Country Towns*, Australian Government Publishing Service for the Commission of Inquiry into Poverty, Canberra, 1975.

Hirst, John, 'How Sorry Can We Be?', in *Sense & Nonsense in Australian History*, Black Inc. Agenda, Melbourne, 2005, pp. 80–103.

Hodge, Bob and John O'Carroll, *Borderwork in Multicultural Australia*, Allen & Unwin, Crows Nest, NSW, 2006.

Holding, Clyde, 'Federal Government Policies and Initiatives', in K. Baker (ed.), *The Land Rights Debate: Selected Documents*, Institute of Public Affairs, Melbourne, 1985. [Originally presented to a conference on Aborigines and International Law, Canberra, November 1983]

——, 'Land Rights Policy Merely a Model', *Bulletin*, 26 March 1985, pp. 39–41.

Horne, Donald, *The Lucky Country*, Penguin, Ringwood, Vic., 1965.

——, *Looking for Leadership: Australia in the Howard Years*, Viking, Ringwood, Vic., 2001.

Howard, John, 'Speech to Reconciliation Convention', 26 May 1997.

HREOC, *Bringing Them Home: Report of the National Inquiry Into the Separation of Aboriginal and Torres Strait Children and Their Families*, Human Rights and Equal Opportunity Commission, Sydney, 1997.

[Inglis, Judy], 'The Outback Aborigines', *Current Affairs Bulletin*, vol. 23 no. 3, 1958, pp. 35–48.

——, '"The Dark People"', *Current Affairs Bulletin*, vol. 29 no. 4, 1961, pp. 50–64.

Jackman, Simon, 'Pauline Hanson, the Mainstream, and Political Elites: The Place of Race in Australian Political Ideology', *Australian Journal of Political Science*, vol. 33 no. 2, 1998, pp. 167–86.

Jacobs, Lawrence R., and Robert Y. Shapiro, *Politicians Don't Pander: Political Manipulation and the Loss of Democratic Responsiveness*, University of Chicago Press, Chicago, 2000.

Jaensch, Dean, *The Hawke–Keating Hijack: The ALP in Transition*, Allen & Unwin, Sydney, 1989.

Jennett, C., 'Politics, the Law and Aborigines: Modern Politics', in J. Jupp (ed.), *Australia: Its People and Their Origins,* Angus & Robertson, Sydney, 1988, pp. 228–33.

Johnson, Jeanette, *Unfinished Business: Australians and Reconciliation*, Australian Government Publishing Service, Canberra, 1996.

Jones, F. L., 'Changing Attitudes and Values in Post-War Australia', in K. Hancock (ed.), *Australian Society*, Cambridge University Press, Cambridge, 1989, pp. 94–118.

Jones, Roger, Ian McAllister, David Denemark and David Gow, 'Australian Election Study, 1993', User's Guide for the Machine-Readable Data

File, Social Science Data Archives, Australian National University, Canberra, 1993.

Jopson, Debra, 'Howard's Far Horizon', *Sydney Morning Herald*, 29 February 2000.

Kelley, Jonathan, Clive Bean and M. D. R. Evans, 'National Social Science Survey 1988–89: Family and Lifestyles', Second edition, User's Guide for the Machine-Readable Data File, Australian Social Science Data Archives, Australian National University, Canberra, 1996.

Kelley, Jonathan, Clive Bean, M. D. R. Evans and Krzysztof Zagorski, 'National Social Science Survey 1993: Inequality II', User's Guide for the Machine-Readable Data File, Australian Social Science Data Archives, Australian National University, Canberra, 1996.

——, 'International Social Science Surveys: Australia 1994', User's Guide for the Machine-Readable Data File, Australian Social Science Data Archives, Australian National University, Canberra, 1996.

Kelly, Caroline, 'The Reactions of White Groups in Country Towns of New South Wales to Aborigines', *Social Horizons*, July 1943, pp. 34–40.

Kelly, Paul, *The End of Certainty: Power, Politics and Business in Australia*, Allen & Unwin, St Leonards, NSW, revised edition 1994.

——, 'Howard's Views on Aborigines Shared by Majority of Public', *Australian*, 3 March 2000.

——, 'We Want to Get it Right on Race', *Australian*, 8 March 2000.

——, *100 Years: The Australian Story*, Allen & Unwin, Crows Nest, NSW, 2001.

Kingston, Margot and Amanda Vaughan, '"Failure" on Blacks Puts PM on Notice', *Sydney Morning Herald*, 29 February 2000.

Lake, Marilyn, *Faith: Faith Bandler, Gentle Activist*, Allen & Unwin, Crows Nest, NSW, 2002.

Latham, Mark, *The Latham Diaries*, Melbourne University Press, Carlton, Vic., 2005.

Lawrence, Carmen, *Fear and Politics*, Scribe, Carlton North, 2006.

Legge, Kate, 'Coombs Stamp on Land for Aborigines', *Age*, 14 September 1985.

Libby, Ronald T., *Hawke's Law: The Politics of Mining and Land Rights in Australia*, University of Western Australia Press, Nedlands, WA, 1989.

Lippmann, Lorna, *Words or Blows: Racial Attitudes in Australia*, Penguin, Ringwood, Vic., 1973.

Lippmann, Walter, *The Phantom Public*, Transaction, New Brunswick, New Jersey, 1925/1993.

Little, Graham, *The Public Emotions: From Mourning to Hope*, ABC Books, Sydney, 1999.

Long, J. P. M., 'The Administration and the Part-Aboriginals of the Northern Territory', *Oceania*, vol. 37 no. 3, 1967, pp. 186–201.

Lucy, Niall and Steve Mickler, *The War on Democracy: Conservative Opinion In the Australian Press*, University of Western Australia Press, Crawley, WA, 2006.

MacCallum, Mungo, 'Aborigines Caught in a Holding Pattern', *Herald*, 19 March 1985.

——, 'Clyde Holding Penthouse Interview', *Penthouse*, September 1985.

Mackay, Hugh, *The Mackay Report: Keynote*, 1992.

——, *Turning Point: Australians Choosing Their Futures*, Pan Macmillan, Sydney, 1999.

——, 'Vox Populi', in M. Grattan (ed.), *Reconciliation: Essays on Reconciliation in Australia*, Black Inc., Melbourne, 2000, pp. 45–52.

Maddock, Kenneth, *Your Land Is Our Land: Aboriginal Land Rights*, Penguin, Ringwood, Vic., 1987.

Maddox, Graham, *The Hawke Government and the Labor Tradition*, Penguin, Ringwood, Vic., 1989.

Manne, Robert, 'In Denial: The Stolen Generations and the Right', *The Australian Quarterly Essay*, No. 1, 2001, pp. 1–113.

——, 'The Howard Years: A Political Interpretation', in R. Manne (ed.), *The Howard Years*, Black Inc., Melbourne, 2004, pp. 3–53.

——, *Left, Right, Left: Political Essays 1977–2005*, Black Inc., Melbourne, 2005.

Markus, Andrew, *Race: John Howard and the Remaking of Australia*, Allen & Unwin, Crows Nest, NSW, 2001.

Marr, David, *The High Price of Heaven*, Allen & Unwin, St Leonards, NSW, 1999.

Mayman, J., 'Land Rights Opponents in Racial Con: Holding', *Age*, 12 September 1984.

——, 'Prominent Aborigine Hits Rights "Fiasco"', *Age*, 27 September 1984.

McAllister, Ian, Roger Jones, Elim Papadakis and David Gow, 'Australian Election Study, 1990', User's Guide for the Machine-Readable Data File, Social Science Data Archives, Australian National University, Canberra, 1990.

McAllister, Ian and Rhonda Moore, *Party Strategy and Change: Australian Electoral Speeches Since 1946*, Longman Cheshire, Melbourne, 1991.

McCourt, J., 'Holding Hits at "Racist" WA Libs', *Daily News*, 14 December 1983.

McGarty, Craig, Anne Pedersen, Colin Wayne Leach, Tamara Mansell, Julie Waller and Ana-Maria Bliuc, 'Group-based Guilt as a Predictor of Commitment to Apology', *British Journal of Social Psychology*, vol. 44, 2005, pp. 658–80.

McGregor, Craig, *Profile of Australia*, Hodder & Stoughton, London, 1966.

——, *Australian Son: Inside Mark Latham*, Pluto Press, North Melbourne, 2004.

McGuinness, P. P., 'Slow, Gradual Path to Reconciliation', *Sydney Morning Herald*, 4 March 2000.

McQueen, Humphrey, *Social Sketches of Australia*, Third edition, University of Queensland Press, St Lucia, Qld, 2004.

Megalogenis, George, 'Reality Check', *Australian*, 11 March 2000.

——, *Faultlines: Race, Work and the Politics of Changing Australia*, Scribe, Melbourne, 2003.

——, *The Longest Decade*, Scribe, Melbourne, 2006.

Miller, M., *Report of the Committee of Review of Aboriginal Employment and Training Programs*, Australian Government Publishing Service, Canberra, 1985.

Millett, Michael, Margo Kingston and Minh Bui, 'It Hurt Us, Unapologetic PM Admits', *Sydney Morning Herald*, 13 December 1997.

Mills, Stephen, 'Holding Pledges Land Rights', *Age*, 27 April 1983.

——, *The Hawke Years: The Story from the Inside*, Viking, Ringwood, Vic., 1993.

Milne, Glenn, 'Community Divided on Native Title but Most Oppose Compensation', *Australian*, 14 June 1993.

Morgan Gallup Poll, Finding No. 1096; *Bulletin*, 2 August 1983.

Morgan Poll Finding No. 2370; *Time*, 25 January 1993.

——, Finding No. 2405; *Time,* 5 April 1993.

——, Finding No. 2425; *Time,* 7 June 1993.

——, Finding No. 2434; *Sunday Sun-Herald,* 13 June 1993.

——, Finding No. 2467; *Time,* 6 September 1993.

——, Finding No. 2543; *Time*, 14 February 1994.

——, Finding No. 2993; *Bulletin*, 17 June 1997.

Mulgan, Richard, 'Citizenship and Legitimacy in Post-colonial Australia', in N. Peterson and W. Sanders (eds), *Citizenship and Indigenous Australians: Changing Conceptions and Possibilities*, Cambridge University Press, Cambridge, 1998, pp. 179–95.

Muller, Denis, 'Treatment of Aborigines Leads to Conflict: Survey', *Sydney Morning Herald,* 20 March 1992.

——, 'Most Say Blacks Lack Equality', *Age,* 23 March 1992.

——, 'Two out of Three Support a Treaty', *Sydney Morning Herald*, 24 March 1992.

Murphy, John, *Imagining the Fifties: Private Sentiment and Political Culture in Menzies' Australia*, University of New South Wales Press, Sydney, 2000.

Native Welfare Conference, *The Policy of Assimilation. Decisions of the Commonwealth and State Ministers at the Native Welfare Conference,*

Canberra … 1961, Commonwealth Government Printer, Canberra, 1961.

Neill, Rosemary, *White Out: How Politics is Killing Black Australia*, Allen & Unwin, Crows Nest, NSW, 2002.

Newspoll, 'Quantitative Research into Issues Relating to a Document of Aboriginal Reconciliation: Stage 1—Tables', Prepared for Office of Indigenous Policy, Department of Prime Minister and Cabinet, January 2000.

——, 'Quantitative Research into Issues Relating to a Document of Aboriginal Reconciliation: Stage II—Tables', Prepared for Office of Indigenous Policy, Department of Prime Minister and Cabinet, February 2000.

——, 'Quantitative Research into Issues Relating to a Document of Aboriginal Reconciliation: Summary of Findings', Prepared for Council for Aboriginal Reconciliation, March 2000.

Newspoll, Saulwick & Muller and Mackay, 'Public Opinion on Reconciliation: Snap Shot, Close Focus, Long Lens', in M. Grattan (ed), *Reconciliation: Essays on Reconciliation in Australia*, Black Inc., Melbourne, 2000, pp. 33–45.

Nihill, Grant, 'Holding Plans WA Land-rights Talks', *Advertiser,* 18 April 1985.

Nossal, Gustav, 'The Next Steps in the Long March to Reconciliation', *Age*, 16 February 2000.

O'Callaghan, M-L., 'Land Rights Gone Wrong', *Sydney Morning Herald*, 5 March 1986.

O'Neill, Margot, 'Holding Hires an Expert to Fight League of Rights', *Age*, 17 July 1984.

——, 'Ad Campaign Will Fight Land Rights Backlash', *Age*, 25 July 1984.

——, 'Holding to Blame for Attitude to Blacks: Lib', *Age*, 13 November 1984.

——, 'Holding Goes on a Talkabout', *Age*, 12 March 1985.

Osborne, Thomas and Nikolas Rose, 'Do the Social Sciences Create Phenomena? The Example of Public Opinion Research', *British Journal of Sociology*, vol. 50 no. 3, pp. 367–96.

Parkin, Andrew and John Summers, 'Ethnic Groups and Aborigines', in J. Summers, D. Woodward and A. Parkin (eds), *Government, Politics and Power in Australia*, Fourth edition, Longman Cheshire, Melbourne, 1990, pp. 275–88.

Parliament [of the Commonwealth of Australia], 'Report from the Select Committee on Voting Rights of Aborigines', *Parliamentary Papers,* Vol. II, No. H of RI [Group H], 1961.

Peake, Ross, 'Howard Denies Being Poll-Driven on Reconciliation', *Canberra Times*, 4 March 2000.

Pedersen, Anne, Jamie Beven, Iain Walker and Brian Griffiths, 'Attitudes Toward Indigenous Australians: The Role of Empathy and Guilt', *Journal of Community & Applied Social Psychology*, vol. 14, 2004, pp. 233–49.

Pedersen, Anne, Pat Dudgeon, Susan Watt and Brian Griffiths, 'Attitudes Toward Indigenous Australians: The Issue of "Special Treatment"', *Australian Psychologist*, vol. 41 no. 2, 2006, pp. 85–94.

Perkins, Charles, 'The Administration of Aboriginal Development: Address by Charles Perkins, Secretary, Department of Aboriginal Affairs' (to the Royal Australian Institute of Public Administration, ACT'), nd, unpublished typescript, AIATSIS Library.

Ponting, J. Rick, 'Processing Public Opinion on Reconciliation in Australia', in *The Nisga'a Treaty: Polling Dynamics and Political Communication in Comparative Context*, Broadview Press, Peterborough, Ontario, 2006, pp. 97–120.

Povinelli, Elizabeth A., *The Cunning of Recognition: Indigenous Alterities and the Making of Australian Multiculturalism*, Duke University Press, Durham, North Carolina, and London, 2002.

Pratt, Angela, *Practising Reconciliation? The Politics of Reconciliation in the Australian Parliament, 1991–2000*, Parliamentary Library, Canberra, 2005.

Pusey, Michael, *The Experience of Middle Australia: The Dark Side of Economic Reform*, Cambridge University Press, Cambridge, 2003.

Reay, Marie and G. Sitlington, 'Class and Status in a Mixed-Blood Community (Moree, New South Wales)', *Oceania*, vol. XVIII no. 3, 1948, pp. 179–207.

Reynolds, Henry, *This Whispering in Our Hearts*, Allen & Unwin, St Leonards, NSW, 1998.

Rickard, John, *Australia: A Cultural History*, Second edition, Longman, London, 1996.

Riley, R., 'Reconciliation?' *Wikaru,* no. 15, July 1987, p. 25.

Rowley, C. D., 'Aboriginals in Australian Society', in *Anatomy of Australia*, Sun Books, Melbourne, 1968, pp. 113–31.

——, *Outcasts in White Australia: Aboriginal Policy and Practice—Volume II*, Australian National University Press, Canberra, 1971.

Rowse, Tim, 'Middle Australia and the Noble Savage: A Political Romance', in J. R. Beckett (ed.), *Past and Present: The Construction of Aboriginality*, Aboriginal Studies Press, Canberra, 1988, pp. 161–77.

——, 'How We Got a Native Title Act', in M. Goot and T. Rowse (eds), *Make a Better Offer: The Politics of Mabo,* Pluto, Leichhardt, NSW, 1994, pp. 111–32.

——, *White Flour, White Power: From Rations to Citizenship in Central Australia*, Cambridge University Press, Cambridge, 1998.

——, 'The Modesty of the State: Hasluck and the Anthropological Critics of Assimilation', in T. Stannage, K. Saunders and R. Nile (eds), *Paul Hasluck in Australian History: Civic Personality and Public Life*, University of Queensland Press, St. Lucia, Qld, [1998], pp. 119–32.

——, *Obliged to be Difficult: Nugget Coombs' Legacy in Indigenous Affairs*, Cambridge University Press, Cambridge, 2000.

——, 'Introduction' in T. Rowse (ed.), *Contesting Assimilation*, API Network, Perth, 2005, pp. 1–24.

Roy Morgan Research Centre, 'Defer Mabo to Full Senate Hearing', 9 December 1993 [Morgan Poll Finding No. 2527].

Rump, Eric E., 'Comparing Australia and New Zealand on Colour Prejudice', *International Journal of Psychology*, vol. 7 no. 1, 1972, 39–45.

Ryan, Lyndall, 'Aboriginals and Islanders', in B. W. Head and A. Patience (eds), *From Fraser to Hawke: Australian Public Policy in the 1980s*, Longman Cheshire, Melbourne, 1989, pp. 394–408.

Saulwick *Age* Poll, 27 July 1993: A. [computer file]. Canberra: Australian Social Science Data Archive, The Australian National University; *Age* and *Sydney Morning Herald*, 4 August 1993.

Saulwick, Irving and Associates, *Age* Poll, November 1978 [computer file]. Canberra: Australian Social Science Data Archive, Australian National University, 1982; *Age* and *Sydney Morning Herald,* 2 January 1979.

——, *Age* Poll, October 1980 [computer file]. Canberra: Australian Social Science Data Archive, Australian National University, 1982; *Age* and *Sydney Morning Herald*, 11 October 1980.

Saulwick, Irving & Associates in association with Denis Muller & Associates, 'Research into Issues Related to a Document of Reconciliation: A Report Prepared for the Council for Aboriginal Reconciliation', 2000.

——, 'Research into Issues Related to a Document of Reconciliation: Report No 2 Indigenous Qualitative Research, Prepared for the Council for Aboriginal Reconciliation', 2000.

Sawer, Geoffrey, 'The Australian Constitution and the Australian Aborigine', *Federal Law Review*, vol. 2 no. 1, 1966–67, pp. 17–36.

Scalmer, Sean, and Murray Goot, 'Elites Constructing Elites: News Limited's Newspapers, 1996–2002', in M. Sawer and B. Hindess (eds), *Us and Them: Anti-elitism in Australia*, API Network, Perth, 2004, pp. 137–59.

Schultz, Julianne, *Reviving the Fourth Estate: Democracy, Accountability and the Media,* Cambridge University Press, Cambridge, 1998.

Scott, Evelyn, 'The People Will Have the Final Say', *Australian*, 29 February 2000.

Seccombe, Mike, 'Kookaburra', *Sydney Morning Herald*, 11 March 2000.

——, 'The PM's Man Who is Master at Massaging Words', *Australian*, 13 April 2000.

Shanahan, Dennis, 'Howard Abandons Deadline—No Reconciliation by Centenary', *Australian*, 28 February 2000.

Shaw, A. G. L., *The Story of Australia*, Faber, London, 1962.

Smith, L., *The Aboriginal Population of Australia*, Australian National University Press, Canberra, 1980.

Smith, Robert, 'Racial Attitudes in the Junior Grades of a Boy's Boarding School in Australia', *Journal of Intercultural Studies*, vol. 1 no. 2, 1980, pp. 40–9.

Sniderman, Paul, Joseph F. Fletcher, Peter Russell, and Philip E. Tetlock, *The Clash of Rights: Liberty, Equality, and Legitimacy in Pluralist Democracy*, Yale University Press, New Haven, Connecticut, 1996.

Stanner, W. E. H., *After the Dreaming*, Australian Broadcasting Commission, Sydney, 1968.

Stokes, Geoff, 'Special Interests or Equality?—The Mining Industry's Campaign Against Aboriginal Land Rights in Australia', *Australian-Canadian Studies*, vol. 5 no. 1, 1987, pp. 61–78.

Strehlow, T. G. H., *Nomads in No-Man's Land*, Aborigines Advancement League Inc. of South Australia, Adelaide, 1961.

——, *Assimilation Problems: The Aboriginal Viewpoint*, Aborigines Advancement League Inc. of South Australia, Adelaide, 1964.

Summers, John, 'Federalism and Commonwealth–State Relations', in J. Summers, D. Woodward and A. Parkin (eds), *Government, Politics, Power and Policy in Australia*, Seventh edition, Longman, Frenchs Forest, NSW, 2002, pp. 89–117.

Sweeney, Brian & Associates, 'A New Beginning: Community Attitudes Towards Aboriginal Reconciliation', South Melbourne, 1996.

——, 'Report on Supplementary Qualitative Research Study on Community Attitudes to Indigenous Citizenship Rights & A Document of Reconciliation', South Melbourne, 1996.

——, 'A Report on a National Quantitative Survey of Community Attitudes Towards Aboriginal Reconciliation', South Melbourne, 1996.

Taffe, Sue, 'The Role of FCAATSI in the 1967 Referendum: Mythmaking about Citizenship or Political Strategy?', in T. Rowse (ed.), *Contesting Assimilation*, API Network, Perth, 2005, pp. 285–98.

Taft, Ronald, 'Attitudes of Western Australians Towards Aborigines', in R. Taft, J. L. M. Dawson and P. Beasley, *Attitudes and Social Conditions*, Australian National University Press, Canberra, 1970, pp. 1–72.

Taft, Ronald, and Kenneth F. Walker, 'Australia', in A. M. Rose (ed.), *The Institutions of Advanced Societies*, University of Minnesota Press, Minneapolis, 1958, pp. 131–92.

Tatz, Colin, 'The Aborigines', in V. G. Venturini (ed.), *Australia: A Survey*, Otto Harrassowitz, Weisbaden, 1970, pp. 27–40.

Taylor, Kerry, 'Show Courage, Howard Told', *Age*, 29 February 2000.

Taylor, Lenore, 'Newspoll: People Turn Against Mabo Plan', *Australian*, 27 October 1993.

——, 'Majority Back Referendum on Native Title Issue', *Australian*, 24 November 1993.

Terry, P., 'Govt to Introduce National Land Rights Within a Year', *Australian*, 6 August 2003.

——, 'Trouble for Govt. on Land Rights Law', *Australian,* 27 March 1985.

Tickner, Liz, 'Mabo a Mystery to Most of WA', *West Australian*, 21 May 1993.

——, 'WA Learns What Mabo is All About', *West Australian*, 30 July 1993.

Tickner, Robert, *Taking a Stand: Land Rights to Reconciliation,* Allen & Unwin, Crows Nest, 2001.

Tiffen, Rod, *Communications and Politics: The Press, the Public and the Third World*, Australian Council for Overseas Aid, Canberra, 1974.

——, Symbolic Processes of Out-Group Politics: The Press, the Public and the Third World, Unpublished PhD thesis, Monash University, 1976.

Uren, Tom, *Straight Left*, Random House, Milsons Point, NSW, 1994.

Victorian Council of Social Service, *Dark People of Melbourne: A Study of Aborigines and Part-Aborigines in Melbourne Conducted by Members of the Melbourne University Psychology Department and Department of Social Studies,* VCOSS, Melbourne, 1950.

Walker, Iain, 'Attitudes to Minorities: Survey Evidence of Western Australians' Attitudes to Aborigines, Asians, and Women', *Australian Journal of Psychology*, vol. 46 no. 3, 1994, pp. 137–43.

Western, John, 'The Australian Aborigine: What White Australians Know and Think about Him', *Race*, vol. 10 no. 4, 1969, pp. 411–34; reprinted as 'What White Australians Think', in G. E. Kearney, P. R. de Lacey and G. R. Davidson (eds), *The Psychology of Aboriginal Australians*, John Wiley, Sydney, 1973, pp. 244–68.

——, 'The Attitudes of White Australians to Australian Aborigines—Some Survey Results', in D. Tugby (ed.), *Aboriginal Identity in Contemporary Australian Society*, Jacaranda Press, Brisbane, 1973, pp. 53–74.

Western, J. S., K. Davan, and Z. Kebenay, 'The Importance of Visibility for Social Inequality Research', *Australian Journal of Social Issues*, vol. 40 no. 1, 2005, pp. 125–41.

Williams, Ross, '"Why Should I feel Guilty?" Reflections on the Workings of Guilt in White-Aboriginal Relations', *Australian Psychologist*, vol. 35 no. 2, 2000, pp. 136–42.

Wilson, John, 'Assimilation to What? Comments on the White Society', in
    M. Reay (ed.), *Aborigines Now: New Perspective in the Study of Aboriginal
    Communities*, Angus & Robertson, Sydney, 1964, pp. 151–66.

Woodward, A. E., *Aboriginal Land Rights Commission: First Report*, Australian
    Government Publishing Service, Canberra, 1973.

——, *Aboriginal Land Rights Commission: Second Report*, Australian
    Government Publishing Service, Canberra, 1974.

——, 'Land Rights and Land Use: A View from the Sideline', *Australian
    Law Journal,* vol. 59 no. 8, 1985, pp. 413–26.

Wright, Tony, 'Howard Is Single-minded About Changing His Views', *Age*,
    4 March 2000.

Wright, Tony, and Caroline Overington, 'PM Backs Survey on Aborigines',
    Age, 4 March 2000.

Yankelovich, Daniel, *Coming to Public Judgment,* Syracuse University Press,
    Syracuse, New York, 1991.

2008 Short, Damien Reconciliation and
Colonial Power: indigenous rights
in Australia.
        Ordered to
        Exeter Library

Index